Sports and Politics

Sports and Politics

Commodification, Capitalist Exploitation, and Political Agency

Edited by
Frank Jacob

ISBN 978-3-11-099263-2
e-ISBN (PDF) 978-3-11-067939-7
e-ISBN (EPUB) 978-3-11-067948-9

Library of Congress Control Number: 2020937021

Bibliographic information published by the Deutsche Nationalbibliothek
The Deutsche Nationalbibliothek lists this publication in the Deutsche Nationalbibliografie; detailed bibliographic data are available on the Internet at http://dnb.dnb.de.

© 2022 Walter de Gruyter GmbH, Berlin/Boston
This volume is text- and page-identical with the hardback published in 2020.
Cover image: akg-images/picture-alliance/dpa
Typesetting: Integra Software Services Pvt. Ltd.
Printing and binding: CPI books GmbH, Leck

www.degruyter.com

Contents

Frank Jacob
1 Sports, Politics, and Capitalism or: The Immoral Corruption of a Human Pleasure —— 1

Section I: Sports, Politics, and Corruption

Steven A. Riess
2 Politics, Corruption, and Urban Sport in Chicago Racing: The Paul Powell Shoebox Scandal and the Bribery of Otto Kerner —— 11

Tom Heenan
3 The Great Australian 'Sting': How and Why Melbourne Became the World's Sporting Capital —— 37

Section II: Sports, Politics, and Racism

Thomas Aiello
4 In the Land of Dreamy Dreams: Tennis and the Nexus of Class and Race in New Orleans, 1876–1976 —— 69

Nicole Hirschfelder
5 "Change Starts with Us": The Issue of Media Representation of Athletes' Activism for Black Lives —— 101

Steve Marston
6 The Revival of Athlete Activism(s): Divergent Black Politics in the 2016 Presidential Election Engagements of LeBron James and Colin Kaepernick —— 119

Section III: Sports, Politics, Sexual Abuse and Homophobia

Kathleen Bachynski
7 #MeToo, Larry Nassar, and Sexual Abuse in Youth Sports —— 143

Francesco Collura
8   Hegemonic Masculinities and the Fear of Being Gay in the NHL —— 167

Contributors —— 185

Index —— 187

Frank Jacob
1 Sports, Politics, and Capitalism or: The Immoral Corruption of a Human Pleasure

Sports are anything but simply sports. Sports represent the human ambition of achievement, the regional or national pride in this achievement, the display of female or male capacities, as well as the fulfillment of a dream to be recognized for. After his protest against racial inequalities and injustices in the US during football games, as well as later in a Nike commercial after the end of his sports career due to his activism, Colin Kaepernick, the former NFL (National Football League) quarterback of the San Francisco 49ers, declared, while highlighting what a dream is worth, that people should "Believe in something. Even if it means to sacrifice everything."[1] While it was a way for him to continue his protest against the social deficits of and discrimination against the weak, e.g. African American victims of police violence, Nike was able to use the advertisement to increase its sales by 31%.[2] Capitalist interest might have determined Nike's decision to work with Kaepernick for the advertisement spot, as much as the quarterback might have matched the company's slogan, "Just do it," quite well. Whatever the interest might have been, the presented case already shows how closely sports and capitalism, especially due to the commodification of the first, are related to each other, and it was the capitalization of sports that turned the original ideals that the latter ones might have represented once into commodifications, including those active in professional sports as well.

Sports clubs were commodified in such a way that they now rather represent wealth than anything else, while they sell a feeling of community to the fans that is close to a religious cult.[3] Real Madrid, as the American scholar Stefan Szymanski argues, "is the closest thing in the world to football royalty" and the "most valuable

---

[1] Charisse Jones, "Nike Goes All In: Colin Kaepernick Voices 'Just Do It' Ad to Air During NFL's Kick-Off Game," *USA Today*, September 6, 2018. Accessed October 31, 2019. https://eu.usatoday.com/story/money/2018/09/05/nike-backs-colin-kaepernick-ad-set-debut-during-season-kickoff/1204599002/
[2] Gina Martinez, "Despite Outrage, Nike Sales Increased 31% After Kaepernick Ad," *TIME*, September 8, 2018. Accessed October 15, 2019. https://time.com/5390884/nike-sales-go-up-kaepernick-ad/
[3] US sociologist Michael Stein emphasized this interrelation already in the 1970s. Michael Stein, "Cult and Sport: The Case of Big Red," *Mid-American Review of Sociology* 2, no. 2 (1977): 29–42.

https://doi.org/10.1515/9783110679397-001

football 'franchise' in the world."[4] Broadcast rights are related to income, which is spent on the recruitment of new players, who then secure sporting success and an increased share of broadcast rights when these are renewed. Of course, players in the top teams and the top leagues, be it soccer, football, basketball or any other sport, are well paid – if they are male – but the countless rank and file of players who will never reach the top level are exploited while trying to get there and are forgotten relatively quickly, once they have failed to do so. In some regions of the world, a career in professional sport still seems to be the only way out of a life determined by poverty and sorrow, while dubious scouts and managers, as well as colleges, are able to tempt promising talents with high numbers. The exploitation strategies in place are, in addition, also very often accompanied by classism, racism, and gender biases.[5]

Due to the latter issue, women still struggle to be fully accepted in professional sports,[6] not to mention their rights for equal pay that are rarely matched, while broadcasting companies and others make a lot of money when millions of fans watch women's sports on television or in sports stadiums around the world.[7] Yet barriers for women, not only to gain equality but even to get access to the world of professional sports, are created by myths that, according to former swimmer and activist Donna de Varona, still seem to dominate the minds of so many:

1. Participating in sport will make women unfeminine.
2. Participating in elite sport will harm women's reproductive organs and will result in the inability to produce children.
3. Women do not need to learn about the lessons of life on the playing fields of sport, but men do.

---

4 Stefan Szymanski, *Money and Soccer: A Soccernomics Guide* (New York: Nation Books, 2015).
5 Krystal K. Beamon, "'Used Goods': Former African American College Student-Athletes' Perception of Exploitation by Division I Universities," *The Journal of Negro Education* 77, no. 4 (2008): 352–364; Komanduri S. Murty, Julian B. Roebuck, and Jimmy D. McCamey, Jr., "Race and Class Exploitation: A Study of Black Male Student Athletes (BSAS) on White Campuses," *Race, Gender & Class* 21, 3/4 (2014): 156–173. From a historical perspective with regard to US College Football since the 1960s see: Michael Oriard, *Bowled Over: Big-Time College Football from the Sixties to the BCS Era* (Chapel Hill, NC: University of North Carolina Press, 2009), 191–232. For a more detailed analysis of European soccer see Frank Jacob and Alexander Friedman, eds. *Fußball: Identitätsdiskurse, Politik und Skandale* (Stuttgart: Kohlhammer, 2020).
6 Marizanne Grundlingh, "Boobs and Balls. Exploring Issues of Gender and Identity Among Women Soccer Players at Stellenbosch University," *Agenda: Empowering Women for Gender Equity* 85 (2010): 45–53.
7 Timothy F. Grainey, *Beyond Bend It Like Beckham: The Global Phenomenon of Women's Soccer* (Lincoln, NE/London: University of Nebraska Press, 2012), xvii.

4. Women will never be accepted as real athletes because they are not as strong, fast and muscular as men are.
5. Women athletes will never be as popular as male athletes; therefore, they will not attract audiences large enough to make women's sport financially profitable and viable.
6. Women are not as interested in sport as men are; therefore, opportunities should not be wasted on them.[8]

The last three arguments in particular will continue to stimulate the exploitation of female athletes until they are accepted as equals by society as a whole, which is why Megan Rapinoe and other members of the US Women's Soccer Team decided to fight for their rights and sued the US Soccer Federation.[9]

Exploitation in the world of sports not only affects the athletes, however, but also the fans, who are supposed to finance their team or star of choice by buying not only tickets, but also merchandise and other forms of related products.[10] The stadium nevertheless provides a last refuge for those otherwise uprooted, where they hope to find authenticity and a community they can attach themselves to.[11] Regardless of the reality of such feelings and their existent or imagined value, it is the fans who pay the price for the commodification of sports, be it due to higher ticket prices or due to the money spent on all kinds of club- or team-related goods. Capitalism, however, goes even further than this. The ways in which sports lead to exploitation are manifold.

Activists have criticized "poor labour standards in the factories, cottage industries, and home-based workshops"[12] of sub-contractors for Nike and other sports companies, and the import and sales of sports-related commodities, like soccer balls, creates a surplus for capitalist companies, while their workers have to produce

---

[8] Donna de Varona, "Introduction – 'M's' in Football: Myths, Management, Marketing, Media, and Money – A Repise," in *Soccer, Women, Sexual Liberation: Kicking off a New Era*, eds. Fan Hong and J.A. Mangan (London: Routledge, 2004), 8.
[9] Andrew Das, "U.S. Women's Soccer Team Sues U.S. Soccer for Gender Discrimination," *The New York Times*, March 8, 2019. Accessed October 12, 2019. https://www.nytimes.com/2019/03/08/sports/womens-soccer-team-lawsuit-gender-discrimination.html
[10] Mel Stanfill, *Exploiting Fandom: How the Media Industry Seeks to Manipulate Fans* (Iowa City: University of Iowa Press, 2019), 77–103.
[11] Richard Gebhardt, "'Kampf um das Stadion', Fußball als gesellschaftliches Konfliktfeld und Einflusszone der extremen Rechten," in *Kritik und Leidenschaft: Vom Umgang mit politischen Ideen*, eds. Henrique Ricardo Otten and Manfred Sicking (Bielefeld: Transcript, 2011), 104.
[12] Karin Astrid Siegmann, "Soccer Ball Production for Nike in Pakistan," *Economic and Political Weekly* 43, no. 22 (2008): 57.

and live in precarious situations. Workers are also exploited when the stadiums for the Olympic Games, World Cups in soccer, or other sports events need to be built as fast as possible, often to be used only for a short period of time.[13] The Olympic Games in particular, which the American scholar, activist, and former athlete Jules Boykoff calls a form of "celebration capitalism,"[14] combine the different forms of exploitation named so far. The cities that host the Olympics – no matter if it is the summer or winter games – are also often exploited. The host cites, often built with taxpayers' money, are left unpopulated after a few weeks of use, while the city's finances are forced to deal with debts for years.[15]

Since sports events represent many options for capitalist investment and exploitation, they also become a political issue. The present volume is particularly interested in this relationship, i.e. how sports are shaped by politics, whose representatives at the national or local levels are involved in diverse roles when it comes to the organization of sports as such in general, and related issues like corruption, racism, and gender-related issues. The focus of the volume is first pointing to historical continuities of political corruption with regard to sports, as analyzed by Steven A. Riess, Tom Heenan, and Thomas Aiello, as well as second to contemporary issues related to several levels of exploitation in sports that are made possible by political intervention or non-intervention, often stimulated by the wish to not damage capitalist interests of politicians and investors alike. The contributions of the present volume are divided into three sections that focus on different levels of exploitation and interrelations between sports and politics. The first section will deal with the interrelationship of sports, politics, and corruption. Well-known US sports historian Steven A. Riess provides a discussion of historical cases of corruption in racing sports in Chicago. He will analyze the Paul Powell shoebox scandal and the bribery of Otto Kerner to emphasize how the bribery of politicians in the US was responsible for internal developments within the racing sports of that metropolis in Illinois. That such interrelations between sports and political corruption are not exclusive American phenomena will be shown by Tom Heenan, whose

---

[13] Sean Ingle, "Amnesty Says Migrant Workers Still Being Exploited in Qatar," *The Guardian*, September 19, 2019. Accessed October 15, 2019. https://www.theguardian.com/football/2019/sep/19/amnesty-says-migrant-workers-still-being-exploited-in-qatar

[14] Jules Boykoff, *Celebration Capitalism and the Olympic Games* (London/New York: Routledge, 2013). For the relation between the Olympic Games, "celebratio capitalism," and activism, see: Jules Boykoff, "The Olympics, Celebration Capitalism, and the Activist Response," *Journal of Sport and Gender Studies* 16 (2018): 62–84.

[15] Jennnifer Wills, "The Economic Impact of Hosting the Olympics," *Investopedia*, June 25, 2019. Accessed October 31, 2019. https://www.investopedia.com/articles/markets-economy/092416/what-economic-impact-hosting-olympics.asp

contribution will explain how and why Melbourne was turned into the "Great Australian Sting," one of the sports capitals of the world. The chapter will highlight how politicians were responsible for the development of Melbourne into a sports center while exploiting public funds and ignoring the rights of the city's population.

The second section then focuses on the question of racism within sports and how politics reacted to it, or even created these issues in the first place, ignoring the exclusion of ethnic groups due to racist stereotypes and prejudices. A long durée approach by Thomas Aiello will focus on the triad of tennis, class, and race in New Orleans between 1876 and 1976. While looking particularly at New Orleans, this chapter highlights the relations between tennis and racial identity in the American South, and also explains the extent to which tennis was related to local politics. It is, therefore, a regional case study, which nevertheless must be seen as being embedded in the larger picture of US sports in general. Nicole Hirschfelder will then look at political activism within sports and show how the media represents athletes with an activist agenda. The case of Colin Kaepernick and other athletes who participate in the Black Lives Matter movement will be taken into closer consideration and critically discussed. Hirschfelder thereby not only shows that "sports constitutes a highly dynamic industry that brings together body, mind, social practices, capitalism, entertainment and politics in a high-pressure environment with a significant amount of public attention" but at the same time how it "both crystallizes and initiates debates about political issues faster and sooner than most other professional fields." Steve Marston concludes the second section with another perspective on athlete activism, namely the political engagements of LeBron James and Colin Kaepernick during the 2016 presidential election. He consequently highlights that athletes are no longer limited to protests within their sports-related sphere, but that they are also able to use the attention they receive, especially on the social media channels of the 21st century, to become active political voices as well. His chapter offers an important insight into the relationship between sports and politics, as it delivers "an examination of political currents' overlapping iterations within the rhetoric of two major athlete-activists."

The final section will consider sports and politics in their relations with sexual abuse and homophobia that are also stimulated by a lack of political countermeasures due to a resistance based on capitalist interest and the actions of the main exploiting parties, i.e. club owners or investors. Kathleen Bachynski "explores the relationship between #MeToo as a broader political movement and its effects on conversations about athlete welfare and sexual abuse in sports," and discusses the Larry Nassar case and the sexual abuse of young athletes. She analyzes the case's relation to the #MeToo movement and thereby shows how the media was shaping the national discussion about sexual violence in general. Cases like this, however, only present the tip of the iceberg, as many cases are not even brougth to light, because those in charge look the other way and protect sexual predators, because they fear a loss of reputation and/or sponsors. Finally, Francesco Collura will take the "hegemonic masculinities" of the National Hockey League (NHL) into closer consideration. By dealing with determinant factors like "masculinity, homophobia, locker-room talk, media reception, societal and political policies and negative implications and repercussions that may surface from coming out," Collura's chapter increases awareness about "mediated sports culture" and provides a better explanation as to why "the NHL is the only league [in North America] without an openly gay player."

Taken together, the papers assembled in the present volume provide a glimpse of the interrelationship between sports and politics, as they reflect continuations of the past or as the represent contemporary issues. Although they mostly focus on the United States, the presented insights will hopefully stimulate further research dealing with the role that politics has in sports, while also highlighting the capitalist roots of this special relationship. The immoral corruption of a human pleasure like sports can probably never be fully reversed, as the role of sports in society is quite important; however, a return to some sporting ideals and the end of the exploitation that relates to the commodification of soccer, football, hockey, tennis, etc. should be achievable if politicians begin to reshape their relationship with sports in a more responsible way. Such an achievement would be worth dreaming of, and in order to reach it, one has to believe in it. Even if it means to sacrifice everything.

Works Cited

Beamon, Krystal K. "'Used Goods': Former African American College Student-Athletes' Perception of Exploitation by Division I Universities." *The Journal of Negro Education* 77, no. 4 (2008): 352–364.
Boykoff, Jules. *Celebration Capitalism and the Olympic Games*. London/New York: Routledge, 2013.
Boykoff, Jules. "The Olympics, Celebration Capitalism, and the Activist Response." *Journal of Sport and Gender Studies* 16 (2018): 62–84.
Das, Andrew. "U.S. Women's Soccer Team Sues U.S. Soccer for Gender Discrimination." *The New York Times*, March 8, 2019. Accessed October 12, 2019. https://www.nytimes.com/2019/03/08/sports/womens-soccer-team-lawsuit-gender-discrimination.html
Gebhardt, Richard. "'Kampf um das Stadion', Fußball als gesellschaftliches Konfliktfeld und Einflusszone der extremen Rechten." In *Kritik und Leidenschaft: Vom Umgang mit politischen Ideen*, eds. Henrique Ricardo Otten and Manfred Sicking, 95–115. Bielefeld: Transcript, 2011.
Grundlingh, Marizanne. "Boobs and Balls. Exploring Issues of Gender and Identity Among Women Soccer Players at Stellenbosch University." *Agenda: Empowering Women for Gender Equity* 85 (2010): 45–53.

Ingle, Sean. "Amnesty Says Migrant Workers Still Being Exploited in Qatar." *The Guardian*, September 19, 2019. Accessed October 15, 2019. https://www.theguardian.com/football/2019/sep/19/amnesty-says-migrant-workers-still-being-exploited-in-qatar

Jacob, Frank and Alexander Friedman, eds. *Fußball: Identitätsdiskurse, Politik und Skandale*. Stuttgart: Kohlhammer, 2020.

Jones, Charisse. "Nike Goes All In: Colin Kaepernick Voices 'Just Do It' Ad to Air During NFL's Kick-Off Game." *USA Today*, September 6, 2018. Accessed October 31, 2019. https://eu.usatoday.com/story/money/2018/09/05/nike-backs-colin-kaepernick-ad-set-debut-during-season-kickoff/1204599002/

Martinez, Gina. "Despite Outrage, Nike Sales Increased 31% After Kaepernick Ad." *TIME*, September 8, 2018. Accessed October 15, 2019. https://time.com/5390884/nike-sales-go-up-kaepernick-ad/

Grainey, Timothy F. *Beyond Bend It Like Beckham: The Global Phenomenon of Women's Soccer*. Lincoln, NE/London: University of Nebraska Press, 2012.

Murty, Komanduri S., Julian B. Roebuck, and Jimmy D. McCamey, Jr. "Race and Class Exploitation: A Study of Black Male Student Athletes (BSAS) on White Campuses." *Race, Gender & Class* 21, 3/4 (2014): 156–173.

Oriard, Michael. *Bowled Over: Big-Time College Football from the Sixties to the BCS Era*. Chapel Hill, NC: University of North Carolina Press, 2009.

Siegmann, Karin Astrid. "Soccer Ball Production for Nike in Pakistan." *Economic and Political Weekly* 43, no. 22 (2008): 57–64.

Stanfill, Mel. *Exploiting Fandom: How the Media Industry Seeks to Manipulate Fans*. Iowa City: University of Iowa Press, 2019.

Stein, Michael. "Cult and Sport: The Case of Big Red." *Mid-American Review of Sociology* 2, no. 2 (1977): 29–42.

Szymanski, Stefan. *Money and Soccer: A Soccernomics Guide*. New York: Nation Books, 2015.

Varona, Donna de. "Introduction – 'M's' in Football: Myths, Management, Marketing, Media, and Money – A Repise." In *Soccer, Women, Sexual Liberation: Kicking off a New Era*, eds. Fan Hong and J.A. Mangan. 7–13. London: Routledge, 2004.

Wills, Jennnifer. "The Economic Impact of Hosting the Olympics." *Investopedia*, June 25, 2019. Accessed October 31, 2019. https://www.investopedia.com/articles/markets-economy/092416/what-economic-impact-hosting-olympics.asp

Section I: **Sports, Politics, and Corruption**

Steven A. Riess
2 Politics, Corruption, and Urban Sport in Chicago Racing: The Paul Powell Shoebox Scandal and the Bribery of Otto Kerner

Tammany politician George Washington Plunkitt (1842–1924) declared around the turn of the 20th century that "I [have] seen my opportunities and I took 'em." He did not believe that politicians should steal from the public trough but supported the concept of honest graft – pursuing the public welfare and enhancing his personal interests at the same time, such as employing their clout and access to inside information to make money. In his day many of the promoters of the three major professional sports – thoroughbred racing, prize fighting, and Major League Baseball – were professional politicians or their close associates, who employed their clout to protect these investments and their access to inside information to make astute business decisions.[1]

New York's Tammany politicians at mid-century often got their first involvement with boxers by employing them on Election Day as "shoulder hitters" to make sure their constituents voted "correctly." Bouts then were universally illegal, and promoters needed clout to arrange that the authorities did not interfere with secret matches. It was not until 1890 that New Orleans boxing promoters used their clout to secure a state law legitimizing prize fights, Six years later Big Tim Sullivan, a leading boxing promoter, and the number two man in Tammany, led the fight in New York to pass the short-lived Horton Act that temporarily legalized prize fights. Professional bouts remained largely banned until 1920 when New York's Democratic Governor Al Smith (1873–1944) signed the Walker Act that legalized the sport under the control of the first state boxing commission. A number of other states soon followed.[2]

Nearly all major league teams in 1900 were owned by men with political clout, including Charles Ebbets of the (1859–1925) Brooklyn Dodgers, Andrew Freedman (1860–1925), and Charles Stoneham (1876–1936) of the New York Giants, popularly

---
[1] William L. Riordan, ed. *Plunkitt of Tammany Hall: A Series of Very Plain Talks on Very Practical Politics* (New York: Dutton, 1963), 3.
[2] Steven A. Riess, "In the Ring and Out: Professional Boxing in New York, 1896–1920," in *Sport in America: New Historical Perspectives*, ed. Donald Spivey (Westport, CT: Greenwood Press, 1985), 95–128.

https://doi.org/10.1515/9783110679397-002

known as "Tammany's team," and the New York Highlanders (renamed the Yankees in 1913), whose first owners included William Devery (1854–1919), the former police commissioner and New York's top gambler, Frank J. Farrell (1856–1926). The sport's legality was never at question, but owners used their political ties to protect themselves from potential interlopers, secure inside information about sites for fire resistant ballparks, to block rising license fees, and fight for Sunday baseball.³

Thoroughbred racing was an elite sport in early America, but starting in the Revolutionary Era, encountered considerable public opposition, at first because of its perception as a British sport with aristocratic pretensions. Racing in the early 19th century encountered growing opposition, mainly because of the gambling aspect, which led to many states outside the South to ban the sport.⁴

Post-Civil War racing revived in the North, dominated by prestigious elite racing clubs like New York's American Jockey Club, whose leaders had enormous political clout, abetted by politically connected owners of proprietary tracks who worked together to legalize the sport in New York in 1887. However, gambling opponents, mainly small-town Republican Protestant moralists who considered wagering sinful, and urban social reformers, who saw gambling as a first step to criminality and the rise of organized crime, successfully fought against the turf. By 1910 thoroughbred racing was banned in nearly every state, with the main exceptions Maryland and Kentucky.⁵

The tide first changed in New York in 1913, with a court decision legalizing on-track gambling, and then in the 1920s racing made a huge comeback during the "Golden Age of Sports" as the American public became more interested in expanding their leisure time and options, and less concerned with the morality of gambling. Several state governments in the 1920s voted to legalize pari-mutuel betting to provide a new source of entertainment for their residents, and also raise funds for state revenue. Racing struggled in the early Depression, but remained very popular, and by 1936, 22 states had racing commissions to supervise the sport which brought in record revenues. After World War II, thoroughbred racing drew more spectators than any other sport.⁶

---

3 Steven A. Riess, *Touching Base: Professional Baseball and American Culture in the Progressive Era*, rev. ed. (Urbana, IL: University of Illinois Press, 1999).
4 Steven A. Riess, "The Cyclical History of Horse Racing: The USA's Oldest and (Sometimes) Most Popular Spectator Sport." In *American National Pastimes – A History*, eds. Mark Dyreson and Jaime Schultz (New York: Routledge, 2014), 30–34.
5 Steven A. Riess, *The Sport of Kings and the Kings of Crime: Horse Racing, Politics, and Crime in New York, 1865–1913* (Syracuse: Syracuse University Press, 2011).
6 Riess, "Cyclical History of Horse Racing," 38–40.

This article focuses on the corrupt connections between the Chicago harness and thoroughbred racing businesses entrepreneurs and local political brokers. Illinois thoroughbred racing was banned in 1905 but made a huge comeback in the late 1920s after betting at the tracks was legitimized by court decisions and the 1927 Lager Act. Greater Chicago had six courses by 1932. Illinois racing was for years among the most successful in the nation.[7]

The widespread popularity of racing led to the introduction of urban harness racing in New York just before World War II, followed by Illinois after the war. Harness racing soon flourished across the country. It did not require expensive thoroughbreds, and races were staged in the evenings when working class fans had free time. Harness racing in Illinois drew more spectators than flat racing from 1969 through 1976. Nationally they collectively outdrew other American sports from the early 1950s to the mid 1980s. Political involvement by ownership was vital in racing states whose racing boards licensed breeders, owners, jockeys, track officials, and track owners, regulated legal gambling and the treatment of horses, determined racing seasons, collected taxes on racing operations, and prevented fixed races.[8]

Illinois track owners spent heavily to garner the support of state politicians to promote their sports, donating funds to political campaigns of influential politicians and selling them shares at below market prices if not giveaway prices. They often hired prominent politicians as managers and consultants. The close relations between Illinois harness racing and state politicians received considerable public attention during the Kefauver hearings on organized crime in 1951 and from press reports, but the problems were largely forgotten until the early 1970s following the death of Illinois Secretary of State Paul Powell (1902–1970), when $850,000 was found in his hotel room that came from his involvement in horse racing. Then one year later, corruption in thoroughbred racing became a national issue when former Governor Otto Kerner (1908–1976), by then a federal judge, was convicted for taking bribes to advance the interests of racing mogul Marge Lindheimer Everett (1922–2012), lying to the FBI, and falsifying his income tax statements.

American harness racing in the late 19th century was mainly contested in heat races at rural county and state fairs, and the prestigious Grand Circuit, first staged in 1873 in Buffalo, Cleveland, Springfield, MA, and Utica. The sport was identified as a more democratic sport than aristocratic thoroughbred racing, employing cheaper working horses instead of expensive blooded stock used exclusively for

---

[7] Ibid., 39.
[8] Steven A. Riess, "Horse Racing in the Windy City, 1945–1980," paper read at the American Historical Association, 4 January 2019; "NCAA Football Attendance Records." Accessed 23 May 2019. http://fs.ncaa.org/Docs/stats/football_records/DI/2010/Attendance.pdf.

racing. Purses were typically modest, and the gambling was mainly between spectators, not professional bookmakers.[9]

Harness racing made few in-roads into major American cities, but entrepreneurs closely tied to prominent politicians and underworld figures in the late 1930s began recognizing the sport's potential as an evening working class entertainment and local governments began identifying the sport as a potential source for badly needed revenue. Harness racing then was governed by three private regional organizations, but in 1938 the U.S. Trotting Association was formed to rationalize and bring order to the sport. In 1939, shortly before New York legalized pari-mutuel racing, George M. Levy (1888–1977), a prominent mob attorney, whose clients included a Long Island dog racing track, and who regularly played golf with mobster Frank Costello (1891–1973), and bookmaking kingpin Frank Erickson (1896–1968), leased a site at Hempstead, Long Island in conjunction with the Old Country Trotting Association (OCTA), of which he owned 39 percent. The syndicate spent $125,000 to rebuild an old car racing track and grandstand and began single heat night racing in 1940 at Roosevelt Raceway. Levy admitted in 1951 to paying Costello $60,000 over four years to keep the bookmakers away from Roosevelt.[10]

Roosevelt struggled at first, drawing just 75,000 spectators in its first year, with a total handle of $1.2 million, losing $100,000, followed by over $50,000 in 1941, and $225,000 in 1942. But, beginning in 1945, Roosevelt's daily average attendance reached 9,743, with a daily handle of $240,951. The Long Island facility became a national model for the sport. By 1950 Roosevelt was drawing 1.5 million, and its pari-mutuel handle skyrocketed to $68 million. Its major innovation was the Phillips starting gate where starters lined up behind car pulled metal gate that folded and drove off once the trotters were up to speed.[11]

Metropolitan New York's second trotting course was the old Empire City track in Yonkers, which hosted a 34 day meet of all the state's harness clubs to cope with wartime travel restrictions. It also hosted the prestigious 1943 Hambletonian, the first event in harness racing's Triple Crown for three-year-olds. In 1950 the facility was sold to William H. Cane (1874–1956), a real estate tycoon, who bought

---

9 Dwight Akers, *Drivers Up: The Story of American Harness Racing* (New York: G.P. Putnam's Sons, 1947), 136–166, esp. 140–141; Dean Hoffman, *Harness Racing in New York State: A History of Trotters, Tracks and Horsemen* (Charleston, SC: The History Press, 2012), 22–23.
10 *New York Times* (hereafter *NYT*), July 20, 1977, 35; Hoffman, *Harness Racing*, 39–43; Tom Bojarski, "The Man Behind the Race," *Hoof Beats Magazine*, March 21, 2013. Accessed 31 January 2019. http://xwebapp.ustrotting.com/absolutenm/templates/hoofbeats_blog.aspx?articleid=52729&zoneid=75; "Harness Racing and New York's Ethics Laws." Accessed 1 February 2019. http://www.albanylaw.edu/media/user/glc/harnessracingandnewyorksethicslaws.pdf.
11 *NYT*, September 3, 1940, S26, July 20, 1977, 35, July 16, 1988,1; Hoffman, *Harness Racing*, 39, 43, 46.

Good Time Park in Goshen in 1926, host of the Hamiltonian from 1930 through 1956. In its inaugural season, after the racing surface was cut from a mile by half, Yonkers hosted about one million spectators (14,766 nightly) who bet over $50 million.[12]

Yonkers was sold in 1952 to Levy's OCTA, shortly before harness racing was recognized as the nation's fastest growing sport. Two years later, OCTA tracks' handle reached $218 million, and New York's eight tracks collectively drew 5 million spectators who bet $272 million, and Levy's original $25,000 investment was worth $14 million. In 1956 Roosevelt was forced to sell off Yonkers following an investigation into widespread corruption and labor racketeering at Yonkers.[13]

Levy protected and promoted his tracks by selling stock at bargain prices to supportive politicians, especially state legislators who helped pass essential bills, including pari-mutuel laws, created a state racing board, and granted harness tracks a larger share of the handle than thoroughbred tracks. The legislators also enacted laws to improve public transportation and highways and thereby increase access to the courses. The state racing board was also a target of gifts from the racing operators who selected racing dates and licensees. These deals were done secretly, often employing the names of friends or relatives, to keep the transactions out of the public eye.[14]

In 1946 Levy opposed the efforts of Nassau County to secure a 2 percent tax on Roosevelt's pari-mutuel revenues. He met with long-time County President J. Russell Sprague (1938–1953) and Irwin Steingut (1893–1952), the Brooklyn Democratic boss and the minority leader in the Assembly, and Levy got his way, after amply rewarding them. Four years later when OCTA wanted a law to prevent the state from increasing the number of licenses, the legislature came through. Steingut owned three-fourths of Batavia Downs, and his daughter held 200 shares of Yonkers Trotting.[15]

Sprague in 1945 paid $2,000 for 40 percent of the Cedar Point Trotting Association (the predecessor of the Nassau Trotting Association which conducted racing at Roosevelt Raceway as a tenant of Old Country). He sold his shares less than a year later for $195,000. In 1947 he bought $1,000 worth of shares in the NNTA in the name of his broker which he sold for $64,000 in 1953. Finally, in 1950 he bought $80,000 worth of stock in the Yonkers track, and earned $88,000 in

---

12 *NYT*, September 3, 1940, S26, July 2, 1943, 24, July 19, 1943, 20, July 27, 1986, S1, July 16, 1988, S1; Hoffman, *Harness Racing*, 33, 39, 46, 48.
13 *NYT*, March 7, 1954, 62, March 25, 1970, 47.
14 Steven A. Riess, *City Games: The Evolution of American Urban Society and the Rise of Sports* (Urbana: University of Illinois Press), 190–191.
15 *NYT*, September 27, 1952, 1; March 14, 1954, E8

dividends in three years. George M. Levy admitted that he bought $2,000 in stock for Sprague's daughter in his own name "so that people wouldn't think that Sprague owned it." She sold it before the 1953 state racing hearings for $150,000.[16]

Several assemblymen and senators who backed Levy, including past Democrat Minority leader John J. Dunnigan (1883–1965), whose family owned Buffalo Raceway, opened in 1942, and Assemblyman Norman Penny, the Nassau County Republican party chairman, who co-authored the constitutional amendment legalizing pari-mutuel gambling, obtained stock openly, often through their families, or secretively.[17]

Albert DiMeo was another politician prominent in harness racing. He was a former Levy associate and an 18-year veteran ex-Nassau County Assistant District attorney, whose salary had never surpassed $6,000. Currently vice president of Maywood Park, he owned with his wife 8,028 shares in the OCTA, worth over $200,000, 700 shares the Nassau TA, worth $13,000, and 6,000 shares in the Columbus Trotting Association, in Hilliard, Ohio. Furthermore, DeMeo and labor racketeer William C. DeKoning were said to get 10 percent of the profits of Harry M. Stevens, Inc., the concessionaire at Roosevelt Raceway.[18]

In the summer of 1953 Tom Lewis, a labor leader who controlled over half of Yonkers' 1,800 employees, including ex-cons, was murdered. This led to a big investigation and to disclosures of shady mob deals, political favoritism, mafia ties and political corruption at New York State's racetracks. Gov. Thomas Dewey got the State Harness Commission to suspend Yonkers' license.[19]

Newsday, a popular Long Island newspaper won a 1954 Pulitzer Prize for its coverage of the murder and the political machinations involving harness racing. It reported that 35 percent of all stock in New York state harness tracks belonged to local politicians, including 30 percent of the Nassau TA, 40 percent of Yonkers, and 100 percent of the Buffalo Trotting Association.[20]

The outcome of the investigations were state laws passed in 1954 creating a code of ethics for public officers and employees and other laws specific to harness racing. It increased the racing commissioner's control over stock transfers and licensees, raised the level of taxes, and made it very hard for political leaders and government employees to obtain racing licenses.[21]

---

16 Riess, *City Games*, 190–191; *NYT*, October 25, 1953, 1, March 6, 1954, 1, March 7, 1954, E2 (quote), March 14, 1954, E8.
17 *NYT*, March 7, 1954, 62.
18 *NYT*, October 25, 1953, 1, March 19, 1954, 17.
19 *NYT*, September 5, 1953, 28, September 23, 1953, 1.
20 *NYT*, 4 May 1954, 26.
21 "Harness Racing and New York's Ethics Laws," 9–10.

Harness racing in Illinois in the 1930s was prominent only at county and state fairs. The sport got a big boost in 1941 when the less than highly regarded Illinois Racing Commission was reorganized into the Illinois Racing Board (IRB), and given responsible for all equine racing sports. Journalists Bill Barnhart and Gene Schlickman described members as "horse-racing dilettantes and rich businesspeople who fancied themselves in the horsey set . . . [or] well-meaning but naive political appointees who were no match for shrewd entrepreneurs . . . and politicians."[22]

The coming of World War II put aside efforts to get harness racing underway. However, a big breakthrough occurred in 1945 when the state created a racing commission to regulate and license harness racing with pari-mutuel betting. Harness racing began to flourish over the next few years, emulating the rise of Roosevelt and Yonkers Raceways which set a model for the confluence of harness racing and politics in Illinois, Ohio, and Michigan. Six-term Representative Paul Powell (D-East St. Louis) was most responsible for securing the legalization, and subsequent expansion of harness racing in Illinois. Powell's power base was in far southern Illinois, and his racing interests centered in and around East St. Louis, where turf sports and illegal horse race gambling had a long history. Thoroughbred racing there had close connection to the old Capone mob and the powerful St. Clair and Madison County Democratic machines.[23]

Powell negotiated with legislators, breeders and racing officials to secure pari-mutuel betting on harness racing under the IRB. Downstater Henry T. "Heinie" Knauf (D-Ladd), president of the U.S. Trotting Association, one of the state's top breeders of standardbreds, and chairman of the Assembly's Agriculture Committee that dealt with racetrack and county fair measures, drew up a bill to legalize pari-mutuels except for July and August to prevent competition with county fairs. The parks got 9 percent of the bets, plus breakage. The state also got to levy a daily $250 license fee on tracks and received 2 percent of the handle. By comparison, thoroughbred tracks then paid a daily $2,500 license fee, and 2 percent of the betting action, while keeping 8 percent of the handle. The new law led to larger purses that would help attract top harness horses and also encourage the breeding industry.[24]

Two tracks opened in 1946 to take advantage of legalized pari-mutuel harness racing. The first was 36-acre Maywood Park, 17 miles west of the Loop, owned by

---

[22] Bill Barnhart and Gene Schlickman, *Kerner: The Conflict of Intangible Rights* (Urbana: University of Illinois Press, 1999), 272.
[23] *CT*, June 21, 1945, 26; Barnhart, and Schlickman, *Kerner*, 88; Robert E. Hartley, *Paul Powell of Illinois: A Lifelong Democrat* (Carbondale: Southern Illinois University Press, 1999), 119–120, 126.
[24] Barnhart and Schlickman, *Kerner*, 89.

Chicagoan Arthur T. Galt, Sr. (1876–1968), an attorney, real estate developer and amateur sulky driver, who constructed a track and grandstand. His partners included several well-known New Yorkers and Chicagoans who put up $350,000, including track president Robert J. Johnson, a New York stockbroker, member of the Chicago Board of Trade, and founding president of Roosevelt Raceway, plus his Long Island racing partner, John DeMeo, who served as vice president. Other New Yorkers involved with Maywood included George M. Levy, his secretary Mrs. Amanda Dooley Abrahams, William Weisman, a Manhattan attorney, and his law partner, legislator Irwin Steingut.[25]

Maywood's breakeven point was a daily take of $75,000, so management was elated on Opening Day, June 6, when 11,320 fans bet $154,977. Maywood was the only Chicago area track used exclusively for harness racing, and was soon considered one of the top half-mile harness tracks in North America, The inaugural 51 day meet was attended by 306,088, $281,000 in purses, and a $5,885,085 handle (a daily average of $115,948), of which the state got $120,741.10. Maywood became so popular that in June 1947 it hosted the first full harness race program televised anywhere. One year later, 414,191 attended the 58 days of racing, wagering $7,702,050, resulting in another profitable meet.[26]

Aurora Downs was the second harness track in metropolitan Chicago. M.G. Farnsworth, CEO of a large Chicago medical supply company headed the Fox Valley Trotting Club that ran the inaugural 39-day meet. The FVTC reopened an old running track following a $200,000 refurbishment. The meet had 81,977 spectators, a mutual handle of $1,690,541, with $36,485.82 to the state, and purses of $166,450. Management indicated it needed a $60,000 daily handle to break even, but only pulled in an average of $43,347.[27]

Aurora enjoyed excellent fall weather in 1947 when it drew 231,426 spectators, over 58 days. The $4,661,316 handle, or more than $80,000 each night, @ @produced a profit of under $12,000. Aurora Downs again finished in the black in 1948, but the tide turned the following year though the 55-day meet drew about 250,000 spectators and a handle of around $6.5 million ($122,000 a day). Expenses rose significantly because of higher administrative costs, larger purses,

---

25 *CT*, October 25, 1953, 1, March 19, 1954, 17.
26 *CT*, June 14, 1971, 16, July 16, 1949, A3; John Hervey, *American Harness Racing* (New York: Ralph Hartenstein, 1948), 2–169; "Chicago Harness: Maywood Park History." Accessed October 27, 2015 http://www.maywoodpark.com/pages/History.cfm; Illinois Harness Racing Commission, *First Annual Report of the Illinois Harness Racing Commission to the Honorable Dwight H. Green, Governor of Illinois*, 1946 (Springfield, IL: Illinois Harness Racing Commission, 1946), 9.
27 Illinois Harness Racing Commission, *First Annual Report*, 26; *CT*, June 2, 1946 A4, June 6, 1946, 29, June 7, 1946, 31, September 17, 1946, 27, September 18, 1946, 29.

and five rainouts, but the bigger problem was the 40-mile commute for Chicago racing fans. Aurora was considered a "flop," and closed. By comparison Maywood in 1949 had a huge handle of $13,359,164, nearly double the previous year.[28]

In 1949 the Democrats took over the Assembly for the first time since 1938, and Powell became its speaker. Powell was closely connected to rich and powerful power brokers looking for good deals, regardless of political persuasion, He employed his clout to become "the state's most powerful booster of horse racing," and would be elected in 1981 to the Illinois Harness Horseman's Association Hall of Fame.[29]

Powell's top associate was Irwin S. "Big Sam" Wiedrick, a sportsman with a spotty career. Wiedrick purchased the Rochester Tribe (later, the Royals) of baseball's International League in the mid-1920s after stealing $110,000 in stocks from a widow. He was arrested and found guilty of a felony which led to him serving 27 months in prison. He was also convicted of failing to pay $10,000 in amusement taxes in 1926 and 1927.[30]

Wiedrick got into harness racing in 1944 when he established the Northville Downs Association, about thirty miles from Detroit. However, the Michigan Racing Board soon barred him from the sport because of his shady past. He moved to Illinois, where he made valuable connections with Paul Powell, William H. Johnston (1901–1977), CEO of Sportsman's Park, a thoroughbred track located in Cicero, a working class town that bordered Chicago, John Stelle (1891–1962), a former lieutenant governor, who had briefly served as governor following the death of Governor Henry Horner (1878–1940). Wiedrick managed operations Maywood from 1946 to 1949 though he was never designated as an officer of the club. This enabled him to circumvent state law that barred anyone from getting a license to run a harness track that had violated a state or federal law.[31]

In 1949 William Johnston sought Powell's help to end restrictions on harness racing so he could book Sportsman's Park for harness events. Powell helped him out by gaining support from the powerful county fair lobby that had considerable clout with downstate legislators, which he needed to end the historic opposition to summer pari-mutuels that limited urban racing, in return for various benefits for breeders and county fairs.[32]

---

28 Hervey, *American Harness Racing*, 143; *CT*, March 5, 1949, A2, July 16, 1949, A3.
29 Hartley, *Powell*, 95.
30 Ibid., 93.
31 *CT*, June 14, 1971, 16; *NYT*, August 29, 1951, 42; Hartley, *Powell*, 93, 119–120, 126; Illinois Harness Racing Commission, *Sixth Annual Report of the Illinois Harness Racing Commission* (Springfield, IL: Illinois Harness Racing Commission, 1951), 20.
32 Hartley, *Powell*, 95.

New pro-harness racing bills were approved virtually unanimously in the 1949 session. Powell's political ally and business partner, Clyde Lee (D-Mt. Vernon), the newly appointed chair of the Agricultural Committee, was very interested in breeding, harness racing, and making county fairs strong. Lee, along with fellow downstaters Clifford C. Hunter (R-Taylorville), and W.P. Westbrook (R-Harrisburg), sponsored a bill empowering the IRB to license harness tracks and raise the takeout from the purses from 11 to 14 percent, and increase the state's share from 2 to 5 percent. The original bill also included an unusual provision to end limitations on the rights of ex-cons to work in the industry, which was aimed at protecting Wiedrick, but it created a furor and was dropped.[33]

Heinie Knauf pushed a bill to permit evening races at pari-mutuel tracks between mid-April and mid-November, which meant legalizing summer harness racing during July and August when county fairs flourished. The measure also eliminated the ban on harness racing within five miles of a flat racing track, enabling Sportsman's Park to add harness racing, but the law still required harness tracks be at least fifty miles apart. Knauf's bill also gave the IRC authority to license tracks when it the served public interest and to tax admissions.[34]

Critics demeaned these quietly introduced measures as "sneaky bills" introduced late in the session so they would attract little or no press coverage. The measures sped through the legislature and were sent to Gov. Adlai Stevenson (1900–1965), a renowned reformer, and future Democratic presidential nominee for final approval. Stevenson needed Powell's support for his own programs and signed the racing acts, promising the new higher tax would bring the state an additional $2.4 million.[35]

Powell biographer Paul Hartley indicates these bills opened the floodgates for Chicago area harness stock owners by permitting pari-mutuel racing at evening harness races at flat tracks. Even before the new laws were enacted, Sportsman's Park incorporated Chicago Downs Association (CDA) on May 4, forming a trust with 100,000 shares held by Johnston and Wiedrick. Sportsman's Park got a license in June to run a 24 day meet under the seemingly ubiquitous Wiedrick, who worked for the CDA until 1971, and soon installed a 700,000-watt lighting system for evening racing. The harness meet began on July 18, with 11,789 fans in attendance, betting $237,812, both opening day records for North American harness racing.[36]

---

33 Ibid., 97–98; *CT*, June 28, 1949, B1.
34 Hartley, *Powell*, 101.
35 *NYT*, August 26, 1951, 42.
36 *CT*, June 28, 1949, B1, July 17, 1949, 4; Hartley, *Powell*, 94–95, 102.

Chicago Downs was a success from the start, quickly securing racing dates previously set aside for downstate tracks. Since the CDA leased Sportsman's Park, it did not need a lot of operating capital to construct a new facility. Johnston and Wiedrick each acted as trustee for one-half of the CDA's stock, which they sold to over 40 carefully chosen individuals, including friends, relatives, business associates, and supportive legislators.

Wiedrick's sales pitch involved wining and dining a legislator and his wife, and then offering a deal to buy stock. The legislator typically begged off, claiming he could not afford the offer. The IRB required that the names of all track's common stock be made public, but state law allowed stockholders to evade that rule by assigning their securities to another person who collected dividends and paid taxes. Wiedrick would turn to the wife and offer her 100 shares at a mere ten cents a share, which could not be turned down. Three months later, a $100 dividend check would arrive, matching the cost of the purchase. The largest share holders were Mrs. Daisy Powell, who bought 16,900 shares for $1,690, producing in four years a 4,000 percent return. The next biggest stockholder was Wiedrick with 15,850 shares. The CDA was extremely successful right from the start, producing a $7,802,851 handle in 1950 and $10,018,953 a year later. Each share then paid $1.75, a return of 1,650 percent.[37]

Chicago's insider trading received national attention in August 1951 during the hearings of the U.S. Senate's Special Committee on Organized Crime, chaired by Tennessee Senator Estes Kefauver (1903–1963) produced a lengthy list of insiders who held stock in Chicago Downs, including nine legislators (or their wives), who had helped pass laws promoting harness racing, including Representatives Powell and Lee, and Senators Frank Ryan (D-Chicago), Everett Peters (R-St. Joseph), Raymond Libonati (D-Chicago), and John W. Fribley (D-Pena). The Kefauver Committee reported that other stockholders included former state attorney general George F. Barrett (1941–1949), Democratic committeeman and former county treasurer Thomas D. Nash, long-time Chicago alderman James "Paddy" Bowler (1875–1957), renowned for his quote "Chicago ain't ready for reform yet." James W. Mulroy, a Pulitzer Prize winning journalist, and assistant to Gov. Stevenson, who bought 1,000 shares (he resigned after the disclosure), Other insiders cited included Powell's secretary and close friend Lucille E. Koval, (1000 shares), Sportsman's Park's auditor, Hugo Bennett (who loaned $80,000 to his pal Chicago mob boss Paul Ricca), and the heirs of the prominent sportsman Charles Bidwill (1895–1947), his sons Charles, Jr., and Bill Bidwill, who each bought 1,000 shares.

---

37 *CT*, June 14, 1971, 16; *NYT*, August 2, 1951, 42.

The IRC and the Sangamon County district attorney followed up the Kefauver Committee with its own investigations, but with negligible results.[38]

Charles Bidwill was an extremely prominent Chicagoan who oversaw the Chicago Business Men's Racing Association that ran Hawthorne Racecourse from 1924 to 1945. He was extremely politically well connected as son of an alderman, and brother of a Republican state senator and clerk of the Chicago Circuit Court. Bidwill was a successful businessman and a wealthy lawyer who was a co-owner of dog tracks in Miami Beach, Tampa and Jacksonville, proprietor of the NFL's Chicago Cardinals from 1932 until his death in 1947, and in the 1940s established the Chicago Bluebirds, a women's professional softball team. More importantly, Bidwill was part of a National Jockey Club group that took over Al Capone's (1899–1947) former dog track in Cicero, and converted it into Sportsman's Park, long identified in the public mind with bootleggers and other gangsters. Following the Kefauver Committee's revelations, the Illinois Harness Racing Commission and the state's attorney of Sangamon County staged their own investigations, but with negligible results.[39]

Powell used his clout for over twenty years to regularly pass major track bills while rejecting those he opposed. In 1955, although no longer Assembly speaker, he got the legislature to reduce the state tax on the racing handle from 6 percent to 4 percent whenever it fell below $300,000, as often happened at the smaller southern Cahokia and Fairmount tracks. Back as speaker in 1960, he passed a bill adding fifteen days to the racing season to ostensibly support state universities which actually received only minor assistance from the additional revenues, and one year later, got a bill passed to enable Marje Everett, the Chicago racing magnate, to move seamlessly into harness racing. Powell's final gift to the sport came in 1968 when as secretary of state he reduced license fees, saving tracks nearly $450,000.[40]

Powell was on the Chicago Downs payroll from 1956–63 for $10,000 a year as a consultant/lobbyist, and later doubled his fee. He regularly corresponded with racing board officials like William Miller, the former long-time chairman of the IRB, who resigned when his syndicate bought Balmoral, and current IRB chairman Thomas Bradley, and also provided friends with passes, stalls, patronage jobs, and invitations to cocktail and dinner parties.[41]

---

38 Hartley, *Powell*, 94, 106–09; *NYT*, August 26, 1951, 42.
39 *CT*, April 20, 1947, A1; *NYT*, August 2, 1951, 42; Hartley, *Powell*, 102–103; Virgil Peterson, *Barbarians in Our Midst: A History of Chicago Crime and Politics* (Boston: Little, Brown, 1952), 290.
40 Hartley, Powell, 117.
41 Ibid., 111–112, 115, 127; Hank Messick, *The Politics of Prosecution: Jim Thompson, Marje Everett, Richard Nixon and the Trial of Otto Kerner* (Ottawa, Ill.: Caroline House Books, 1978), 64.

Powell was heavily involved in downstate harness racing. Cahokia Downs opened in 1954 near Allerton in St. Clair County, with a three-quarter mile track for harness and thoroughbred racing. The meet was hosted by the East St. Louis Jockey Club, whose president John Stelle, had secretly bought stock when the track opened. He and Wiedrick shared consulting fees and took large stock positions in Cahokia Downs, the Fox Valley Trotting Club, and the Mississippi Valley Trotting Association, as well as Sportsman's Park, Suburban Downs, and Maywood.[42]

The Cahokia Downs track was heavily financed as a land trust, a rare, enticing, and unusual investment opportunity unique to Illinois which had the power to issue bonds. Cahokia Downs was an Illinois corporation that owned a landsite, which empowered it to issue $1,400,000 in 10-year first mortgage bonds to build the track and buildings and $600,000 in 19-year debenture notes for operating expenses. Bond holders got 6 percent interest for building projects, and debenture holders got 8 percent for operating expenses.[43]

Powell was deeply involved in the Egyptian Trotting Association (ETA), a paper racing organization that promoted events at established tracks beginning in 1957 at Cahokia Downs. Cahokia's founders organized the ETA to keep their involvement in organizing harness meets kept hidden. The ETA had a poor start, losing $94,228 in its first eight months, mainly because of start up expenses like advertising, and repairs and maintenance at Cahokia. However, the ETA took off in the 1958 season, and then was permitted by the racing commission to transfer its affairs to Maywood Park. By the end of 1963, the ETA had $430,000 in the bank. *Tribune* reporters Ronald Koziol and Thomas Powers argue that it had more political clout than any other state racing association due to such stockholders as Paul Powell, long-time Republican legislator state John W. Lewis, who succeeded Powell as secretary of state, long-time Democratic Congressman Dan Rostenkowski (1928–2010), and Clyde Choate (D-Anna), a Powell disciple, who served 30 years in the state house, including many years as a party leader. Choate was steered by Powell into a stock deal in 1961 that netted him $36,000 in four years. Rostenkowski became a secret stockholder in the ETA in 1957 when he was a state legislator. He went on to serve 36 years in the U.S. House, including 13 as chair of the Ways and Means Committee, his career ended by the Congressional Post Office scandal, a conspiracy to launder Post Office money through stamps and postal vouchers. Rostenkowski pled guilty to mail fraud and received an 18-month sentence.[44]

---

42 Hartley, *Powell*, 93, 119–120, 126; *NYT*, August 26, 1951, 42.
43 Hartley, *Powell*, 102, 122, 131.
44 One source claimed that Rostenkowski made $42,000 on a secret $500 investment on a trotting association; *CT*, September 21, 1971, 1, October 2, 1971, 1, December 2, 1972, W2, February 21, 1973, 7, August 12, 2010, 1; Hartley, *Powell*, 130–133.

Powell was very protective of his secret investments and those of his friends. His own stock certificates were written in Stelle's name, though Powell took the dividends and paid all the taxes. His friends' involvement in racing was secret and legal but reflected their inside position and would be very embarrassing for any politician running for election or holding an appointive position. Track management also wanted the financial arrangements kept secret, worried the IRC would penalize them with crummy racing dates for having humiliated it.[45]

Powell was a particularly good friend to Marje Everett, the owner of Arlington Park and Washington Park. In 1961 he helped pass Senate Bill 717, sponsored by Sens. Arthur J. Bidwill (R-River Forest), and Everett Peters that permitted out-of-state corporations to hold a state racing license and enabled track operators to have more than one license and permitted racing groups to hold meets at another track besides their own. This act was especially advantageous to Everett since her Chicago Thoroughbred Enterprises was already incorporated in Delaware, which provided advantageous tax laws, and she was the only track operator owning multiple tracks. The new law enabled Everett to move thoroughbred dates from Washington Park to Arlington Park.[46]

One year later Marje created the Washington Park Trotting Association (also known as the Washington Park Trotters Association) (WPTA) under president Charles H. Wacker III, a noted horseman, whose father was a wealthy industrialist, and whose grandfather was chairman of the Chicago Plan Commission from 1909 to 1926. The WPTA's first tenant was the politically powerful ETA, which moved over from Maywood in 1961. In the future the pro-Everett IRB consistently granted the WPTA choice racing dates like Labor Day.[47]

Marje gave 49 percent of the stock to Powell to divide among key legislators who between 1961 and 1963 bought stock at $1 a share, which was worth $8.80 a share by the end of 1968. Among the original stockholders, attorney Lynch made $120,000, Wacker, $105,000, and her husband Webb Everett, general manager of California's Golden Gate Fields, in Berkeley, CA., who made $100,000. Share holders who were legislators included Powell ($35,000), Republican Assembly speaker John Lewis, ($15,000), Republican Arthur Bidwill, president pro tem of the Senate (1961–1963) ($72,000), William Pollock Republican minority leader of

---

45 Hartley, *Powell*, 131–132.
46 Ibid., 114–115, 142.
47 *CT*, November 16, 1962, D1, November 17, 1972, 3, December 7, 1972, 2. Wacker was eventually indicted for avoiding $1.9 million in taxes. See David Silverman, "LARGEST TAX-EVASION CASE IN AREA HISTORY," *CT*, August 18, 1983, 1.

the Assembly in 1961 ($35,000) and George Dunne (D-Chicago), Assembly majority leader in 1963 ($20,000). By 1970, the legislators made $446,000.[48]

The biggest winner was James L Hayes, a former Washington Park director, appointed in 1961 to the IRB. In late 1961 after he obtained stock in the CTE, he signed the order granting WPTA racing dates for 1962. He subsequently got more stock that eventually made him $600,000, even though it was illegal for IRB members from owning racing stock while on the board.[49]

Legislators were not made responsible for disclosing stock ownership of $5,000 or more in a company regulated by the state until passage of the Ethics Act of 1967. The first cases were tried four years later in Springfield involved state senators Everett Peters, and Bernie Neistein (D-Chicago) who allegedly held stock in the name of his wife, Alice, but both were found innocent.[50] Just prior to the indictments, Liberal House Democrats introduced legislation to abolish secret land trusts and require public disclosure of ownership of horse racing interests. The goal was to prevent secret racetrack holdings, including by a trust or nominees, and to prohibit political campaign contributions by racetrack interests, including track concessionaires. Penalties included a fine of up to $20,000 and loss of racing dates. The bill passed the House, 159–0, but never got through the Senate.[51]

Two months after Powell died on October 10, 1970, his executor announced the discovery of $750,000 in a shoe box, two leather briefcases, and three steel strongboxes in the closet of the secretary of state's suite in Springfield's St. Nicholas Hotel. An additional $50,000 was found in his state office. When the estate was finally added up two years later, Powell's assets were worth more than $3 million, plus 61,290 shares of stock in seven Illinois racetracks, although he never earned a salary of over $30,000 during his long governmental career.[52]

The shoe box scandal led to a year long IRS probe in 1971 and investigations by four federal grand juries to discover if politicians were getting discounted horse racing stock in exchange for favors. They targeted an investment company operating out of an attorney's La Salle Street offices and a secret bank trust in Alton, where they uncovered evidence of past and current politicians holding racing stock in hidden trusts and dummy names. The Federal Agents found that 25,000 shares of Chicago Horse Racing, Inc. (CHR), which raced at Washington Park, listed in the name of Holders Investment, Inc. in care of its president,

---

48 *CT*, November 16, 1972, 3; Messick, *Politics of Prosecution*, 63–64.
49 Messick, *Politics of Prosecution.*, 62, 64.
50 *CT*, December 9, 1971, 1, December 12, 1971, B6, July 20, 1972, 3.
51 *CT*, November 11, 1971, A3.
52 *CT*, February 24, 2013, 1.

attorney Leo Arnstein, worth $154,500 ($6.18 a share), and another 7,500 shares in a local bank.[53]

The investigators also found that other prominent politicians still had major holdings in the Chicago turf. Joseph E. Knight, former director of the Illinois Department of Financial Institutions, had 12,000 shares in CHR and 3,000 shares of the Balmoral Jockey Club (BJC). A federal grand jury discovered that two former law partners of Mayor Daley, Circuit Court Judge George J. Schaller and Federal District Court Judge William J. Lynch, still had substantial holdings. Schaller had 1,000 shares in the CHR, 6,200 shares of the BJC and 1,000 in Washington Park, while Lynch had 725 shares of the BJC. In addition, the grand jury learned that former representative Clyde Lee held 7,000 shares of Washington Park in the name of Judge Schaller.[54]

On September 27, 1971 Gov. Richard Ogilvie indicated widespread public concern over recent disclosures of "questionable regulation of racing in past years," and demanded that the General Assembly and IRB "lift the veil of secrecy" that shielded immense profits to politicians. He wanted to ban the ownership of racing associations by elected and appointed government officers and prohibit nominees or require disclosure of beneficial owners. Ogilvie sought a central registry for stock transfer records and periodic publication of ownership interests, the banning of secret trusts and political contributions, and warned that without strong remedies, he might try to either ban racing or have the state take it over. However, no major legislative reforms were achieved for years to come in harness racing.[55]

In 1971 Federal Judge Otto Kerner, Jr., the former governor of Illinois was indicted for pressuring racetrack owner Marje Lindheimer Everett to sell him stock in the Chicago Thoroughbred Enterprise. Kerner came from a political family. His father had served as the state's Attorney General and as a judge on the United States Court of Appeals for the Seventh Circuit, while his father-in-law was former Chicago mayor Anton Cermak, the man who made the modern Cook County Democratic machine but was assassinated in 1933. Kerner graduated from Brown University and Northwestern University Law School, rose to major general in the reserves, and served with distinction as United States Attorney for the Northern District of Illinois (1947–1954), and judge in the Cook County Circuit Court. In 1960 he defeated incumbent William G. Stratton in the gubernatorial election and was re-elected in 1964 over moderate Republican

---

53 *CT*, June 10, 1971, 1, June 5, 1971, 1, June 7, 1971, 12, June 12, 1971, 4, June 14, 1971, 16, June 25, 1971, 8, February 21, 1973, 7.
54 *CT*, June 10, 1971, 1.
55 *CT*, September 28, 1971, N4. See also *CT*, May 24, 1975, W5, June 14, 1975, W_B24.

Charles H. Percy. Kerner promoted economic development, education, mental health services, and equal access to jobs and housing. In July 1967, he chaired the National Advisory Commission on Civil Disorders, and the following year was appointed to the United States Court of Appeals for the Seventh Circuit. He left the governor's mansion with a reputation for integrity and leadership.[56]

The main figure in Chicago racing in the 1960s was Marje Lindheimer Everett, whose father Ben Lindheimer had groomed her to take over his racing empire comprised of Arlington, Washington Park, and Balmoral. Marje, like her father, was an aggressive marketer and a ruthless and demanding boss, who in 1968 pushed out bothersome minor stockholders even though they were her father's friends. Marje continued many of her father's policies, such as employing a slush fund to develop valuable relations with politicians and journalists to support her interests. According to journalists Bill Barnhart and Gene Schlickman, "she cast herself as a victim of those who would do her – and therefore Illinois racing – wrong."[57]

Journalists Steve Corman and Jack Swanson worked for Marje from 1965 to 1968 when they ghostwrote stories for Chicago journalists: "Marje Everett handled the press as she handled politicians, wooing them not with stock profits, but with gift certificates, Christmas presents, sumptuous luncheons, cash payments for participation in promotional events, and summer jobs for reporters' children"[58]

Marje's financial arrangements with politicians were not secret. In the fall of 1960, Marje donated $45,000 to Otto Kerner's first gubernatorial campaign, and also hired Theodore Isaacs, Kerner's chief advisor, and future Director of Revenue, to close her father's estate. Her intent was to get their undivided attention and make it clear that she represented the best interests of Illinois and horse racing. She expected that Kerner would promote her racing enterprises by pushing the IRB for special treatment, particularly the awarding of choice racing dates racing dates.[59]

Marje's chief advisor at the time was William Miller, an attorney and self-made millionaire horse breeder, who Gov. Adlai Stevenson appointed to the IRB in 1951. She also had important support from William Miller, whose power over racing

---

[56] For an excellent biography of Kerner, see Bill Barnhart and Gene Schlickman, *Kerner*.
[57] Ibid., 269 (quote), 272, 275; Whitney Tower, "The Racing Lady of Chicago," *Sports Illustrated* (August 20, 1962): 38–40, 45–46; Steve Anderson, "Everett, former Hollywood Park chairwoman, dies at age 90." *Daily Racing Form*, March 23, 2012. Accessed May 17, 2014. http://www.drf.com/news/everett-former-hollywood-park-chairwoman-dies-age-90; Messick, *Politics of Prosecution*, 28–29.
[58] Steven Corman and Jack Swanson, "Cozy Times in the Press Box," *Chicago Journalism Review* 4 (December 1971): 3–6.
[59] Barnhart and Schlickman, *Kerner*, 110, 112, 269, 272

increased after the state merged the IHRC into the IRB in 1965 to achieve regulatory efficiently, leaving him in charge of both harness and thoroughbred racing.[60]

Miller and Everett agreed that the time had come to break off from the Republicans, and so she fired her legal representatives, the prestigious, venerable and very Republican Kirkland law firm, and replaced them with Democrats like George J. Schaller and William J. Lynch[61]

In 1966, Kerner and Revenue Director Theodore Isaacs each bought 25 shares CTE for $25,000 from Everett, the stock price back in 1962. However, when the sale was consummated, the shares were actually worth $150,000. Marje drew up a "letter of intent" at the time of transaction which falsely carried a 1962 date. Neither Kerner nor Isaacs placed any undue pressure on her to complete the deal. Her intent was to get favored treatment from the state, including choice racing dates and construction of extra highway exits for Arlington Park. Everett's sale of stock at a bargain price was unseemly, had all the look of a bribe, and her falsification of the transfer date was a crime. Marje later claimed she thought that trading stock for political favors was simply business as usual in her industry. Marje subsequently filed a loss on her 1966 taxes on these transactions, but the IRS disallowed it since her paperwork indicated the transaction occurred in 1962.[62]

Six months later, Kerner and Isaacs traded their CTE holdings for 5,000 shares each in Everett's Balmoral Jockey Club. One year later they sold that stock for $30 a share, collecting a profit of $125,000 each on their original $25,000 investment. Kerner and Isaacs also turned a profit of $22,400 apiece within a ten-month period on other Everett investments.[63]

Marje regularly sold stock to legislators for their support. The one politician who rejected her offer was Abner Mikva (1926–2016), a distinguished Chicago attorney who served five terms in the state house in the 1960s because he considered it a bribe. Mikva later served four-terms in the Congress and fifteen years on the Court of Appeals for the District of Columbia, retiring to become White House Counsel under Bill Clinton. Mikva wanted to raise the state tax on pari-mutuel betting and ran afoul of Governor Kerner who felt such a tax would hinder track patronage and lower state revenues.[64]

---

60 Ibid. 129, 269–70, 272.
61 Ibid., 111, 129, 269–70, 272; "Balmoral Park History." Accessed May 17, 2014. http://www.balmoralpark.com/History.cfm?Cat=G; Messick, *Politics of Prosecution*, 53, 57; Barnhart and Schlickman, *Kerner*, 269.
62 "Chicago: The Racing Scandal," *Time* 98 (December 13, 1971): 29–30 Barnhart and Schlickman, *Kerner*, 303, 309; Robert E. Hartley, *Big Jim Thompson of Illinois* (Chicago: Rand McNaly, 1979), 52.
63 Hartley, *Big Jim Thompson*, 52; Messick, *Politics of Prosecution*, 91.
64 Barnhart and Schlickman, *Kerner*, 270.

Illinois's racing's attendance and gross receipts had stagnated in the 1950s, but once Marje took over, both grew steadily. The state profited from the admission tax on spectators, its share of the handle, and half of the breakage fee. State revenues more than doubled from $18 million in 1960 to $40 million eight years later, a handsome appreciation compared to other racing states.[65] Everett did very well with the IRB, the governor, and the legislature when it came to getting favored treatment. For example, bills passed on her behalf permitted her to employ the CTE, an out of state corporation for her racing enterprises that consolidated her harness and thoroughbred businesses. In addition, legislative proposals that would hurt her financial interests were regularly defeated.[66]

Marje sold control of the CTE in 1968 to Gulf & Western Industries, an American conglomerate formed in 1958 by Charles Bluhdorn, in an exchange of stock valued at over $25 million. She remained as CEO, signing a ten year a contract that paid her a salary between $50,000 and $150,000 a year, plus expenses, but would be eased out of the company by February 1970.[67]

One year after Marje traded her CTE stock, she developed a mentee-mentor relationship with George Mahin, former head of the Better Government Association, a reform organization founded in 1923 to investigate municipal corruption and promote efficient government. Mahin then was running incoming Governor Richard Ogilvie's transition team, and went on to his Director of Revenue. Marje complained to Mahin that ruthless forces in racing were oppressing her, compelling her to pay tribute to prominent politicians in return for favorable racing dates, a violation of the Hobbs Act of 1947, a federal anti-racketeering act that criminalized the use of extortion to hinder interstate commerce. Marje blamed Miller for making her sell stock to Kerner and Isaacs to influence them. Mahin introduced her to FBI agent Jack Walsh, then involved in the Chicago Special Project, President Richard Nixon's program to investigate the Cook County Democratic machine, renamed in 1970 Project CRIMP (Crime, Racketeering, Influence, Money, and Politics). The allegations against Kerner stoked interest in Washington, but since nearly everyone had high regard for him, the investigation proceeded very slowly.[68]

---

65 Ibid., 270–272. On Powell, see *CT*, February 26, 1973, C15.
66 Barnhart and Schlickman, *Kerner*, 129, 269–70, 272.
67 *CT*, February 27, 1970, C1.
68 Better Government Association, "History," https://www.bettergov.org/history. Accessed September 21 2019; Barnhart and Schlickman, *Kerner*, 260–261, 273, 275; *CT*, July 30, 1971, 1. Journalist Hank Messick argues that the effort to get Kerner was largely propelled by Nixon's hatred of the Daley machine, a view supported by Nixon aide Charles Colson. See Messick, *Politics of Prosecution*, 4–5; "Interview with James Thompson," # IST-A-L-2013-054.06 Interview # 6: June 12, 2014, 238, Abraham Lincoln Presidential Library (ALPL). Accessed August 17, 2018. Https://www2.illinois.gov/alplm/library/collections/oralhistory/illinoisstatecraft/Thompson/

Federal tax agents were already aware of the Kerner-Everett nexus. A routine 1970 audit of Kerner's 1967 tax return listed a big profit from the "Chicago Company" actually the CTE. Their suspicions aroused, the IRS then checked Isaacs's return, which also reported a profit from his sale of Chicago Company stock. The IRS audited Everett, and questioned some of her business expense write offs, which she justified as part of the culture of Illinois race track business. However, the agents considered this bribery, and not a legitimate deduction. When Marje was asked to explain this, she blew the whistle on Kerner and Isaacs. On January 7, 1971 she signed an affidavit, admitting to having paid the governor and his chief advisor with undervalued stock to gain favored treatment for her racing investments.[69]

A federal investigation was instigated in late spring, with Kerner twice testifying before a Chicago federal grand jury investigating the alleged racing scandal. The Justice Department was very cautious about going after a sitting federal judge in a case rated only a 50 percent chance of conviction.[70] Kerner insisted that he had not intervened in the allocation of racing dates on behalf of Everett or helped her secure nearby highway exits. The racing investigation was not limited to Kerner and uncovered a long list of politicians holding racing stock, but not Mayor Richard Daley, who explained: "I never have and I never will." Some 100 witnesses were called, including Miller, Isaacs, Judges Lynch and Schaller, and Joseph Knight.[71]

On December 15, 1971, Attorney General John N. Mitchell and U.S. Attorney for the Northern District of Illinois James Thompson announced that Kerner, Isaacs, Knight, Miller and his personal secretary, Faith McInturf, were indicted on charges of conspiracy, using the mail with intent to distribute the proceeds of bribery, and using interstate facilities to further bribery and mail fraud. Kerner was also charged with perjury before a grand jury, making false statements to the IRS, and tax evasion.[72]

Documents/ThompsonJam/Thompson_Jam_PFNL_Vol_II.pdf. However, Thompson and John Mitchell always denied this, and other researchers familiar with Nixon's archives have never found any evidence. See Hartley, *Big Jim*, 43–44; and Nicholas Sarantakes, Luke Nichter and Rick Moss, e-mails to the author, 5 March 2019.

69 Barnhart and Schlickman, *Kerner*, 284. Mayor Richard Daley in an interview claimed he had been offered the same deal as Kerner. See Frank Sullivan, *Legend: The Only Inside Story about Major Richard J. Daley* (Chicago: Bonus Books, 1989), 221.

70 "Chicago: The Racing Scandal," 30; Messick, *Politics of* Prosecution, 47; Barnhart and Schlickman, *Kerner*, 306.

71 *CT*, June 9, 1971, 1, June 10, 1971, 1, June 11, 1971, 1; Messick, *Politics of Prosecution*, 105, 127; Adam Cohen and Elizabeth Taylor, *American Pharaoh: Mayor Richard J. Daley – His Battle for Chicago and the Nation* (New York: Warner Books, 2000), 517 (quote).

72 Barnhart and Schlickman, *Kerner*, 315.

Marje Everett was the state's star witness, having personally participated in the alleged bribery. Though there was not much question about her culpability, Thompson made a deal with her to testify for the state in return for immunity, because, from his perspective, Kerner was the big fish in the case. Marje at the time of the investigation was deeply involved with California's Hollywood Park in Ingleside, having received 10 percent of its stock (65,000 shares, worth $3 million) from G&W as part of the sale of CTE. She applied to become a track director late in 1971, but the California Racing Board (CRB) was worried about her reputation, and specifically about her involvement with Kerner. Thompson responded to inquiries from the board, explaining that "Mrs. Everett was a public minded citizen and that certain facts of the investigation could not be disclosed because of the pending trial." Her application was approved.[73]

Two months prior to going to trial, Thompson dropped indictments against Joseph Knight because of illness, and also Miller and Faith McInturf, because Miller promised to testify for the state in return for immunity. Miller was facing his own criminal indictment and an IRS bill for $2.8 million for back taxes and penalties. Thompson originally intended to argue that Miller had been Everett's agent enabling the racing queen to "ingratiate herself on a continuing basis" with the political elite but dropped that theory to concentrate on just Kerner and Isaacs.[74]

As the trial unwound, with Kerner testifying on his own behalf, Assistant Prosecutor Sam Skinner argued that Kerner had lied to the IRS and later lied on the witness stand to conceal the bribery conspiracy that enabled him to put up $15,079 of his own money and end up with a 401 percent return ($144,721). Skinner also showed that in 1961 Kerner approved a racing bill designed to enable Everett to organize the CTE, move all flat racing to Arlington, and open Washington Park for trotting. The first payoff came in 1966 when Kerner paid 40 cents a share for his stock, one-fifth of fair market value. The stock seven months later paid a 20-cent dividend and was sold in May 1967 for $2 a share. Kerner later exchanged that stock for BJC stock of equal value, that he sold for $150,000.[75]

---

[73] *CT*, April 12, 1972, 1; Bill Dwyer, "Marje Everett Dies at 90; Legendary Figure in Horse Racing," *Los Angeles Times*, March 24, 2012; "Interview with Thompson," 238–240, ALPL. Accessed August 17, 2018. Https://www2.illinois.gov/alplm/library/collections/oralhistory/illinoisstatecraft/Thompson/Documents/ThompsonJam/Thompson_Jam_PFNL_Vol_II.pdf; "Kerner: The Trial and Conviction." Governor's Conference on Otto Kerner, November 2, 2013, ALPL, Springfield, IL. Accessed March 22, 2019. https://www.youtube.com/watch?v=PxMNahvgSG
[74] *CT*, January 18, 1973, 10. February 20, 1973, 6 (quote); 315. Barnhart and Schlickman, *Kerner*, 315;
[75] *CT*, September 12, 1972, 1, February 15, 1973, 3.

Kerner and Isaacs were convicted on February 19, 1973 of all 19 counts. Kerner was found guilty of receiving lucrative racing stock in return for valuable favors for the racing interests, evading income tax on $87,000 of profits money made from the sale of stock, and lying about that matter to the IRS, and lying to a federal grand jury about his stock purchases and his role in the allocation of racing dates. Kerner and Isaacs both received 3-year prison sentences and a $50,000 fine. Kerner shortly thereafter resigned his judgeship to avoid the ignominy of impeachment. Kerner was released after just seven months because of ill health (he died of lung cancer one year later), and the empathy of the prosecutors who felt he had stained his exceptional career, had served as much time as others convicted of a similar crime, and that his sad example would become a sufficient deterrent for future white collar criminals.[76]

The politics of Illinois racing in the early 1970s was an embarrassment. A 1973 legislative investigation asserted that "the State's system of regulation is outdated, inefficient, and fraught with potentialities for mismanagement and abuse ... Since its inception, the Illinois racing board has ruled racing in Illinois with an iron hand. Unfortunately, the board has never possessed the requisite degree of racing experience to temper its positions and to plan its own actions." The assertion that the IRB "employed an iron hand" was laughable. A second investigation one year later concluded that Illinois racing was "a forum for three vested interests—the state, the racing associations and the horsemen. Each ... followed a course of self enrichment." Frederick C. Klein, sports columnist for the *Wall Street Journal* added a fourth element – many individual legislators and state officials. According to Klein, "No state ... surpasses Illinois in the variety and mischievousness of political involvement in horse racing."[77] Yet nothing was done to compel public disclosure that racing associations disclose a list of all stockholders, or that of office holders disclose their non salary sources of income.

The Kerner scandal and all the dicey politics behind Illinois racing was a local and national embarrassment. When an outstanding public servant like Kerner was convicted of crimes in office, the public's confidence in their public officials becomes very shaky. Unfortunately, Illinois did not seem to learn. Three subsequent Illinois governors have ended up in prison. Democrat Dan Walker (1973–1977) was sentenced to prison for seven years for bank fraud and served 18 months.

---

[76] *CT*, May 10, 1976, 1, April 1, 1973, 1, February 1, 1998.
[77] Illinois Legislative Investigating Commission, "Illinois Horse Racing: A Study of Legislation and Criminal Practices, 1974; Illinois Racing Board Controversy: A Report to the Illinois General Assembly," March 1973, quoted in Barnhart and Schlickman, *Kerner*, 272–273; Frederick C. Klein, "A State Squeeze on Racing," *Wall Street Journal*, June 1, 1972, 16.

Republican George H. Ryan (1999–2003) served five years in prison for obstructing an investigation into the licensing of unqualified truckers while secretary of state, as well as lying to federal agents, and trading state contracts for personal gifts. Finally, Democrat Rod Blagojevich (2003–2009), was impeached for corruption in office, and sentenced to prison for 14 years for soliciting bribes for political appointments and extorting bribes from a children's hospital and racing interests seeking state financing. He shook down John Johnston, an owner of Maywood and Balmoral Park racetracks for a $100,000 campaign donation in return for a supporting bill to benefit the racing industry.[78]

The Kerner case did not have as big an impact on Chicago politics as Project CRIMP, one of the most successful efforts to fight urban machine corruption. Several prominent Cook County machine Democrats were indicted and sent to jail including City Councilman Ed Keane, the number two man in the machine, who served 22 months for mail fraud. County Clerk Edward J. Barrett (1955–1973) was convicted of taking kickbacks from a voting machine company, income tax evasion, and mail fraud, sentenced to three years in jail. Circuit Court Clerk Matt Danaher (1968–1974), Daley's point man on patronage, was indicted in a case involving a $400,000 bribery payment from two South Side builders but died before his guilt was determined. Thompson went on to become governor of Illinois in 1977.[79]

Regrettably, Chicago political corruption continues. Since 1972, 30 aldermen have been convicted of crimes related to official duties.[80]

Works Cited

Akers, Dwight. *Drivers Up: The Story of American Harness Racing*. New York: G.P. Putnam's Sons, 1947.
Anderson, Steve. "Everett, former Hollywood Park chairwoman, dies at age 90." *Daily Racing Form*, 23 March 2012. Accessed May 17, 2014. http://www.drf.com/news/everett-former-hollywood-park-chairwoman-dies-age-90.
"Balmoral Park History," http://www.balmoralpark.com/History.cfm?Cat=G. Accessed 17 May 2014.

---

[78] Jeff Coen, and Bob Secter. "Pal Outlines Horse Track Plot," *Chicago Tribune*, June 15, 2010, 11a.
[79] John Kifner, "Investigation of Chicago's No. 2 Democrat Appears to Pose a Serious: Threat to the Daley Machine," *NYT*, April 8, 1973, 68; *CT*, December 16, 1974, 1, April 5, 1977, 1, February 4, 1978, 1; James L. Merriner, *Grafters and Goo Goos: Corruption and Reform in Chicago* (Carbondale: Southern Illinois University Press, 2004), 195–201.
[80] *CT*, March 22, 2019, 4.

Barnhart, Bill, and Gene Schlickman, *Kerner: The Conflict of Intangible Rights* (Urbana: University of Illinois Press, 1999).

"Blagojevich Trial Scorecard." *Chicago Tribune*. June 27, 2010, 11.

Bojarski, Tom. "The Man Behind the Race." *Hoof Beats Magazine* 21 March 2013. Accessed 31 January 2019. http://xwebapp.ustrotting.com/absolutenm/templates/hoofbeats_blog.aspx?articleid=52729&zoneid=75.

"Chicago Harness: Maywood Park History." Accessed October 27, 2015. http://www.maywoodpark.com/pages/History.cfm.

"Chicago: The Racing Scandal." *Time* 98 (December 13, 1971): 29–30.

Chicago Tribune, 1945–1974.

Coen, Jeff, and Bob Secter. "Pal Outlines Horse Track Plot." *Chicago Tribune*, June 15, 2010, 11a.

Cohen, Adam, and Elizabeth Taylor. *American Pharaoh: Mayor Richard J. Daley – His Battle for Chicago and the Nation*. New York: Warner Books, 2000.

Corman, Steven, and Jack Swanson. "Cozy Times in the Press Box." *Chicago Journalism Review* 4 (December 1971): 3–6.

Hartley, Robert E. *Big Jim Thompson of Illinois*. Chicago: Rand McNaly, 1979.

Hartley, Robert E. *Paul Powell of Illinois: A Lifelong Democrat*. Carbondale: Southern Illinois University Press, 1999.

"Harness Racing and New York's Ethics Laws." Accessed 1 February 2019. http:///www.albanylaw.edu/media/user/glc/harnessracingandnewyorksethicslaws.pdf.

Hervey, John. *American Harness Racing*. New York: Ralph Hartenstein, 1948.

Hoffman, Dean. *Harness Racing in New York State: A History of Trotters, Tracks and Horsemen*. Charleston, SC: The History Press, 2012.

Illinois Harness Racing Commission. *First Annual Report of the Illinois Harness Racing Commission to the Honorable Dwight H. Green, Governor of Illinois, 1946*. Springfield, IL: Illinois Harness Racing Commission, 1946.

Illinois Harness Racing Commission. *Sixth Annual Report of the Illinois Harness Racing Commission*.Springfield, IL: Illinois Harness Racing Commission, 1951.

Illinois Legislative Investigating Commission. "Illinois Horse Racing: A Study of Legislation and Criminal Practices." 1974.

Illinois Racing Board Controversy. "A Report to the Illinois General Assembly." March 1973.

"Interview with James Thompson." # IST-A-L-2013-054.06. Interview # 6: June 12, 2014. Abraham Lincoln Presidential Library. Accessed August 17, 2018. https://www2.illinois.gov/alplm/library/collections/oralhistory/illinoisstatecraft/Thompson/Documents/ThompsonJam/Thompson_Jam_PFNL_Vol_II.pdf.

"Kerner: The Trial and Conviction." Governor's Conference on Otto Kerner." November 2, 2013, Abraham Lincoln Presidential Library, Springfield, IL. Accessed March 22, 2019. https://www.youtube.com/watch?v=PxMNahvgSGM.

Kifner, John. "Investigation of Chicago's No. 2 Democrat Appears to Pose a Serious. Threat to the Daley Machine." *New York Times*, April 8, 1973, 68.

Klein, Frederick C. "A State Squeeze on Racing." *Wall Street Journal*, June 1, 1972, 16.

"MARJE EVERETT RECALLED ON HRTV'S INSIDE INFORMATION: MARJE EVERETT THIS SUNDAY, JULY 1 AT 11:30 P.M. ET." Accessed January 26, 2017. http://www.tvg2.com/marje-everett-recalled-on-hrtvs-inside-information-marje-everett-this-sunday-july-1-at-1130-pm-et/.

Merringer, James L. *Grafters and Goo Goos: Corruption and Reform in Chicago*. Carbondale: Southern Illinois University Press, 2004.

Messick, Hank. *The Politics of Prosecution: Jim Thompson, Marje Everett, Richard Nixon & the Trial of Otto Kerner*. Ottawa, IL: Caroline House Books, 1978. *New York Times*, 1945–1972.

"NCAA Football Attendance Records." Accessed May 23, 2019. http://fs.ncaa.org/Docs/stats/football_records/DI/2010/Attendance.pdf.

Peterson, Virgil. *Barbarians in Our Midst: A History of Chicago Crime and Politics*. Boston: Little, Brown, 1952.

Riess, Steven A. "The Cyclical History of Horse Racing: The USA's Oldest and (Sometimes) Most Popular Spectator Sport." In *American National Pastimes – A History*, eds. Mark Dyreson and Jaime Schultz, 29–54. New York: Routledge, 2014.

Riess, Steven A. "Horse Racing in the Windy City, 1945–1980." Paper read at the American Historical Association. January 4, 2019.

Riess, Steven A. "In the Ring and Out: Professional Boxing in New York, 1896–1920." In *Sport in America: New Historical Perspectives*, ed. Donald Spivey. Westport, CT: Greenwood Press, 1985.

Riess, Steven A. *City Games: The Evolution of American Urban Society and the Rise of Sports*. Urbana: University of Illinois Press, 1989.

Riess, Steven A. *The Sport of Kings and the Kings of Crime: Horse Racing, Politics, and Crime in New York, 1865–1913*. Syracuse: Syracuse University Press, 2011.

Riess, Steven A. *Touching Base: Professional Baseball and American Culture in the Progressive Era*, rev. ed. Urbana, IL: University of Illinois Press, 1999.

Riordan, William L. Riordan, ed. New York: Dutton: 1963.

Sarantakes, Nicholas, Luke Nichter and Rick Moss. e-mails to author, March 5, 2019.

Silverman, David. "LARGEST TAX-EVASION CASE IN AREA HISTORY," *Chicago Tribune*, August 18, 1983, 1.

Sullivan, Frank. *Legend: The Only Inside Story about Major Richard J. Daley*. Chicago: Bonus Books, 1989.

Tower, Whitney. "The Racing Lady of Chicago." *Sports Illustrated*, August 20, 1962: 38–40, 45–46.

Tom Heenan
3 The Great Australian 'Sting': How and Why Melbourne Became the World's Sporting Capital

In April 2016, *SportBusiness International* selected Australia's second city and the Victorian capital, Melbourne, as the decade's Ultimate Sports Business City. For many local politicians and sports industry boosters, it confirmed Melbourne's place as the world's sporting capital. The Victorian state government gloated that Melbourne was awarded "the one-off gong ahead of Berlin, London, New York and, of course, [its great rival] Sydney." Melbourne won *SportsBusiness'* annual awards in 2006, 2008 and 2010, and in 2016 added 'gongs' in the Ultimate Sports Large City and Best Venues categories. Sports Minister, John Eren, was not holding back. "The eyes of the world are on Melbourne all-year round," he suggested, and the city was "top of the bucket list of sports fans right around the globe."[1] Melbourne does stage a Grand Slam and Grand Prix, and the world's richest handicap horserace, the Melbourne Cup, but it is not a London, New York or even a Manchester; cities that house global sporting brands with global followings. Nonetheless, Melbourne's media, sports administrators and public swallowed Eren's line. Melbourne's sports 'Mafia' can throw a good sports party on the public credit card, but the city is hardly top of most people's "bucket list" and certainly not the world's sporting capital.

So why have so many Melburnians fallen for this spin? The answer lies in Melbourne's rich sporting heritage which has been packaged and commodified by a private-public clique of entrepreneurial spin-doctors. Melbourne was once Australia's capital, and financial and manufacturing heartland, but by the 1980s money and political power had moved to Sydney. Like a fading grandee, Melbourne was left with its sporting memories. It retained the mantle of Australia's sporting capital based on its past glories. The Melbourne Cricket Ground (MCG), arguably the city's most famous landmark, staged the first cricket Test match between Australia and England, and Olympic and Commonwealth games. Melburnians invented their own football code, Australian rules, and exported it across Australia's south. Melbourne has been the Australian Open tennis tournament's traditional home since 1972, and houses some of the

---

[1] John Eren, "Melbourne: The Sporting Capital of the World," Media Release, Victorian State Government Printer, April 21, 2016.

https://doi.org/10.1515/9783110679397-003

world's finest sand-belt golf courses. Despite this rich sporting history, Melbourne is a peripheral player, globally. Since the early 1980s, politicians, sports industry boosters and property developers have drawn on this heritage to re-image Melbourne around sport. To justify splurging public monies on sporting infrastructure and events, this cabal has peddled the sporting capital line to a largely unquestioning public.

Like many traditional manufacturing cities, Melbourne was hit by the recessions and neoliberal economic shock therapies of the 1970s and 1980s. In the early 1970s, protected and high labor-cost manufacturing industries employed 30% of Victoria's workforce. With the economy stagnating and Britain entering the European Common Market, the Whitlam Federal Labor government, seeking stronger trade ties with Asia, slashed tariffs by 25%. The impact was immediately felt across Melbourne's heavily protected manufacturing industries. Between 1971–1981 manufacturing jobs declined by 33%. By 1982, another 33% disappeared as the economy slid into recession, and the impact spread to other sectors. Between 1972–82, approximately 7000 jobs were lost in Melbourne's retail sector. Particularly effected were the inner city shopping strips, where retail jobs declined by 25%. By the early 1980s, these strips and their surrounding neighborhoods were emptying, leaving growing numbers of abandoned shops and warehouses.[2]

In 1981, a reformist state Labor government under John Cain was elected in Victoria after almost 30 years of conservative Liberal Party rule. Though predisposed to Keynesianism, Cain came to power as neoliberal shock therapies were being introduced to spark Western economies after a decade of stagflation. Restrictive trade practices and controls on global capital flows were liberalized, while governments decreased their tax-bases to stimulate business and attract footloose capital. In 1983, the Hawke Labor Government was elected, nationally. Unlike Cain, Bob Hawke (1929–2019) and his treasurer, Paul Keating, embraced neoliberal reforms, cutting tariffs, further gutting Melbourne's manufacturing base, while deregulating the banking system. Foreign banks entered the Australian market, with the majority being located in Sydney, causing financial sector jobs to flow from Melbourne to the more globally connected harbor city. These developments impacted Melbourne's CBD and inner-city industrial neighborhoods. Post-war suburbanization had seen the city sprawl outwards. This movement, coupled with inner-city manufacturing's decline,

---

[2] Seamus O'Hanlon, "The Events City: Sport, Culture and the Transformation of Inner Melbourne, 1977–2005," *Urban History Review* 37, no. 2 (2009): 30–31.

saw Melbourne's inner suburban population drop to 75% of 1971 levels by the mid-1980s.[3]

Fearing that Melbourne faced the economic deterioration and social dislocation of North American and British cities, the Cain Government sought to reinvigorate the CBD and inner suburbs by reinventing Melbourne as a 'bread-and-circus' city. The groundwork was laid by the preceding Hamer Liberal Government and Victoria's main planning authority, the Melbourne and Metropolitan Board of Works (MMBW). In 1977, it released two reports forecasting that manufacturing's demise could push Melbourne's unemployment levels to 20%, resulting in the inner urban decay and "social unrest" of rustbelt British and American cities. As Seamus O'Hanlon explains, a new strategy was devised centered on the provision of "services, spectacle and consumption," which was implemented by the Cain government.[4] Outlined in the 1984 report, *Victoria, the next step*, the strategy focused on Melbourne's strengths, which included culture and sport, and recommended they be integrated with tourism and the wider economy.[5] Given Melbourne's rich heritage, sport was earmarked for investment. As the report noted, Melbourne housed the headquarters of five of the six largest sports in Australia and world-class facilities. It envisaged that the local football code's Grand Final, the Australian Open and the Melbourne Cup could be used to place-market Melbourne nationally and internationally, create employment, and lure tourists and footloose capital to the city. The government would pump public monies into revitalizing and gentrifying the city center through arts festivals and sport spectaculars. Abandoned industrial sites would be redeveloped within a five-kilometer radius of the CBD. A major focus was the Yarra River's southern bank. Bordering the CBD, it was a largely abandoned industrial-maritime area. The Hamer government had located there the National Gallery and Arts Center, but it remained an under-utilized part of the city. In 1986, the Cain Government announced that Southbank – as it became known – would be redeveloped for housing, commerce, tourism and the arts. It was to become the city's tourism and cultural hub, as the government sought to promote Melbourne as a "festival city."[6]

But sport was the main game. As Melbourne was considered Australia's sporting capital, the strategy played to its competitive strength. Though Melbourne housed the country's best sporting infrastructure, many sites were well past

---

[3] Ibid., 36.
[4] Ibid., 30–31.
[5] State Government of Victoria, *Victoria: The Next Step: Economic Opportunities and Initiatives for the 1980s,* April 9, 1984.
[6] O'Hanlon, "The Events City," 34.

their used-by-dates. The landmark MCG had no light towers and was ringed by ageing grandstands. The then Victorian Football League (VFL) – the forerunner of the Australian Football League (AFL) – was planning to shift the Australian Rules' Grand Final to its ground, Waverley Park, on Melbourne's outer suburban eastern fringe. It was poorly serviced by public transport, but owned outright by the VFL. Revenues from matches played there were not split with the Melbourne Cricket Club, as occurred at the MCG, but were retained by the VFL. Football drew large crowds and consumed much local media space, and therefore, it was essential in the government's strategy of reinvigorating the city-center. To stop the drift of showcase games to the ground, the government refused a VFL request for a rail link to Waverley, installed lights at the MCG and initiated plans for the latter's redevelopment. The government secured an agreement with the VFL that a minimum of 45 games would be played at the MCG each season, and a commitment that the Grand Final would stay at the ground.[7]

The Cain government's greatest coup, however, was saving the Australian Open tennis tournament. It was the basket-case Grand Slam until the tournament relocated from leafy suburban Kooyong to Flinders Park on the CBD's edge in 1988. A private members' club, Kooyong had been the Open's permanent home since 1972, but it and the Open had seen better days. The facilities were poor and tennis' big names by-passed the tournament, prompting warnings from the International Tennis Federation that it would remove the tournament's Grand Slam status. Tennis Australia (TA) gave Kooyong an ultimatum; invest in upgrading the facilities or lose the tournament. In July 1983, members rejected the proposal and TA revoked the club's contract to host the tournament long-term.

Faced with mounting international pressure and rumors that Sydney wanted the tournament, the Cain government announced in March 1984 the construction of a stadium at Flinders Park. Cain recognized the tournament's economic potential and its role in promoting Melbourne internationally as one of the world's foremost sports cities, alongside "the big players" – Paris, London and New York.[8] The Flinders Park development would be publicly funded and cutting-edge. The main stadium would have a retractable roof, a first for Grand Slam venues. The project's costs were initially estimated at $AUD 53 million, but promptly blew-out to $AUD 83 million.[9] To lessen costs, the government and TA

---

[7] Alistair John, *Sport City: A Critical Analysis of Melbourne's Sportscape* (PhD diss., Victoria University, 2015), 186.

[8] Ibid., 105.

[9] Alistair John, Bob Stewart and Brent McDonald, "Mixed Doubles: Political Hegemony, Urban Entrepreneurialism and the Australian Open Tennis Championship," *The International Journal of the History of Sport* 20, no. 2 (2013): 169.

agreed that the main stadium must be multipurpose, and capable of hosting other sporting and entertainment events.

The development saved the Open, but at the expense of public parkland which was appropriated without public consultation. Flinders Park was zoned crown land for public parks. Therefore, it was outside the jurisdiction of the *Crown Lands (Reserves) Acts* of 1958 and 1978. The latter was particularly important because it decreed that crown land could be used for public purposes, such as "a national tennis centre" and for "other sports and entertainment." In 1985, the Cain government passed the *National Tennis Centre Act* which rezoned Flinders Park, not as public parkland, but as crown land reserve. Without public consultation, or planning and environmental assessments, the Tennis Centre could now be built in the park. Despite protests from environmental groups, the development proceeded, impacting on amateur sporting clubs that had used the park.[10] The Act established a precedent for future sporting infrastructure developments that would see public parks transformed into privatized sporting spaces. Legislation protecting city parkland would be over-ridden, while community consultation and environmental impact statements dismissed as too messy and time-consuming. The 1985 *Act* cut-through such humbug and established the National Tennis Centre Trust to administer the site. Members were appointed by the Sports Minister and limited to parliamentarians, individuals from other sporting trusts and organizations, and a Melbourne City Councilor. As Cain emphasized, restricting membership gave the government "some capacity . . . to exercise control over the Tennis Centre."[11] It ensured the Open's interests overrode wider community concerns on the parkland's uses.

The Centre opened in 1988. With Melbourne's own Pat Cash playing Sweden's Mats Wilander in the men's Open final, the new venue was judged a huge success by an unquestioning media and public. Despite appearances, the Tennis Centre was in financial trouble and required an injection of public money. The initial tournament recorded a $AUD 4.3 million loss caused by hefty interest rate payments stemming from the Centre's financing. As the Victorian Auditor-General found, from 1989 until June 1991 the Centre lost $AUD 35 million because of high interest rates and low returns from non-tennis activities. To ease the burden, the Labor government sought to inject $AUD 144 million over the next 12 years in exchange for an agreement from TA that the tournament remain at Finders Park for 25 years.[12]

---

10 Ibid.
11 John, *Sport City*, 115.
12 Ibid., 116–17.

But the government had its eye on bigger circuses. Melbourne's sporting cabal yearned for the glory days of the 1956 Olympic Games. Melburnians' memories of the Games, however, are fuzzy. Dubbed the "friendly games," preparations were so poorly advanced by 1955 that the International Olympic Committee (IOC) president, Avery Brundage (1887–1975), threatened to strip Melbourne of the Games and award them to Rome.[13] However, the Games did proceed and heralded television's arrival in Australia, the modernization and Americanization of the country,[14] and the misguided conviction that Melbourne had the sporting culture, prowess and infrastructure to host another Olympics.[15] The city bid for the 1988 Games, but it floundered without federal and state government support.[16] Brisbane secured Australian Olympic Committee (AOC) support to bid for the 1992 Games, but was beaten by Barcelona. Melbourne got its chance in the late-1980s, beating arch-rival Sydney for the right to bid for the 1996 Olympics in an acrimonious campaign that split the AOC along state lines.

The bid was based on Melbourne's sporting heritage, and extensive and expensive sports infrastructure development program, but it flopped. Despite the Cain government's investment in sport, Melbourne was still a rustbelt city with an economy on the skids. The government's sales-pitch focused on the pipedream $AUD 79–86 million in revenue, and the 31,000 jobs that would supposedly flow from the Games.[17] But Melbourne could not compete with Atlanta, the home of Olympic sponsor, Coca-Cola, and was on the wrong side of the Pacific for the lucrative US television market. Most importantly, it was financially bust. When IOC president, Juan Antonio Samaranch (1920–2010), toured the city in the early 1990s, it was riddled with industrial unrest. The state bank and a major building society had collapsed, and interest rates were running at 17%. The state's credit rating had been downgraded and the city's construction sites had ground to a halt. Writing in the *Washington Post*, Melbourne journalist Peter Stephens trashed his hometown's chances. Melbourne's public transport was "dirty, inefficient and unreliable" in comparison to Atlanta's, he asserted, while the city had been "battered" by financial mismanagement and powerful

---

[13] Richard Baka, "Melbourne's Status as an Olympic City: Past, Present and Future Perspectives," *The International Journal of the History of Sport* 35, no. 9 (2019): 875.
[14] Graeme Davison, "Welcoming the World: The 1956 Olympic Games and the Representation of Melbourne," *Australian Historical Studies* 27, no. 109 (1997): 65.
[15] Baka, "Melbourne's Status," 5.
[16] Ibid., 16.
[17] John, *Sport City*, 129.

trade unions.[18] The IOC agreed, concluding that Melbourne could not afford the Games.[19]

Behind closed doors the bid was being scuttled by the AOC's Sydney members who realized that a Melbourne victory would ruin Sydney's chances of securing the 2000 Games. Some, such as the AOC executive board member Phil Coles, advised the Atlanta bid, while the future AOC president, John Coates, offered only lukewarm support for Melbourne. So too did the former IOC vice-president, Kevan Gosper. A Melburnian, Gosper later stated that he "worked very hard for Melbourne," but "hadn't really a full commitment" to the bid.[20] Acrimony from the bid has continued to shape AOC politics. Under Coates' presidency, the AOC was restructured in the 1990s which saw power move from state councils to the national federation controlled by Coates. Melbourne was again sidelined as power and the AOC headquarters shifted to Sydney.[21] The acrimony surfaced during the 2006 Commonwealth Games in Melbourne. The organizing committee declined to invite either Coles or Coates.

In 1990, Joan Kirner (1938–2015) replaced Cain as Labor premier and inherited a state in financial tatters. The Hawke Government had cut the share of federal government revenues to the states. Whereas revenues had comprised 49% of the Victorian state budget in 1986–87, it had dropped to 42% by 1992–93.[22] Coupled with manufacturing's demise, this meant that governments had to become more entrepreneurial in finding other funding sources. Consequently, Kirner launched a $AUD 1 billion road project and invited bids for a casino.[23] She also established the Victorian Major Events Corporation (VMEC) in 1991, appointing as its chair the Melbourne property developer, Ron Walker (1939–2018).

The VMEC emanated from Melbourne's failed Olympic bid which was also headed by Walker. Its brief was to secure major sporting and other events that would promote the city internationally and attract tourists and investment. Walker was very well-connected in business and political circles. His early wealth stemmed from the chemical industry. His company, Brooks Barmer, developed chemicals used in banknotes. Walker sold Barmer to Monsanto for $AUD

---

18 Peter Stephens, "Purse Strings May Hang Melbourne's Bid," *Washington Post*, September 17, 1990, C15.
19 John, *Sport City*, 131.
20 Ron Reed, "Retiring Kevan Gosper Admits Melbourne's 1996 Olympic Bid Wasn't Winnable," *Herald Sun*, November 23, 2013.
21 Baka, "Melbourne's Status," 16 & 23.
22 Benno Engels, "State Entrepreneurialism and Place Promotion: Lessons from Victoria," *Journal of Australian Political Economy* 43, (June 1999): 91.
23 Graeme Davison, *Car Wars: How the Car Won our Hearts and Conquered our Cities* (Crow's Nest, NSW: Allen & Unwin, 2004), 240.

11 million and teamed with Lloyd Williams to form the property development company, Hudson Conway, in 1986. A Liberal Party member, Walker had served as the city's Lord Mayor from 1972–74, but his business acumen was admired across party political lines. As a Labor appointment, he had chaired Melbourne's Olympic bid, but he remained staunchly Liberal, serving as the Party's treasurer from 1987–2001. Regularly on the *Business Review Weekly's* rich list, Walker had interests in property development, equities and media.[24] In the early 1990s, he led Hudson Conway's failed take-over bid for *The Age* and Melbourne radio station, 3AW. He later chaired the Fairfax Media Group – publisher of *The Age* – from 2005–2009.[25] Given his range of business interests and political connections, Walker cut a powerful figure in Melbourne.

In October 1992 Labor was swept from office. The incoming Liberal Coalition government was led by Jeff Kennett. A friend of the premier, Walker would profit from the new government's major construction and special events programs. Few questions would be asked about Walker's obvious conflicting interests as VMEC chair, property developer and political insider. Kennett was a bash-and-crash neoliberal 'heavy' who saw government as the entrepreneurial arm of business. But he was a selective neoliberal. Kennett often used public revenues and state power to assist business at the community's expense. McChesney defines neoliberalism as a set of "policies and processes whereby a relative handful of private interests are permitted to control as much social life in order to maximize their personal profit."[26] This occurred under Kennett between 1992–99.[27] The Kennett government commodified and corporatized public spaces without community consultation or regard for planning and environmental processes, while public monies were used to absorb costs in public-private ventures that involved Kennett's business and political cronies, the most notable of whom was Walker.

As has been documented, Kennett was a product of the 1980s era of Australian 'larrikin entrepreneurs' who helped popularize the public's perception of big business.[28] Kennett exuded a 'can-do' gruffness and larrikinism that broadened his electoral appeal. He disliked red-tape, big government and interventionist economic policies that restricted the free market; but he was prepared to intervene

---

24 Anne Hyland, "Walker's War in Cancer," *Australian Financial Review*, January 30, 2015, 14.
25 Damon Kitney and James Chessell, "Fairfax Rejects Walker's Bid for *The Age* and radio 3AW," *The Advertiser*, June 14, 2011.
26 Robert W. McChesney, "Noam Chomsky and the Struggle Against Neoliberalism," *Monthly Review* 50, no. 11, (April 1999): 40.
27 Mark Lowes, "Neoliberal Power Politics and the Controversial Site of the Australian Grand Prix. Motor Sport Event in an Urban Setting," *Society and Leisure* 27 no. 1, (March 2004): 69–88.
28 John, Stewart and McDonald, "Mixed Doubles," 163–164.

in the market to further his political or business agendas. His government inherited a state debt of $AUD 29.5 billion.[29] By May 1993, Kennett declared that the debt had blown-out to $AUD 60 billion which provided the impetus for public sector cuts. In its first budget, the government had slashed the state budget by 9%.[30] The Victorian public service was cut by 20%, while state-run schools were closed, public housing slashed, healthcare rationalized, and publicly-owned assets sold to foreign interests.[31] To ensure that labor costs were competitive with those in developing Asian economies, the government reformed the state's industrial relations system, passing the 1993 *Employee Relations Act*. It attacked workers' rights to collectively bargain with employers through trade unions, and opened labor relations to the market through the introduction of individual common law contracts between employers and employees.[32] As negotiating power shifted in employers' favor, Melbourne moved towards a service economy based on a growing casual and short-term contract labor-force. As Melbourne historian Graeme Davison notes, Kennett recognized that the "the old production line manufacturing industries, and the model of Keyneisan economic management on which they rested" were being replaced by a service economy with "ever accelerating global flows of money, goods, information and people."[33] Attracting these footloose flows of money to Melbourne required a new entrepreneurial approach to government, and so city planning and development based on public-private partnerships and market mechanisms replaced rational planning by centralized authorities. This was most evident in Melbourne's $AUD 1.8 billion CityLink road project. Linking Melbourne's eastern and western suburbs, the road's construction involved a public-private partnership with the international toll-road developer and operator, Transurban. It covered the construction costs in exchange for a 34-year concession to operate the road.[34]

CityLink was more than a road. It symbolized Kennett's obsession to transform Melbourne into a city of iconic structures and eye-catching spectacles. The urban geographer David Harvey argues that the after-effects of "deindustrialization . . . left most major cities in the advanced capitalist world with few options except to compete with each other" for finance, spectacles and as sites of conspicuous

---

29 Engels, "State Entrepreneurialism," 93.
30 Davison, *Car Wars*, 247.
31 John, Stewart and McDonald, "Mixed Doubles," 167.
32 Engels, "State Entrepreneurialism," 96–7.
33 Davison, *Car Wars*, 242.
34 Royce Millar and Ben Schneiders, "Transurban; The Making of a Monster," *The Age*, May 14, 2016. https://www.theage.com.au/national/victoria/transurban-the-making-of-a-monster-20160512-gotjm9.html.

consumption.[35] Melbourne was no exception. Kennett sought to re-image the city, distinguishing his post-industrial Melbourne from its rust-belt past. His government pumped public money into iconic building projects and spectacles to promote Melbourne as an international arts, sport and entertainment center. Kennett used symbols and structures to alter public perceptions of the city. Car number plates were changed. Victoria was no longer the staid "Garden State," but was now "On the Move," and sport was particularly important in promoting this mantra. As Smith notes, sport was central in the re-imaging of rustbelt British and North American cities. "The media coverage devoted to sport, its intrinsic popularity in contemporary culture and its supposed positive connotations . . . resulted in the adoption of sporting initiatives by industrial cities as a means of image enhancement," he contends.[36] Kennett adopted a similar strategy, but for the benefit of his cronies and at great cost to the wider community.

Kennett's Melbourne provides a case-study in crony capitalism which has shaped the city's approach to sports business. Cronyism was glaringly apparent in one of the government's iconic developments; the construction of a casino, hotel and entertainment complex that would form the centerpiece of Southbank's redevelopment. The contract was awarded in 1994 to a Hudson Conway-led consortium. The decision was controversial given Walker's role in the bid, his and business partner Lloyd Williams' close relationship with Kennett, and his numerous conflicting political and business interests. The other short-listed candidate was the international consortium, Sheraton-Leighton. Leighton was Australia's largest construction company, while Sheraton's parent company, ITT Corporation, numbered amongst the world's largest multinationals. In contrast, Hudson Conway was locally owned by Williams, Walker and Roderick Carnegie, with media mogul, Kerry Packer (1937–2005), holding a 10% stake. Its consortium comprised the Tasmanian casino operator, Federal Hotels, the Victorian state gambling concern, the TAB, and Carlton & United Breweries; but it lacked the muscle of the Sheraton-Leighton bid. The weak link was Federal Hotels. Hudson Conway was to fund its contribution through a $AUD 41 million preference share deal.[37]

---

[35] David Harvey, *The Conditions of Postmodernity: An Enquiry into the Origins of Cultural Change* (Oxford, England; Cambridge, Mass., USA: Blackwell, 1990), 92.

[36] Andrew Smith, "Sporting a new Image? Sport-based Regeneration Strategies as a Means of Enhancing the Image of the City Tourist Destination," in *Sport in the City, The Role of Sport in Economic and Social Regeneration*, eds. Chris Gratton and Ian P. Henry (London: Routledge, 2001), 128.

[37] Mark Forbes, "Inside the Casino Deal," *Sydney Morning Herald*, October 8, 1994. https://www.smh.com.au/national/inside-the-casino-deal-20090821-etfi.html.

The merchant bank, SBC Dominguez Barry, was appointed to assess the bids. It found that the bids were "similar" and recommended that the contract be awarded on "grounds other than the financial attributes of each applicant." Nonetheless, SBC questioned both TAB and Federal Hotels' capacity to meet their obligations, and the non-inclusion of a builder, and suggested that Hudson Conway had under-estimated the project's cost. According to the Melbourne *Age's* Mark Forbes, Hudson Conway's costings of $AUD 622 million were well below Sheraton-Leighton's $AUD 822 million, yet the former's proposed hotel complex was five times larger than the latter's. Consequently, SBC recommended that Sheraton-Leighton was better equipped to meet with all the project's requirements.[38]

Despite SBC's assessment, the contract was awarded to Hudson Conway. Kennett declared it "a fantastic result" based on the bid's financial superiority. His position contrasted with SBC's analysis and raised questions of cronyism. Forbes contends that Hudson Conway's success stemmed from "a desperate last minute plunge" in which the government allowed the company to increase its costings by $AUD 80 million.[39] Former Kennett adviser, Stephen Mayne, similarly alleges that the government allowed Hudson Conway to change its bid at the last minute.[40] Given Walker's political and business connections, and his VMEC chairmanship, questions were asked about whether Hudson Conway had acted on insider information. At the time, Walker and Kennett were involved in secret negotiations with Formula One's Bernie Ecclestone about relocating the Australian Grand Prix from Adelaide to Melbourne. According to Sheraton-Leighton, Hudson Conway's access to the government gave it an "unfair advantage."[41] The company alleged that Hudson Conway was provided information, enabling it to increase its financial projections and meet SBC's concerns about the bid's strength. Sheraton-Leighton also asked why the bidding process was suddenly reopened on 18 August 1994, two days after it had officially closed. Allegedly, this allowed Hudson Conway to address SBC's concerns. When the decision was announced on 6 September, Sheraton-Leighton claimed that the process lacked probity. It called for the reopening of tenders after Hudson Conway's design altered and its projected costs escalated, but the request was dismissed, prompting

---

38 Mark Forbes, "Casinos Secrets Revealed," *Sydney Morning Herald,* August 9, 1994. https://www.smh.com.au/national/casino-secrets-revealed-20090821-et0m.html
39 Forbes, ibid. and "Inside the Casino Deal."
40 Stephen Mayne, "How Crown Prince Packer Conquered Melbourne", *Crikey,* November 4, 2014. https://www.crikey.com.au/2014/11/04/mayne-how-crown-prince-packer-conquered-melbourne/
41 Forbes, "Casino Secrets" and "Inside."

Williams to remark, "the prizes in this life are for the people who move forward."[42] He and the government had the result they wanted. The process was a triumph for crony capitalism. A handful of vested interests had used the administrative processes of government to increase their personal wealth.

While the cronies counted their chips, spending on health, education and other public services were either cut or privatized. By 1995, the Victorian public service had lost 20% of its workforce since 1992. Publicly funded state schools had been reduced by 260, while 11,400 teachers were now redundant. Around $AUD 300 million had been slashed from healthcare, while state-owned public transport, gas and electricity facilities were now in foreign hands.[43] Nonetheless, the Kennett government's spending splurges continued. In May 1995 it announced a $AUD 23 million infrastructure upgrade of the Tennis Centre and the announcement coincided with its re-branding. No longer was it Flinders but Melbourne Park, place-marketing the city through the Open's capture of a global television audience. In 1998, the government announced the construction of an additional $AUD 70 million, multi-purpose stadium with a retractable roof. As well as tennis, it would house basketball and cycling events and, according to Kennett, add capacity to Melbourne's already crowded sporting calendar and improve the city's chances of hosting the 2006 Commonwealth Games.[44] Kennett and Walker, however, had their eyes on a much bigger sporting circus.

With the South Australian Government's contract for the Australian Formula One Grand Prix due to expire in 1996, Walker, as VMEC chair, and Kennett moved quickly to bring the event to Melbourne. In December 1993, they announced that Victoria had pinched the race from Adelaide. The South Australian Government had expected its contract to be renewed, but Walker, Kennett and Formula One Construction Association chief, Bernie Ecclestone, had sealed the steal in September 1993. Kennett dubbed the Grand Prix the "jewel in Victoria's crown." It will make Melbourne "an international star attraction," he claimed, and "add energy to our society, build confidence among the people, create jobs, add to our economic wealth and position this city as no other event could."[45] Not everyone shared Kennett's optimism. Melburnians in the inner southern suburbs considered the Grand Prix a noisy encumbrance that destroyed public parkland and diminished the quality of their lives.

---

[42] Ibid.
[43] Dave Holmes, "How Kennett Gets Away with It", *Green Left Weekly*, September 28, 1994. https://www.greenleft.org.au/content/how-kennett-gets-away-it.
[44] John, Stewart and McDonald, "Mixed Doubles," 171 and 174.
[45] Sue Neales, "Kennett Unveils Melbourne's Grand Prix Masterplan, "*The Age*, November 16, 1994, 5.

Cities use grand prixs to place-marketed themselves as cosmopolitan, high-end destinations for tourists and investors. As a grand prix city, Melbourne sits in supposedly elite company, though it pays a high price for the privilege. The Kennett government entered the Grand Prix market when both demand and costs were high, and it could tap into Walker's international mates' network. Walker was close to Ecclestone and, seemingly, conducted negotiations on the government's behalf. The friendship did not stop Ecclestone from extracting a substantial annual license fee for the rights to the race. Without parliamentary debate or community consultation, the mates' network signed-off on the deal.

The race would be staged in the inner city parkland of Albert Park with the Melbourne skyline as its backdrop. The site was chosen because it was supposedly the Australian Grand Prix's traditional home, and according to Walker, Ecclestone's pre-condition for Melbourne getting the race.[46] He wanted an inner-city street race, and the Kennett Government agreed. In justifying the decision, the government embellished Melbourne's sporting past, claiming that Albert Park was the Grand Prix's traditional home. The Park had hosted the race in 1953 and 1956, but local residents' complaints saw it moved to Sandown Park on Melbourne's outer south-eastern fringe.[47] Residents would not have the same success in shifting Kennett and Walker's Grand Prix. Situated on the CBD's southern fringe, the park was home to many amateur sporting clubs, a public golf course, and a haven for recreational users. The park's managing authority, Parks Victoria, had developed a Draft Strategy Plan, based on consultation with the community. Under the Plan, the park would accommodate "a variety of recreational experiences including sport, leisure and open space enjoyment"[48] The Grand Prix scuttled the Plan, corporatizing a valued community space without any public consultation.

Like Walker, Kennett was contemptuous of consultative processes. He dismissed "reviews and committees" as for "those who cannot make decisions."[49] By-passing established processes, he barreled through the Victorian Parliament the *Australian Grand Prix Act* in October 1994. It established the Australian Grand Prix Corporation (AGPC) and the ubiquitous Walker was subsequently appointed its chair. The Act gave the AGPC wide-ranging powers that overrode existing environmental, planning and common law rights. As such, the Grand

---

46 Mark Lowes, "Neoliberal Power Politics," 71.
47 Mathew Nicholson, "Motor Sport", in *The Encyclopedia of Melbourne, the City Past and Present*, eds.Andrew Brown-May and Shurlee Swain (Port Melbourne, Vic.: Cambridge University Press), 491.
48 Lowes, "Neoliberal Power Politics," 74.
49 Ibid., 79.

Prix site was excluded from environmental protection and planning laws, and placed solely under the AGPC's authority. It was empowered to restructure the park to meet the race's requirements. Ignoring protests from local residents, trees were cut-down, while spectator mounds and permanent buildings were constructed. The number of sports fields were reduced, while much of the park was unusable for four months each year.[50] Under the Act, residents and the wider community had few avenues to challenge the AGPC's powers. The body was exempt from the 1982 *Freedom of Information Act* so contractural details remained secret. It was even beyond the common law. Under the Act, claims for damages caused during the track's construction were outside the courts' jurisdiction. The government had created a quasi-state within a state under Walker's control.

Though the event was backed by the public and media, and had bipartisan political support, concerns were constantly expressed about the race site's appropriateness and the lack of transparency on costs.[51] Kennett and Walker were more concerned about place-marketing Melbourne globally as a desirable tourist and investment destination, and considered the Grand Prix as the perfect vehicle to achieve this. As Lowes notes, Formula One was perceived as "a glamorous global spectacle" that harnessed great "cultural capital." Melbourne joined a select number of host urban chic and "distinctly cosmopolitan" cities. The re-imaging favored vested political and business interests, and was a momentary mirage that masked the state's gutted public sector and the city's growing social and economic inequalities.[52] For Ecclestone, however, Albert Park was the ideal venue for promoting "Aussie chic."[53] Cosmopolitanism, sophistication and conspicuous consumption were the benchmarks for Grand Prix cities, and "Aussie chic" Albert Park ticked all Bernie's boxes. For Walker, the parkland location highlighted the city's "attractiveness . . . to a global television audience," while the event stamped Melbourne as a world city, trumping Sydney in the race for international tourists and footloose capital.[54] For Kennett, the event enhanced his electoral popularity. He dismissed local resident groups as elitist, claiming

---

50 Ibid., 81–2.
51 John, *Sport City*, 168–169.
52 Mark Lowes, "Towards a Conceptual Understanding of Formula One Motorsport and Local Cosmopolitanism Discourse in Urban Placemarketing Strategies", *Communication and Sport* 6 no.2 (2018): 203–205.
53 Mark Fogarty, "Losing F1 Could Prove the Greatest Cost of All," *Sydney Morning Herald*, February 24, 2013. https://www.smh.com.au/sport/motorsport/losing-f1-could-prove-the-greatest-cost-of-all-20130223-2ey3p.html.
54 John, *Sport City*, 159.

that "[t]he park is not the possession of a few, [but] . . . is for the enjoyment of many."⁵⁵ Three weeks after the 1996 Grand Prix he was returned at the polls.

However, concerns persisted about the race's value for money. Though Walker boasted that the exposure Melbourne gained through the race was in the millions, the Victorian Auditor-General dismissed such claims as unquantifiable, pointing out that the 1996 Grand Prix had registered an overall loss of $AUD 60 million.⁵⁶ The figure did not include Ecclestone's license fee which was commercial-in-confidence, despite being paid from taxpayer revenues. Concerns would persist about the lack of transparency and public accountability surrounding the event; and whether it and the Open were appropriate uses of public monies, especially given the cuts in government services. But Melburnians were not prepared to critically address these questions. They were beginning to believe that Melbourne just might be the world's sporting capital.

By 1999, Victorians had wearied of Kennett's bullying and growing arrogance, electing a Labor government under the more urbane Steve Bracks. Though the leadership style changed, the sports strategy remained the same. One of Kennett's final schemes was orchestrating the construction of the $AUD 460 million Docklands football stadium on the CBD's western waterfront. The ground was to be built on government-owned land in a disused dock area with easy access to public transport and the CBD. Though multi-purpose and with a retractable roof, its main tenants would be AFL clubs. The government had secured the AFL's involvement in 1997, but the latter had driven a hard bargain. AFL CEO, Wayne Jackson, agreed to put $AUD 30 million towards construction costs, and play 30 games per season at the venue, in exchange for full ownership by 2025 on payment of $AUD 30 million. The deal was a steal for the most powerful sporting body in town, and signaled the end of Waverley Park. Though it would survive as an AFL club training ground, the surrounding land was sold to property developers in 2001 for $AUD 110 million.⁵⁷

The Kennett government recognized that developing Docklands would open the city to the waterfront. In 1992, the government established the Docklands Authority which opened the area to private developers, with the proposed stadium as the drawcard. Construction commenced in 1997 on public land gifted to the Dockland Stadium Consortium which was controlled by the media company, the Seven Network. Completed in 2000, the stadium housed the AFL's headquarters and the Seven Network's Digital Broadcast Centre. In June 2006,

---

55 Neales, "Kennett Unveils," 5.
56 John, *Sport City*, 168.
57 Ibid., 188–189.

the stadium's leasehold was sold for $AUD 330 million to the Sydney-based James Fielding Funds Management Group, comprising largely of industry-based superannuation funds.[58] Being privately owned, the stadium did not receive government funds unlike the MCG. This meant that the stadium's AFL tenants were worse off, in comparison to clubs that played at the MCG. While home clubs banked 41% of match day revenues at the MCG, Docklands' tenants retained only 36%.[59] The arrangement particularly disadvantaged clubs with low supporter bases, many of which played at Docklands. Hence, throughout 2015–16 the AFL moved to buy-out the Fielding Group, but negotiations were complicated by a 'thought-bubble' from the Collingwood Football Club President and Melbourne media 'talking head,' Eddie McGuire.[60]

A power in Melbourne's sports-media, McGuire had the ear of government, the public and the AFL. In March 2016, he suggested that Docklands be sold and a $AUD 1 billion, 60,000-seat stadium, with the now obligatory retractable roof, be built on the site of the Australian Open's second showpiece court, Hisense Arena. McGuire had a vested interest in the development. Under his presidency, the Collingwood Football Club had colonized the precinct in 2008, establishing a training ground and administrative facilities opposite the Tennis Centre. Despite being one of the AFL's largest and wealthiest clubs, Collingwood received $AUD 11.3 million from federal government coffers to assist in the development.[61] While the training ground was being laid, the club used nearby Gosch's Paddock which was public parkland. As Melbourne planning academic Michael Buxton noted, the Paddock was "the last large bit of public space in the area," and used by dog-walkers and recreational joggers.[62] The Paddock and its surrounding parkland had been under the Melbourne City Council's control. In 2005, the Bracks Labor government placed the site under the pro-corporate Melbourne and Olympic Park Trust's (MOPT) authority which ensured that the interests of Collingwood and the precinct's other occupants, the National Rugby

---

[58] John Stensholt, "Etihad Stadium Owners Agitate for Sale," *Australian Financial Review*, February 22, 2015. https://www.afr.com/news/etihad-stadium-owners-agitate-for-sale-20150219-13jl2h. Ian McIlwraith, "Grounds and Revenue: Some AFL Clubs Score Goals, Others Behinds," *Sydney Moring Herald*, September 30, 2011, 9.
[59] Ibid.
[60] Stensholt, "Etihad Stadium Owners."
[61] John Kehoe, "Dress it Up as Women's Sport Under the Guise of Women's Sport," *Australian Financial Review*, February 15, 2019, 8
[62] *ABC News*, Melbourne, "Eddie McGuire's Plan to Sell Docklands, Build New Stadium Would 'Plunder' Parkland, Expert Says," (March 9, 2016). https://www.abc.net.au/news/2016-03-09/dump-docklands-stadium-build-a-new-one-eddie-mcguire-tells-afl/7232038.

League's (NRL) Melbourne Storm and the A-League's Melbourne Victory, were prioritized over the community's.

But McGuire also thought there was an opportunity to 'refigure' the city's sports and entertainment precincts, and that "the missing piece" was "a 50,000 to 60,000 seat stadium" at Collingwood's end of town.[63] "Docklands Stadium," he argued, "hasn't quite worked" and selling it would get rid of the restrictive tenancy agreements, ease club debt, and "bulletproof the AFL"[64] Discussions on the proposed stadium were apparently well advanced. McGuire had met with all the major stakeholders, including the Victorian government, and had Walker's full support.[65] Though Victoria's facilities were "world class," Walker warned, "we must not rest on our laurels." He had always "dreamed of a glamorous structure . . . that would finish Melbourne off and form a new gateway to the city."[66] McGuire's stadium would fill the bill. Labor Premier Daniel Andrews agreed, boasting that the sporting precinct was "the envy of the world," but "in a competitive market we can't . . . let others pass us by."[67] Little consideration was given to the costs which would far exceed revenues raised from Docklands' sale; the disruption to major rail and road links; or the impact on the Tennis Centre and the Australian Open. As Kennett cautioned, the government should not "put at risk the Australian Open . . . for a new stadium." The Open, he reminded, is the "biggest sporting event in Australia over two weeks . . . [and] gives us lots of promotion overseas."[68] McGuire's pipe-dream would undermine the essence of Melbourne's sports strategy; using major events to promote the city internationally.

The stadium did not eventuate, but McGuire's thought-bubble highlighted sport's all-pervading place in Melbourne's culture and identity, as well as the trickle-up sports economy. Instead, the AFL bought Docklands in 2017 for $AUD 200 million, funded in part from a $AUD 2.5 billion media rights deal with News Corp, Seven West and Telstra. The AFL promptly received $AUD 225 million from the Andrews Government for 'upgrades' to the ground and the surrounding

---

63 Ibid.
64 Nathan Schmook, "McGuire Leading Push for New Stadium," *AFL.com.au.* March 9, 2016. https://www.afl.com.au/news/2016-03-09/eddie-mcguire-leading-push-for-new-1-billion-football-stadium-near-mcg. Alison Worrall, "Eddie McGuire Proposes $1b New Stadium Near MCG," *The Age,* March 8, 2016. https://www.theage.com.au/national/victoria/eddie-mcguire-proposes-1-billion-new-stadium-near-mcg-20160308-gndzh4.html
65 Ibid.
66 James Frost, "Walker Backs Controversial Stadium," *Australian Financial Review,* March 18, 2016, 11.
67 Schmook "McGuire Leading Push."
68 Ibid.

precinct, as well as $AUD 241 million for suburban football. The payments came as AFL revenues peaked at $AUD 650 million, producing a $AUD 48.8 million surplus. As a not-for-profit organization, the AFL was not taxed on these earnings, yet it had pocketed $AUD 465 million in public monies.[69] In exchange, the Andrews government brokered an agreement with the AFL that the Grand Final would stay at the MCG until 2057.[70]

The AFL and government have partnered to develop the stadium and Docklands precinct. The 'not-for-profit' AFL intends to move into property development, investing the $AUD 225 million on stadium improvements and the construction of an 11-storey retail and hotel complex, with a 1500-seat function room.[71] When the Liberal Opposition questioned if this was an appropriate use of public money, Andrews jumped to the AFL's defense. "If you don't invest in those things others will pass you by," he declared.[72] Since, the AFL has sold the stadium's naming rights to the Disney Corporation in an eight-year deal reportedly worth $AUD 70 million.[73] In September 2018, it was renamed Marvel Stadium, emanating from Disney's 2009 acquisition of Marvel Entertainment. The deal rebranded the stadium and refashioned Docklands as an entertainment precinct. A Marvel store opened, intended to lure a younger demographic to the precinct, stadium and football. With Marvel's superheroes on its side, the AFL solidified its position as the most profitable 'not-for-profit' in town.

When Andrews dismissed Liberal concerns about the AFL's use of public monies in property development, he was singing from a familiar song-sheet. Victorian governments' heavy investments in sport were fueled by persistent fears that Melbourne would lose major events and the world's sporting capital tag if it did not continually build new or upgrade existing sporting facilities. As Andrews emphasized, other Australian cities were now in the market. Adelaide and Perth had invested heavily in stadiums, as was Sydney, while "Queensland

---

[69] John Stensholt, "How Etihad Stadium Has Transformed the AFL into a Financial Powerhouse," *Australian Financial Review*, March 25, 2018, 20.

[70] ABC News, "AFL Grand Final to Stay in Victoria until 2057, MCG and Docklands Stadium to be Upgraded," April 13, 2018. https://www.abc.net.au/news/2018-04-13/mcg-to-keep-afl-grand-final-till-2057-state-government-says/9652420.

[71] Linda Cheng, "Melbourne Stadiums Set for Major Redevelopment," *ARCHITECTUREAU*, April 16, 2018. https://architectureau.com/articles/melbourne-stadiums-set-for-major-redevelopment/.

[72] Ibid.

[73] Peter Farquhar, "Nobody Really Knows How to React to Marvel Winning the Naming Rights to Melbourne's Etihad Stadium," *Business Insider Australia*, May 20, 2018. https://www.businessinsider.com.au/nobody-really-knows-how-to-react-to-marvel-winning-the-naming-rights-to-melbournes-etihad-stadium-2018-5.

will have . . . legacy stadiums and other benefits coming out of the [2018 Gold Coast] Commonwealth Games."[74] Victorian governments feared losing the city's major international events to more globally connected, cosmopolitan cities. These fears have been costly. Governments have invested billions to ensure Melbourne has the cutting-edge infrastructure to retain its showpiece international events.

While the Grand Prix's costs have been heavily scrutinized, Australian Open expenditures have attracted less attention. Costs of keeping the Open at Melbourne Park have now tipped over the billion-dollar mark. In 2009, the Brumby Labor Government announced a $AUD 363 million upgrade of the venue without public consultation. The upgrade included the construction of Margaret Court Arena and 21 new courts which were formerly situated on public land granted to the Tennis Centre under an amendment to the *Melbourne & Olympic Park Act*. According to TA, the upgrade ensured Melbourne would retain the Grand Slam. Reports had circulated that Sydney, Madrid, Shanghai and Dubai wanted the Open. In justifying the expenditure, Labor Premier Brumby stated that the Open "occupied a central role in Melbourne's 'sporting capital' identity which is consistently used in the city's marketing campaigns."[75] Melbourne had invested heavily in creating the illusion that it was the world's sporting capital. Brumby's comment suggests that the $AUD 363 million was a down-payment on keeping the illusion alive.

Another $AUD 338 upgrade was announced in 2014 by the Napthine Liberal government, of which its share was $AUD 298 million. Napthine assured that the upgrade would mean that Melbourne "remains the sporting capital of the world" and "attract[s] the best sporting, music and cultural events." He, too, warned that other cities wanted the Open, but reassured that the investment secured its long-term future.[76] With over a $AUD 1 billion spent on the site, even Walker was having doubts about the Open's impact on the state budget. In 2012, he warned that Victorians faced annual interest rates' payments of $AUD 90 million on borrowings to fund the Tennis Centre's capital works. However, he was less critical of the Grand Prix's impact on the budget's bottom-line.

The race was Walker's chestnut. Though it consistently recorded losses, Walker maintained that the race had brought $AUD 1 billion in intangible economic benefits to the state during its first eight years.[77] The Victorian

---

74 Cheng, "Melbourne Stadiums."
75 John, Stewart and McDonald, "Mixed Doubles," 172.
76 "Australia: Plans Progress Quickly for Melbourne Park Upgrades," *MENA Report*, London, June 12, 2014.
77 John, *Sport City*, 169.

Auditor-General disagreed, contending instead that the Grand Prix's costs far out-weighed its benefits. This was confirmed in the AGPC's annual reports tabled before the Victorian Parliament in 2007. They indicated that from 2003–07, the race had recorded losses of over $AUD 90 million.[78] Clearly, if exposed to free market forces, the Grand Prix would have hit the wall.

Undeterred, the Bracks government extended the grand prix contract in 2008 for another five years. At the time, Ecclestone was driving a hard bargain. He wanted a night race tailored for the European television market. The Singapore Grand Prix was moving to night, and Ecclestone claimed that South Korea, Russia and India were now eyeing a Grand Prix slot. While the Bracks government mulled over the decision, Walker touted that "[e]very country wants a race like this because it advertises the city it's in and that's why it's so valuable."[79] The government rejected Ecclestone's demand, because of the added expense, though the parties settled instead on a later start-time. The deal was clinched at a London meeting in mid-2008 by Walker and Ecclestone and signed-off by the Bracks government. Neither the local Port Phillip Council nor Albert Park residents were consulted about the race's altered start-time.[80]

The major sticking-points remained; the lack of transparency concerning the license fee paid to Ecclestone, and the escalating costs of staging the race. Governments repeatedly spun the line that the event must provide value for money, yet repeatedly it failed to do so. From 2009 to 2011, the accumulated losses totaled $AUD 130 million, raising doubts about whether the contract should be renewed after 2015.[81] But Ecclestone called the Victorian government's bluff. While in New York negotiating a possible street race, he suggested that if Melburnians didn't want the race "they can go." The Grand Prix's old guard jumped to its defense. Kennett insisted that it was "more than just a race" in that it "adds to our reputation as the sporting capital of the world."[82] The AGPC's CEO Andrew Westacott was much blunter, suggesting "if you don't

---

[78] Seven Nightly News (SEVEN Melbourne), "Taxpayers propping up F1 Grand Prix: Victorian Taxpayers have had to Prop Up This Year's Grand Prix," October 30, 2008.

[79] Seven Nightly News (SEVEN Melbourne), "Victorian Government Upset at Claims Grand Prix Could Be Lost to Melbourne," February 3, 2008.

[80] National Nine News (NINE NETWORK Melbourne), "Bernie Sticks to his Guns Over Night Time Melbourne Grand Prix," June 17, 2008; and "Exclusive Details about Twilight Grand Prix," November 24, 2008.

[81] Seven Nightly News (Seven Melbourne), "New Controversy Over Melbourne's Formula 1 Grand Prix," January 24, 2011.

[82] *6pm with George Negus*, (10 Network), March 25, 2011.

have the Grand Prix, you don't have tourists coming to Melbourne."[83] Walker chipped in, claiming "[i]t's the largest single day sporting event in Australia" which "advertise[s] Melbourne to [the] rest of the world."[84] Ecclestone again went on the attack, warning, "[w]e have other cities wanting to take the place of Australia."[85] He realized that Victorian governments needed the race to place-market Melbourne globally, so jettisoning it was unlikely.

He continued to play Victorian governments on a break ably assisted by the canny Walker. Despite concerns over the event's repeated losses, and calls for greater value for money, the Napthine government in 2014 extended the contract until 2020. As in the past, Napthine refused to disclose the license fee paid to Ecclestone, however, details were aired in the media. From 2011 to 2015, Ecclestone had pocketed $AUD 170 million. The disclosure breached the contract's confidentiality clause, causing Kennett to warn that it could "put the state at risk of losing a major event."[86] But it continued and so too did the losses. The 2014 race reported a $AUD 62 million shortfall, bringing overall losses since 2010 to $AUD 280 million. Politicians again blustered about the event's benefits and how Melbourne was now "the major event capital of the world."[87] With the New South Wales government eying the race, Andrews hurriedly extended the contract until 2023 without any community consultation or debate over its value. He refused to divulge details of the deal, claiming it would give "our competitors the number they had to beat."[88] It was new spin on the old 'commercial-in-confidence' line. Though on the Labor Party's left, Andrews was another in a long line of politicians who were merely Walker and Bernie's bunnies.

What commenced as a re-imaging of a rustbelt city, had by 2015 developed into a publicly funded, trickle up, sports-corporate economy. Public revenues were used to benefit the city's sports-corporate elites, while taxpayers covered the costs. As public services were cut or privatized, workforces casualized and inner-city homelessness grew, more public money was spent on sporting infrastructure developments, and sustaining existing or securing greater events. This trickle-up economy is evident at Melbourne's Caulfield and Flemington racecourses, which

---

83 Ten 5PM News (TEN Melbourne), "Revving Up: Melbourne's Grand Prix Organizers Have Used this Year's Launch to Defend its Long-term Viability," February 2, 2012.
84 Ten 5PM News (TEN Melbourne), "Grand Prix's Future," March 1, 2012.
85 Ibid.
86 Seven Nightly News (SEVEN Network), "Race at Risk: Melbourne Could Lose the F1 Grand Prix After Secret License Fees Paid to FI Chief Were Disclosed," January 23, 2013.
87 Jean Edwards, "Melbourne Grand Prix: Victorian Pay Record Price for Formula One Race," *ABC News Victoria*, October 22, 2015. https://www.abc.net.au/news/2015-10-22/melbourne-grand-prix-victorians-pay-record-price-race/6878030
88 John, *Sport City*, 177.

house some of the city's most exclusive and wealthiest sporting clubs. Racing industry apologists often trumpet the sport's battler ethos, but it is structured on strict class lines. Only the wealthy, like Walker's 'mate' Lloyd Williams, can afford a horseracing stable and six Melbourne Cup winners. The racing calendar's highpoint, the Spring Racing Carnival, parades high-end celebrities, fashion and conspicuous consumption.[89] Racing's darker is seen in the doping scandals, the wastage of discarded thoroughbreds, and 199 horse-deaths on Australian tracks between August 2017 and July 2018.[90] In racing's showcase event, the Melbourne Cup, six starters have been destroyed since 2014. The deaths have not spoiled the on-course Cup Day party and the race's nation-wide attraction, or dinted the interests of those who control Victorian racing. Caulfield's Melbourne Racing Club (MRC) and Flemington's Victoria Racing Club (VRC) sit on vast tracts of valuable suburban land and profit from substantial gambling revenues, yet draw on the public purse and political patronage to increase their social and financial capital.

The clubs' power stems from racing's much touted contribution to the Victorian economy. As sports academic Sam Duncan wrote after the 2018 Melbourne Cup, racing is too big to fail. It, supposedly, contributes $AUD 4.3 billion and 33,000 jobs to the Victorian economy, while Melbourne's Spring Racing Carnival's multiplier effects flow into the hospitality, fashion, gambling, and food and drink industries.[91] Governments receive sizeable revenues from gambling, so it is not surprising that Liberal and Labor support the sport. Before the 2018 Victorian state election, the Labor Party committed $AUD 33 million to bolster prize-money. It was part of a $AUD 72 million package to be distributed over the next four years.[92] In November, the Andrews government slashed the MRC's annual rent on the Caulfield Racecourse by 66%. As a not-for-profit organization, the MRC's earnings are not subject to taxation, yet the club recorded a $AUD 1 million surplus in 2017–18, while sitting on real estate projects worth $AUD 1.5 billion.[93]

---

89 Caroline Winter and Ward Yong, "Fashion, Fantasy and Fallen Horses. Alternate Image of Thoroughbred Racing," *Annals of Leisure Research* 17, no. 4, (2014): 363 and 365.
90 Sam Duncan, "Why You Shouldn't Expect Racing to Change its Ways," *The New Daily*, November 7, 2018. https://thenewdaily.com.au/sport/racing/2018/11/07/racing-cliffsofmoher-melbourne-cup/.
91 Ibid.
92 Shane Anderson, "$40m Boost Pledge for Victorian Racing," *Racing.com*, October 11, 2018, https://www.racing.com/news/2018-10-11/news-40m-boost-pledged-for-victorian-racing. Minister for Racing, "Delivering a Stronger Racing Industry for Victoria," October 20, 2018. https://www.premier.vic.gov.au/delivering-a-stronger-racing-industry-for-victoria/.
93 Damien Hughes, "Council Slams Rent Deal for Caulfield Track: Exclusive," *Australian Financial Review*, November 22, 2018, 7.

Meanwhile, the VRC recently built a $AUD 128 million members grandstand at Flemington, partially funded by the government. The grandstand is for the VRC's corporate elites and consists of high-end bars and fine dining areas, as well as a new members' bar and dining room.[94] The Victorian government's contribution of $AUD 10 million was small, but followed a $AUD 131 million splurge to finance – in part – the VRC's other infrastructure projects.[95] The Andrews government justified these expenditures on the $AUD 427 million supposedly generated by Melbourne's Spring Racing Carnival. Few questions were asked of whether these expenditures were appropriate uses of public monies, particularly when spent on an elite, private members' club.

Other revenues were to be raised by the auction of crown lands attached to the racecourse and leased to the club under the 1871 and 1956 *Victoria Racing Club Acts*. Under the acts, the land must be used "for the purpose of a public racecourse." Though these acts were repealed in 2006, this essential precondition has remained in place.[96] Seemingly, it was side-stepped with the grandstand's construction. To partly fund it, the VRC was given permission by the state government to sell two parcels of racecourse land to the Chinese property developer, Greenlands, in 2014. Greenlands intended to build two residential towers, while the VRC would raise $AUD 45 million to cover partially the new grandstand's costs. Community concerns, however, delayed the project, causing Greenlands to withdraw. In February 2017, the Andrews government approved a modified development for the site, and the VRC indicated that it would be seeking partnerships to create a vibrant Flemington precinct.[97] Questions were not asked about whether this was an appropriate use of the land, given the requirements under the Act. There was no discussion about the sale of crown land to a developer; or whether the monies from the sale should go to the state or a private club. The government decided to make a trickle-up welfare payment to one of Melbourne's most exclusive sporting establishments.

In January 2018, Ron Walker died. Tributes flowed from political and business leaders, hailing him as a great Melburnian and Victorian. The Liberal Prime Minster, Malcolm Turnbull, and his predecessor, Tony Abbott, sang Walker's

---

94 Michael Bleby, "Grand Plans Unveiled: Racing's New Facilities Will Aim to Provide a Deluxe Experience," *Australian Financial Review*, March 6, 2014, 37.
95 Minister for Racing, "Boost for the 2017 Melbourne Cup Carnival," October 30, 2017, https://www.premier.vic.gov.au/boost-for-the-2017-melbourne-cup-carnival/
96 *Victoria Racing Club Act* (2006), 1 and 4.
97 Nick Lenaghan, "Victoria Racing Club Considers Next Move for Flemington," *Australian Financial Review*, February 17, 2017. https://www.afr.com/real-estate/victoria-racing-club-considers-next-move-for-flemington-land-20170217-gufc6b.

praises, as did the Victorian Labor Premier, Daniel Andrews who dubbed Walker "a giant of a Victorian and Australia," and a major factor in "why [Melbourne is] known as the sporting capital of the world."[98] Lloyd Williams could not think of "anyone who has done more for the city . . . than Ron Walker,"[99] while the hyperbolic McGuire suggested that not since Victoria's first colonial governor, Charles Latrobe (1801–1875), had "one person had an impact on so many varied institutions." McGuire added that in "his great partner, Jeff Kennett . . . [Walker had] found a Batman to his Superman." Kennett was less effusive. "No individual's unselfish, consistent contribution had delivered so much to what is rightly magnificent Melbourne today," he declared.[100]

Walker was no selfless saint or superhero. He was leader of an entrepreneurial class of local robber barons who had exclusive access to government, and used it to secure rights and funds to benefit their interests. He undoubtedly was instrumental in Melbourne's post-industrial transformation, but he was not alone. Labor and Liberal governments were equally complicit in the creation of a 'trickle-up' robber baron economy, during periods when government budgets and services were being cut or privatized. Walker profited from this economy, manipulating political processes to benefit those involved and the organizations they represented. As a Liberal Party powerbroker, and the chair of both the VMEC and AGPC, Walker secured events intended to increase tourism and attract footloose capital. As this capital flowed into – and inflated – the Melbourne property market, Walker profited, developing an empire from political largesse. By 2015, Walker's empire was valued at just under $AUD 795 million.[101] In 2003, he established the residential property development company, Evolve, with Ashley Williams. By 2012, reportedly, the company had apartment developments worth approximately $AUD 1 billion on its books.[102] In

---

[98] Australian Associated Press, "Ron Walker, Former Grand Prix Boss and Lord Mayor, Dies Aged 78," *The Guardian*, January 31, 2018. https://www.theguardian.com/australia-news/2018/jan/31/ron-walker-former-grand-prix-boss-and-melbourne-lord-mayor-dies-aged-78.

[99] Ebony Bowden & Michael Lynch, "A Generous Visionary in a Hard Time," *The Age*, February 1, 2018, 9.

[100] Dan Harrison, "Ron Walker Fareweled at State Funeral Attended by Jeff Kennett, Daniel Andrews," *ABC News Melbourne*, February 7, 2018. https://www.abc.net.au/news/2018-02-07/mourners-farewell-major-events-maestro-ron-walker/9404932.

[101] Hyland, "Walker's War." Simon Thomsen, "'Mr. Melbourne' Business Giant and GP Boss Ron Walker Has Died aged 78," *Business Insider Australia*, January 30, 2018. https://www.businessinsider.com.au/melbourne-ron-walker-died-2018-1.

[102] Anthony Black, "Ron Walker: Big Money, Big Buildings and Shrinking Media," *Smart Company*, December 18, 2018. https://www.smartcompany.com.au/finance/economy/rich-lister-ron-walker-on-big-buildings-and-a-shrinking-media/.

part, Evolve's success stemmed from foreign investment in the Melbourne property market. By the time of his death, Walker's fortune was pegged at just under $AUD 1 billion, most of which stemmed from property development.[103] The footloose capital which flowed into Melbourne fed his property interests.

Like his 'mate' Jeff Kennett, Walker had no time for democratic or consultative processes, and was not above exaggerating a point. He once claimed the Melbourne Grand Prix attracted an audience of 54 billion, "nine-times the world's population."[104] He was a more refined Donald Trump and, indeed, admired the Queens' property developer. Walker considered Trump "a lifter, not a leaner" who "actually gets things done." Like most developers, Walker added, Trump gets frustrated with bureaucracy which motivated him to become a politician.[105]

The comment explains much about Walker's attitude to government, and indeed the type of robber baron governance that emerged in Victoria over the past 30 years. Entrepreneurial and populist, it privileged capital over labor, and 'can-do' individualism over consultative governance. It ruled for the top-end-of-town, not suburban communities, and used sport to sell illusions that masked growing social and economic inequalities. It used – and abused – public monies to fund sporting infrastructure and spectacles, while privatizing and corporatizing public spaces. It sold the illusion that Melbourne was the sporting capital of the world to justify what was little more than crony capitalism in a peripheral sports city. In many ways, it has been a stunning achievement. Without this illusion Melbourne would be just another rustbelt city. But it has also been a stunning sting conducted by a robber baron cabal of Victorian politicians, sporting administrators, and the ubiquitous Walker.

Works Cited

"Australia: Plans Progress Quickly for Melbourne Park Upgrade." *MENA Report* (June 12, 2014). https://search-proquest-com.epoxy.lib.monsh.edu.au/docview/1535142127?accountid=12528.

Australian Associated Press. "Ron Walker, Former Grand Prix Boss and Lord Mayor, Dies Aged 78." *The Guardian*, January 31, 2018. www.theguardian.com/australia-news/2018/jan/31/ron-walker-former-grand-prix-boss-and-melbourne-lord-mayor-dies-aged-78.

---

103 Thomsen, "Mr. Melbourne."
104 Greg Baum, "All Hail the Grandiose Grand Prix," *Sydney Morning Herald*, March 23, 2018. https://www.smh.com.au/sport/all-hail-the-grandiose-prix-20180323-p4z5yc.htm.
105 Mathew Cranston, "Developers Can Make Good Politicians: Trump's New America," *Australian Financial Review*, November 11, 2016, 15.

Australian Broadcasting Corporation (ABC), Melbourne. "Eddie McGuire's plan to sell Docklands, Build New Stadium Would 'Plunder' Parkland, Expert Says." *ABC News Melbourne*, March 9, 2016. www.abc.net.au/news/2016-03-09/dump-docklands-stadium-build-a-new-one-eddie-mcguire-tells-afl/7232038.

ABC News. "AFL Grand Final to Stay in Victoria until 2057, MCG and Docklands Stadium to be Upgraded." April 13, 2018. https://www.abc.net.au/news/2018-04-13/mcg-to-keep-afl-grand-final-till-2057-state-government-says/9652420.

Anderson, Shane. "$40m boost pledge for Victorian Racing." *Racing.com*, October 11, 2018. www.racing.com/news/2018-10-11/news-40m-boost-pledged-for-victorian-racing.

Baka, Richard. "Melbourne's Status as an Olympic City: Past, Present and Future Perspectives." *The International Journal of the History of Sport* 35 no. 9 (February 2019): 1–24.

Baum, Greg. "All Hail the Grandiose Grand Prix." *Sydney Morning Herald*, March 23, 2018. https://www.smh.com.au/sport/all-hail-the-grandiose-prix-20180323-p4z5yc.htm.

Black, Anthony. "Ron Walker: Big Money, Big Buildings and Shrinking Media." *Smart Company*, December 18, 2018. https://www.smartcompany.com.au/finance/economy/rich-lister-ron-walker-on-big-buildings-and-a-shrinking-media/.

Bleby, Michael. "Grand Plans Unveiled: Racing's New Facilities Will Aim to Provide a Deluxe Experience." *Australian Financial Review*, March 6, 2014: 37.

Bowden, Ebony, and Michael Lynch. "A Generous Visionary in a Hard Time." *The Age*, February 1, 2018: 9.

Cheng, Linda. "Melbourne Stadiums Set for Major Redevelopment." *ARCHITECTUREAU*, April 16, 2018. https://architectureau.com/articles/melbourne-stadiums-set-for-major-redevelopment/.

Cranston, Mathew. "Developers Can Make Good Politicians: Trump's New America." *Australian Financial Review*, November 11, 2016: 15.

Davison, Graeme. "Welcoming the World: The 1956 Olympics Games and the Representation of Melbourne." *Australian Historical Studies* 27 no.109, (October 1997): 64–76.

Davison, Graeme. *Car Wars: How the Car Won Our Hearts and Conquered Our Cities*. Crow's Nest, NSW: Allen & Unwin, 2004.

Duncan, Sam. "Why You Shouldn't Expect Racing to Change its Ways." *The New Daily*, November 7, 2018. https://thenewdaily.com.au/sport/racing/2018/11/07/racing-cliffsofmoher-melbourne-cup/.

Edwards, Jean. "Melbourne Grand Prix: Victorian Pay Record Price for Formula One Race." *ABC News Victoria*, October 22, 2015. https://www.abc.net.au/news/2015-10-22/melbourne-grand-prix-victorians-pay-record-price-race/6878030.

Engels, Benno. "State Entrepreneurialism and Place Promotion: Lessons from Victoria." *The Journal of Australian Political Economy* 43 (June 1999): 88–123.

Eren, John. "Melbourne: The Sporting Capital of the World." *Media Release, Victorian State Government*, April 21, 2016. https://www.premier.vic.gov.au/melbourne-the-sporting-capital-of-the-world/.

Farquhar, Peter. "Nobody Really Knows How to React to Marvel Winning the Naming Rights to Melbourne's Etihad Stadium." *Business Insider Australia*, May 20, 2018. https://www.businessinsider.com.au/nobody-really-knows-how-to-react-to-marvel-winning-the-naming-rights-to-melbournes-etihad-stadium-2018-5.

Fogarty, Mark. "Losing F1 Could Prove the Greatest Cost of All." *Sydney Morning Herald*, February 24, 2013. https://www.smh.com.au/sport/motorsport/losing-f1-could-prove-the-greatest-cost-of-all-20130223-2ey3p.html.

Forbes, Mark. "Casinos Secrets Revealed." *Sydney Morning Herald*, August 9, 1994. https://www.smh.com.au/national/casino-secrets-revealed-20090821-et0m.html.
Forbes, Mark. "Inside the Casino Deal." *Sydney Morning Herald*, October 8, 1994. https://www.smh.com.au/national/inside-the-casino-deal-20090821-etfi.html.
Frost, James. "Walker Backs Controversial Stadium." *Australian Financial Review*, March 18, 2016: 11.
Harrison, Dan. "Ron Walker Fareweled at State Funeral Attended by Jeff Kennett, Daniel Andrews." *ABC News Melbourne*, February 7, 2018. https://www.abc.net.au/news/2018-02-07/mourners-farewell-major-events-maestro-ron-walker/9404932.
Harvey, David. *The Conditions of Postmodernity: An Enquiry into the Origins of Cultural Change*. Oxford England; Cambridge, Mass., USA: Blackwell, 1990.
Holmes, Dave. "How Kennett Gets Away with It." *Green Left Weekly*, September 28, 1994. https://www.greenleft.org.au/content/how-kennett-gets-away-it.
Hughes, Damien. "Council Slams Rent Deal for Caulfield Track: Exclusive." *Australian Financial Review*, November 22, 2018: 7.
Hyland, Anne. "Walker's War in Cancer." *Australian Financial Review*, January 30, 2015: 14.
John, Alistair. *Sport City: A Critical Analysis of Melbourne's Sportscape*. PhD diss., Victoria University, 2015.
John, Alistair, Bob Stewart and Brent McDonald. "Mixed Doubles: Political Hegemony, Urban Entrepreneurialism and the Australian Open Tennis Championship." *The International Journal of the History of Sport* 30 no. 2 (February 2013): 162–178.
Kehoe, John. "Dress it up as Women's Sport Under the Guise of Women's Sport." *Australian Financial Review*, February 15, 2019: 8.
Kitney, Damon, and James Chessell. "Fairfax Rejects Walker's Bid for *The Age* and Radio 3AW." *The Advertiser*, June 14, 2011. https://www.adelaidenow.com.au/business/fairfax-rejects-walker-age-bid/news-story/b303cc6d5e4b4bef8672761f74670858.
Lenaghan, Nick. "Victoria Racing Club Considers Next Move for Flemington." *Australian Financial Review*, February 17, 2017. https://www.afr.com/real-estate/victoria-racing-club-considers-next-move-for-flemington-land-20170217-gufc6b.
Lowes, Mark. "Neoliberal Power Politics and the Controversial Site of the Australian Grand Prix. Motor Sport Event in an Urban Setting." *Society and Leisure* 27 no. 1, (March 2004): 69–88.
Lowes, Mark. "Towards a Conceptual Understanding of Formula One Motorsport and Local Cosmopolitanism Discourse in Urban Placemarketing Strategies." *Communication and Sport* 6 no. 2 (April 2018): 203–218.
Mayne, Stephen. "How Crown Prince Packer Conquered Melbourne." *Crikey*, November 4, 2014. https://www.crikey.com.au/2014/11/04/mayne-how-crown-prince-packer-conquered-melbourne/.
McChesney, Robert W. "Noam Chomsky and the Struggle Against Neoliberalism." *Monthly Review* 50, no. 11, (April 1999): 40–47.
McIlwraith, Ian. "Grounds and Revenue: Some AFL Clubs Score Goals, Others Behinds." *Sydney Moring Herald*, September 30, 2011: 9.
Millar, Royce, and Ben Schneiders. "Transurban; The Making of a Monster." *The Age*, May 14, 2016. https://www.theage.com.au/national/victoria/transurban-the-making-of-a-monster-20160512-gotjm9.html.

Minister for Racing. "Boost for the 2017 Melbourne Cup Carnival." *Media Release, Victorian State Government Printer*, October 30, 2017. https://www.premier.vic.gov.au/boost-for-the-2017-melbourne-cup-carnival/.

National Nine News (NINE NETWORK Melbourne). "Bernie Sticks to his Guns Over Night Time Melbourne Grand Prix." June 17, 2008.

National Nine News (NINE NETWORK Melbourne). "Exclusive Details about Twilight Grand Prix." November 24, 2008.

Neales, Sue. "Kennett Unveils Melbourne's Grand Prix Masterplan." *The Age*, November 16, 1994: 5.

Nicholson, Mathew. "Motor Sport." In *The Encyclopedia of Melbourne, the City Past and Present*, edited by Andrew Brown-May and Shurlee Swain, 491. Port Melbourne, Vic.: Cambridge University Press, 2007.

O'Hanlon, Seamus. "The Events City: Sport, Culture, and the Transformation of Inner Melbourne, 1977-2006." *Urban History Review*, 37 no. 2 (2009): 30–39.

Reed, Ron. "Retiring Kevan Gosper Admits Melbourne's 1996 Olympic Bid Wasn't Winnable," *Herald Sun*, November 23, 2013. https://www.heraldsun.com.au/sport/retiring-kevan-gosper-admits-melbournes-1996-olympic-games-bid-wasnt-winnable/news-story/e41cd7a59b3ed1dd6c2ba742034f5b49.

Schmook, Nathan. "McGuire Leading Push for New Stadium." *AFL.com.au*, March 9, 2016. https://www.afl.com.au/news/2016-03-09/eddie-mcguire-leading-push-for-new-1-billion-football-stadium-near-mcg.

Seven Nightly News (SEVEN Melbourne). "New Controversy over Melbourne's Formula 1 Grand Prix." January 24, 2011.

Seven Nightly News (SEVEN Network). "Race at Risk: Melbourne Could Lose the F1 Grand Prix After Secret License Fees Paid to F1 Chief Were Disclosed." January 23, 2013.

Seven Nightly News (SEVEN Melbourne). "Taxpayers Propping Up F1 Grand Prix: Victorian Taxpayers have had to Prop Up This Year's Grand Prix." October 30, 2008.

Seven Nightly News (SEVEN Melbourne). "Victorian Government Upset at Claims Grand Prix Could Be Lost to Melbourne." February 3, 2008.

Smith, Andrew. "Sporting a New Image? Sport-based Regeneration Strategies as a Means of Enhancing the Image of the City Tourist Destination." In *Sport in the City. The Role of Sport in Economic and Social Regeneration*, edited by Chris Gratton and Ian P. Henry, 127–148. London: Routledge, 2001.

State Government of Victoria. *Victoria, The Next Step: Economic Opportunities and Initiatives for the 1980s*. Melbourne: Victorian Government Printer, 1984.

Stensholt, John. "Etihad Stadium Owners Agitate for Sale." *Australian Financial Review*, February 22, 2015. https://www.afr.com/news/etihad-stadium-owners-agitate-for-sale-20150219-13jl2h.

Stensholt, John. "How Etihad Stadium Has Transformed the AFL into a Financial Powerhouse." *Australian Financial Review*, March 25, 2018: 20.

Stephens, Peter. "Purse Strings May Hang Melbourne's Bid." *Washington Post*, September 17, 1990: C15.

Ten 5PM News (TEN Melbourne). "Grand Prix's Future." March 1, 2012.

Ten 5PM News, (TEN Melbourne). "Revving Up: Melbourne's Grand Prix Organizers Have Used this Year's Launch to Defend its Long-term Viability." February 2, 2012.

The Economist Intelligence Unit. *A Summary of the Livability Ranking & Overview*. August 2015. https://www.eiu.com/public/topical_report.aspx?campaignid=Liveability2015.

Thomsen, Simon. "'Mr. Melbourne' Business Giant and GP Boss Ron Walker Has Died Aged 78." *Business Insider Australia*, January 30, 2018. https://www.businessinsider.com.au/melbourne-ron-walker-died-2018-1.

Winter, Caroline, and Ward Yong. "Fashion, Fantasy and Fallen Horses; Alternate Image of Thoroughbred Racing." *Annals of Leisure Research*, 17, no. 4: 359–376.

Worrall, Alison. "Eddie McGuire Proposes $1b New Stadium near MCG." *The Age*, March 8, 2016. https://www.theage.com.au/national/victoria/eddie-mcguire-proposes-1-billion-new-stadium-near-mcg-20160308-gndzh4.html.

Section II: **Sports, Politics, and Racism**

Thomas Aiello
4 In the Land of Dreamy Dreams: Tennis and the Nexus of Class and Race in New Orleans, 1876–1976

Perhaps the most famous match played at the New Orleans Lawn Tennis Club never actually happened. LaGrande McGruder only agreed to play a match against Roxanne Miller after continued prodding, not wanting to because Miller was, in her conception, "a cripple," and because Miller and her husband were new members, Jews, only admitted because the club had just moved to a new location and needed an infusion of cash. McGruder, whose father had once been president of the United States Lawn Tennis Association, had played at the club her entire life, and was confident that she could easily throttle the crippled, Jewish newcomer. But the newcomer was good. She surprised McGruder with shot after improbable shot, until finally a frustrated McGruder called a ball out that was clearly not out, hoping to gain an advantage. She did, and after that momentum swing, she was able to defeat the interloper, but it was a Rubicon of sorts for McGruder. She was so frustrated with herself that she drove to the Huey P. Long Bridge and dumped her tennis equipment into the Mississippi River.[1]

The McGruder-Miller match occurred in Ellen Gilchrist's (1935-) short story, "In the Land of Dreamy Dreams," McGruder's abandonment of tennis after failure in the face of moral crisis mirrored by the crisis of faith in her mentor, Claiborne Redding, who lamented the infusion of new-money members, Jewish members, and their breach of protocol. Coffee was being served in styrofoam cups with powdered creamer, for example, whereas at the old club waiters had formerly brought café au lait in silver serving. Nailor, the black groundskeeper, was equally wistful about the bygone era. Gilchrist's story, published in 1981 but taking place in 1977, used the coffee cups and the violation of honor to symbolize the passing away of upper-class insulation that was part and parcel of the competitive tennis culture at the club. The old standards of class and culture that had dominated from 1876 to 1976 had seemingly dissolved in a styrofoam cup of stale coffee.

Tennis in New Orleans was, as it was in other urban areas, a vehicle of restrictive exclusivity, but that exclusivity worked in myriad ways across lines of class and race, beginning with the founding of Gilchrist's New Orleans Lawn Tennis

---

[1] Ellen Gilchrist, "In the Land of Dreamy Dreams," in *In the Land of Dreamy Dreams: Short Fiction* (Fayetteville: University of Arkansas Press, 1981), 60–71.

https://doi.org/10.1515/9783110679397-004

Club in 1876 and moving through a century beset by racial and economic turmoil. Post-Reconstruction New Orleans tennis looked much like antebellum Louisiana writ large, with a small exclusive upper class, an also-small upper-middle class with slightly less exclusivity but seeking as much as they could muster, then the majority of white players below who were left to use playing ability rather than social or financial status to gain access. Then there was the black population that was excluded from all of that competition, middle and upper class players participating in a separate world until pioneers came along to push back against that closed system. Black tennis in New Orleans, then, democratized from the top down, those with access working to open doors for themselves, then leading the way for their social and economic inferiors who otherwise would not have access. White tennis, meanwhile, democratized from the bottom up, with players originally priced or classed out of the NOLTC making new opportunities to play the game and creating new access for a new group of players.

The modern version of tennis came about in England in 1873, and the following year, American Mary Ewing Outerbridge (1852–1886) brought the game to Staten Island. In 1877, formal rules for the game would be established by the All-England Croquet and Lawn Tennis Club, Wimbledon. Even before Wimbledon's rules, however, the United States had first developed its own club for the sport in December 1876, the New Orleans Lawn Tennis Club, still the nation's oldest.[2]

December 1876 was an inauspicious time to begin such an endeavor, after the contested presidential election of 1876 and before the Compromise of 1877 two months later that would eventually withdraw the remaining federal troops from New Orleans and restore home rule. The NOLTC was founded at the tail end of a violent Reconstruction process that began with a bloody race riot where mobs of angry whites murdered 44 black victims and wounded 150 more outside of the city's Mechanics Institute. As the NOLTC formed, the city was still reeling from a September 1874 coup known locally as the Battle of Liberty Place, wherein a band of roughly five thousand members of the White League, a paramilitary terrorist organization affiliated with the far right wing of the Democratic Party, attacked the police and held the statehouse for three days before fleeing to escape the arrival of federal troops. If that weren't enough, just a year after the club formed and home rule was restored, a yellow fever outbreak that killed

---

[2] Carolyn Kolb, "For the Love of Tennis," *New Orleans Magazine* 44 (December 2009): 54–55; New Orleans *Times-Picayune*, 25 February 1898, 14; and Elizabeth Wilson, *Love Game: A History of Tennis, from Victorian Pastime to Global Phenomenon* (Chicago: University of Chicago Press, 2014), 9–27.

thousands in the city and even more throughout the lower Mississippi Valley in 1878. Despite political, social, and environmental turmoil, however, the NOLTC forged ahead.[3]

The development of an upper-class tennis culture in New Orleans also came at an inauspicious economic time in the city's history. The NOLTC was founded in between the Panic of 1873, which decimated the city's economy, and the yellow fever epidemic that decimated a portion of its population. Understandably, the city's economic growth rate was not as pronounced as it was in its antebellum heyday, but its economic growth in products traveling by rail and products traveling from the Gulf both more than doubled over the course of the Gilded Age, keeping New Orleans the country's second largest port, though the economic distance between it and New York continued to grow. Throughout the late 19th century, according to historian Joy Jackson, both capital and labor "had organized and centralized their efforts," and despite the interracial cooperation of some of the city's trade unions, the rich continued to get richer.[4]

As Eric Arnesen has demonstrated, the 1880s were a legitimately successful decade for the labor movement in the city, as biracial unions and segregated black and white unions of waterfront workers acting in tandem helped cotton workers and stevedores earn more control over the conditions of their employment, aided by a "Democratic party machine" that helped unions "confront employers in an unfettered way." The 1890s saw that movement decline as racism rose in the wake of Jim Crow and the economy fell in the wake of the Panic of 1893. But it didn't disappear. Strikes littered the New Orleans waterfront in the first decade of the twentieth century, facilitated by interracial unionism that was blamed for all of the unrest. In the decades that followed, the employers, many of whom were members of the NOLTC, would consolidate their control, creating labor stability and less control for workers, which only further highlighted the differentiation between social and economic classes, even after the city's red light district had largely disappeared.[5]

---

3 See James G. Hollandsworth, *An Absolute Massacre: The New Orleans Race Riot of July 30, 1866* (Baton Rouge: Louisiana State University Press, 2004); Justin Nystrom, *New Orleans After the Civil War: Race, Politics, and a New Birth of Freedom* (Baltimore: Johns Hopkins University Press, 2010); and Khaled J. Bloom, *The Mississippi Valley's Great Yellow Fever Epidemic of 1878* (Baton Rouge: Louisiana State University Press, 1993).

4 Joy J. Jackson, *New Orleans in the Gilded Age: Politics and Urban Progress, 1880–1896* (Baton Rouge: Louisiana State University Press, 1969), 204–231. Quote from 231.

5 Eric Arnesen, *Waterfront Workers of New Orleans: Race, Class, and Politics, 1863–1923* (New York: Oxford University Press, 1991), 74, 119–121, 160–1161, 204; and Roger W. Shugg, *Origins of Class Struggle in Louisiana: A Social History of White Farmers and Laborers during Slavery and After, 1840–1875* (Baton Rouge: Louisiana State University Press, 1939), 197–233, 274–314.

The club's first president was Gustaf Westfeldt (1852–1916), of the city's Westfeldt Brothers Coffee empire. He was joined by founding members like Atwood Violett (1847–1932), who was president of the Southern Mineral and Land Improvement Company, the Standard Fireless Engine Company, and the New Orleans Telephone Company, along with several other powerful city businesses. Gilbert Green was a prominent banker. N.D. Wallace was a powerful cotton factor who owned several other companies. They were joined by leaders like Henry Charnock, an import-export magnate who had come to New Orleans from England, bringing his passion for the new game with him, and several other English immigrants. It was an elite group, and their intent was to create an elite club, an organization that catered to those of similar breeding.[6]

The club's location bounced around in the late 19th century from the corner of Jackson and Prytania streets to another Prytania location to the corner of Dryades and Amelia until it finally settled in February 1898 on Saratoga Street, where it would stay until 1973. To secure its Saratoga Street location, members formed a private stock company. Selling stock in the new company facilitated the land purchase and building of its first clubhouse, with a broad viewing gallery that overlooked the playing space. Because of the club's English influence, the gallery always featured afternoon tea. The club's groundskeeper, John Irwin, rolled and graded an area for twelve Bermuda grass courts. With many British immigrants among the membership, space was also set aside for a cricket crease. On its initial founding, women were only allowed to play on Wednesday afternoons, designated Ladies' Day, but upon the purchase of its new space formal ladies' memberships were opened to women (though full "stockholder" memberships would not be open to women until 1998).[7]

Tennis made sense as a southern entity, a region dominated by a wealthy oligarchy who had kept millions of its black citizens enslaved and recently carried the bulk of its poorer white citizens into a costly and devastating war to protect an

---

6 Kolb, "For the Love of Tennis," 54–55; "About Us," Westfeldt Brothers, Inc., Coffee Importers. Accessed January 13, 2018 http://www.westfeldtcoffee.com/about.html; Andrew Morrison, *New Orleans and the New South* (New Orleans: Metropolitan Publishing Co., 1888), 10, 114; T.P. Thompson, "Early Financing in New Orleans, Being the Story of Canal Bank, 1831–1915," in *Publications of the Louisiana Historical Society*, vol. 7, 1913–1914 (New Orleans: Louisiana Historical Society, 1915), 57; *Biographical and Historical Memoirs of Louisiana*, vol. 2 (Chicago: Goodspeed Publishing Co., 1892), 441; and Missouri Pacific Railroad Co. v. International Marine Insurance Co., 84 Texas 149, in *The American and English Railroad Cases*, vol. 55, ed. William M. McKinney (Northport, Long Island: Edward Thompson Co., 1893), 549.
7 Kolb, "For the Love of Tennis," 54–55; Stephen Tignor, "The Survivor," *Tennis* 42 (September 2006): 86–89; and New Orleans *Times-Picayune*, 25 February 1898, 14. See also Ann Maden, "Popular Sports in New Orleans, 1890–1900" (MA Thesis: Tulane University, 1956): 63–64, 80.

investment in which those poor fighters would never participate. "The remarkable interest displayed in lawn tennis throughout the North, and the increasing popularity of the game, as shown each year by the multitude of new players and new clubs, have been fully equaled in the South during the past two seasons," one commentator concluded in 1889. "The Southern interest is an awakening one. The athletes of that section have become aware, only during the last few years, that lawn tennis is a game which fully develops every muscle, and at the same time possesses the elements of excitement and competition which render any athletic game more attractive."[8]

As Larry R. Youngs explains in his study of the intersection of sports and tourism in wintertime Florida in the Gilded Age and Progressive Era, "Having acquired the necessary time and disposable wealth, certain affluent men and women put increasing value on the quality and meaning of their time away from work and home." Youngs is interested in those from northern cities spending winters in Florida and the broader Southeast, but his analysis is fitting for many in New Orleans as well. "Such people increasingly embraced the idea that participating in outdoor recreation, including certain competitive sports, helped to immunize against the unhealthy aspects – both mental and physical – of modern urban life, especially life in an industrial and capitalistic society."[9]

Steven Reiss agrees with Youngs. "As widening income levels, substantial differences in discretionary time, and diverse social values resulted in different leisure options for different social classes" in the late 19th and early 20th centuries, "sport came to mark social boundaries and to define status communities."[10] That was certainly true in New Orleans, but in a place where "diverse social values" and "discretionary time" had always been part of the definition of the city itself, those boundary markers were going to be far more populous and far more intricate, particularly when a game like tennis, which already had its own social and economic boundary lines built into it, came to a city with its own pre-established boundaries.

---

8 H.W. Slocum, "Lawn Tennis in the South," *Outing* 13 (March 1889): 496.
9 Larry R. Youngs, "The Sporting Set Winters in Florida: Fertile Ground for the Leisure Revolution, 1870–1930," *Florida Historical Quarterly* 84 (2005): 59. Pre-revolutionary Cuba was a similar kind of destination for Americans of wealth. A similar argument is made, for example, in Rosalie Schwartz, *Pleasure Island: Tourism and Temptation in Cuba* (Lincoln: University of Nebraska Press, 1997), and, to a lesser extent, in Louis A. Perez, *On Becoming Cuban: Identity, Nationality, and Culture* (Chapel Hill: University of North Carolina Press, 1999).
10 Steven A. Riess, *City Games: The Evolution of American Urban Society and the Rise of Sports* (Urbana: University of Illinois Press, 1989), 53.

As Alecia Long has noted in her study of post-Civil War New Orleans concert saloons, social class and respectability were deeply intertwined among the city's citizens. They bore a particular weight on African Americans and immigrants, most of whom appeared at the mouth of the MIssissippi with far fewer privileges than the English immigrants who helped found the NOLTC. And respectability could easily be shaped by the places one chose to spend his time. Long evaluates an 1893 lawsuit brought against a local concert saloon by its neighboring businesses, each worried that the saloon was a nuisance to the neighborhood and that its presence would decrease property values. Lawyers emphasized that "people of the very lowest class and very lowest order" made up the bulk of the saloon's clientele. "Of course, there are occasions where gentlemen go there, but those are exceptions." One witness openly admitted not attending concert saloons because of the risk to his "good reputation." When one of the plaintiffs admitted that the shows at concert saloons were at least similar to the "ballet at the French Opera House," the lawyer questioning him asked, "One is the rich man's opera, and the other a poor man's opera, is that it?" The plaintiff rejected that comparison, but the implication was clear. Respectability was not alone built on ideology and bank account. It was also a creature of the buildings one frequented and the social codings for what went on inside them.[11]

Inherent in such endeavors was also a celebration of masculinity, as men frequented concert saloons to experience the hospitality of its female employees. While New Orleans was unique in some of its methods of excess, it was not unique in excess, as a working-class rejection of Victorian moral idealism in the postwar 19th century led to a new emphasis on toughness as a better biological standard on which to judge people, in lieu of more culturally constructed and unfair categories like social standing and wealth. Thus developed the saloon bloodsport culture across the country, which also dominated in New Orleans and fed the city's ever-expanding bar scene. Concert saloons themselves served a different purpose, but bar culture, animal bloodsports, and the working-class reaction against Victorianism would give way to a boxing culture that absolutely dominated in New Orleans, a reputation solidified at the city's Olympic Club in September 1892, when Jim Corbett (1866–1933) knocked out John L. Sullivan (1858–1918) in twenty-one rounds to win the heavyweight championship. Boxing was the living embodiment of the social Darwinian ideal, as the strongest survived despite privilege of birth or 'breeding,' and thus leveled the social playing

---

[11] Alecia P. Long, *The Great Southern Babylon: Sex, Race, and Respectability in New Orleans, 1865–1920* (Baton Rouge: Louisiana State University Press, 2004), 66–69, 95–97. The case from which Long's analysis derives, and from which the quotes appear, is *Koehl, et al. v. Schoenhausen*, 47 La. An. 1316, 17 So. 809 (1895).

field. It created, in what Elliot Gorn has described, explaining the draw of the *Police Gazette*, proud progenitor of such amusements, "a democracy of pleasure denied by Victorian culture."[12]

It was hard to argue biology, and so Victorians, in turn, sought to develop their own athletic ethic. Already shunning physical brutality as they had done prostitution and concert saloons, the middle and upper classes sought to cordon off a place for uplifting, beneficial sports. They celebrated amateurism as the ultimate sports experience to counter the pay and professionalization in boxing (and, increasingly, in team sports like baseball). In 1888, for example, the Amateur Athletic Union developed under the original auspices of the New York Athletic Club as an umbrella organization to organize amateur athletic contests – to celebrate pure competition devoid of the professionalism that brought ruin to players and fans.[13] Amateur sports like tennis, golf, and polo generally required a club membership of one kind or another. Thus they solved every Victorian problem in one fell swoop. They taught amateur values, shunned the violence of lower class sports, and had a built-in system for ensuring that only those of a certain class and breeding would be able to participate. The NOLTC was far different than a concert saloon, but it worked the same way socially.

In the 1890s, YMCA leader Luther Halsey Gulick (1865–1918) emphasized the organization's athletic offerings, arguing for what he called "muscular Christianity." Spiritual life rests on the equal development of the mind and the body, he argued, so not developing the body was against the will of God. Gulick became a leader in the Boy Scouts movement and the Playground Association of America, among other similar endeavors. He also teamed with sociologist G. Stanley Hall (1846–1924) of Clark University to develop a pseudobiological response to the "survival of the fittest" mantra of boxing enthusiasts. Their evolutionary theory of play became incredibly influential in the early 20th century, arguing in a roundabout way that humans had developed an impulse to play during evolution and that everyone mimicked the broader stages of human evolution in every phase of their lives. With each person recapitulating the history of humanity through sports, those games were necessarily essential to proper physical, moral, and neural growth. Gulick and Hall used their

---

[12] Elliott J. Gorn, *The Manly Art: Bare-Knuckle Prize Fighting in America* (Ithaca: Cornell University Press, 1986), 83.
[13] Eric Danhoff, "The Struggle for Control of Amateur Track and Field in the United States," *Canadian Journal of History of Sport and physical Education* 6, no. 1 (1975): 43–85; and Richard Wettan and J.D. Willis, "Effect of New York Athletic Clubs on Amateur Athletic Governance, 1870–1915," *Research Quarterly. American Alliance for Health, Physical Education and Recreation* 47, no. 3 (1976): 499–505.

paradigm to argue for the benefit of team sports in particular, but it also provided a greater emphasis on physical activity for those not attending boxing matches and concert saloons.[14]

The bind in which upper class tennis enthusiasts found themselves, however, is that precisely because of its association with wealth and leisure, tennis was not placed on par with other, more democratic physical activities. At the national level, its reputation for effete dandyism even developed among the privileged at times. In 1878, several Harvard men deserted crew for tennis, and the school newspaper was indignant. "Is it not a pity that serious athletics should be set aside by able-bodied men for a game that is at best intended for a seaside pastime?" asked *The Crimson*. "The game is well enough for lazy or weak man, but men who have rowed or taken part in a nobler sport should blush to be seen playing Lawn Tennis."[15]

Still, it was a Harvard man who contributed to the game's rise in national popularity, when in 1900 Dwight F. Davis (1879–1945) established the International Lawn Tennis Challenge Cup to foster international rivalries. A generation later, superstars like Big Bill Tilden (1893–1953) and Suzanne Lenglen (1899–1938) drove an even greater national obsession with the game.[16] What they were unable to do, particularly in places like New Orleans where class and respectability politics were so intertwined, and where the NOLTC was the symbol of both tennis and restrictive exclusivity, was to disassociate the game from its privileged image.

American tennis had always been a decidedly upper-class endeavor. The first United States tennis championship took place in August and early September, 1881 in Newport, Rhode Island. Held at the Casino Club, an institution so exclusive that it denied membership to president Chester Arthur (1829–1886) because he did not have what the club considered to be the proper social standing.[17]

That being the case, tennis clubs like NOLTC created social cues for those who wanted to identify themselves as having become part of the city's elite. In New Orleans, the game's upper class status was cemented not just by club exclusivity,

---

[14] See Clifford Putney, *Muscular Christianity: Manhood and Sports in Protestant America, 1880–1920* (Cambridge: Harvard University Press, 2003).

[15] *Harvard Crimson*, April 5, 1878, 2.

[16] Wilson, *Love Game*, 19, 56–69, 74–79, 113–122. See also Marshall Jon Fisher, *A Terrible Splendor: Three Extraordinary Men, a World Poised for War, and the Greatest Tennis Match Ever Played* (New York: Broadway Books, 2010); Frank Deford, *Big Bill Tilden: The Triumphs and the Tragedy* (New York: Simon and Schuster, 1976); and Larry Engelmann, *The Goddess and the American Girl: The Story of Suzanne Lenglen and Helen Wills* (New York: Oxford University Press, 1988).

[17] Benjamin G. Rader, *American Sports, from the Age of Folk Games to the Age of Televised Sports*, Fifth ed. (Upper Saddle River, NJ: Prentice Hall, 2004), 67.

but by the corresponding disinterest of everyone not included in the club. "Why lawn tennis, one of the most fascinating of out door amusements open to both sexes, has not attained to a more extended popularity in this city, is a mystery," wondered the city's *Times-Picayune* newspaper in 1879. The game's required supplies were relatively inexpensive, costing less "than that of a cheap croquet set." And yet croquet was still more popular, though it was less skillful, athletic, and exciting.[18] What the paper failed to take into account was that in those early days, tennis was associated almost solely with the NOLTC, with wealth, making it anathema to so many without such means.

As if to highlight that disconnect, the paper ran an anonymous piece of fiction in 1880 that told of an idle young wealthy man who still maintained some work at the city's cotton exchange. When asked why, he explained that "it helps me along wonderfully in society, when I talk about my 'June deliveries,' and all the other contracts I have on hand. Really, a fellow can't be playing lawn tennis all the time, you know – really he can't." Another editorial comment that year referred to lawn tennis mockingly as "Presbyterian base ball."[19]

Adding another hindrance and making the rise of New Orleans tennis all the more improbable, the tennis players of early New Orleans entered a climate that was relatively averse to sports. "Exercise for health reasons was not stressed or considered worth promoting," writes historian Joy Jackson. "Most men preferred to spend their hours after work or on Sunday afternoons at their social clubs, or at saloons and beer gardens." By the 1890s, however, that attitude had changed. Baseball and bicycling gained an incredible popularity, along with tennis, golf, crew, and yachting. And their popularity was growing, even among those not of advantageous breeding. In 1880, for example, Seebold's on Canal Street, a store typically dedicated to books, stationery, and art supplies, began advertising the sale of tennis equipment, along with supplies for archery and croquet.[20]

That democratizing trend would exist at the top of the social hierarchy as well. The NOLTC's club championship tournament began in 1890, won twice in its first seven years by plantation owner and sugar magnate C.C. Krumbhaar (1874–1946). In 1901, after substantial debate, the club began an annual interclub tournament. It was not the sort of event that aided restrictive exclusivity, but because of that exclusivity, in the words of the *Times-Picayune*, the club was "comparatively a stranger to the tennis world at large, and must necessarily win its

---

18 New Orleans *Times-Picayune*, July 26, 1879, 4.
19 New Orleans *Times-Picayune*, May 2, 1880, 2, September 7, 1880, 4.
20 Jackson, *New Orleans in the Gilded Age*, 261–268. Quote from 261. The advertisements continued through much of the year. For an example, see New Orleans *Times-Picayune*, March 28, 1880, 8.

own recognition by the excellence of its tournaments and the skill of its members." Much of the benefit of exclusivity, in other words, came from others knowing what they were missing. That first event included teams from the Tulane Tennis Club and Alameda Tennis Club, along with a delegation from Georgia's Atlanta Athletic Club. The Atlantans had only played on clay and came to the NOLTC to test their skills on grass. Still, the club had not become a democracy overnight. No spectators were admitted without a special card that certified them as worthy of watching the tournament.[21]

It was, however, a first step. The following year the club took a second step, aligning officially with the United States Lawn Tennis Association and hosting the Gulf States Championship, which the venue would continue to host annually from 1902 to 1914. The Gulf States awarded prizes in men's and ladies' singles and men's doubles. After winners were declared in the men's divisions, winners played the champions from the previous year for a challenge cup. All matches were decided by two of three sets, with the exception of the men's finals and challenge matches, which were best three of five. The club was also part of the Southern Lawn Tennis Association, organized in 1887 and by the early 1900s comprised of clubs in Atlanta, Memphis, Knoxville, Macon, Montgomery, Mobile, and Greenville, South Carolina. The SLTA's founding document included the express dictum, "No club which is situated north of Wilmington, Delaware, should be admitted to membership in the Association."[22]

Beginning in 1914, the NOLTC graduated to hosting the Southern Championship, a larger event than the Gulf States with the same divisions and rules. To make the club more accommodating to visiting tournament players, in 1925 the NOLTC added four clay courts and a concrete court to compliment its grass offerings.[23]

This emphasis on tournament play may at first seem to cut against the bent toward restrictive exclusivity, but within the cloister of class-restricted tennis,

---

[21] New Orleans *Times-Picayune*, May 23, 1897, 8, June 24, 1901, 8; and "Stenographic Report of the Discussion at the Meeting of the Louisiana Sugar Planters' Association," *Louisiana Planter and Sugar Manufacturer* 56 (17 June 1916): 394–395

[22] The SLTA's first championships, in the 1880s and 1890s, took place on the east coast, rotating between Wilmington, Washington, DC, and Baltimore. Slocum, "Lawn Tennis in the South," 496; and "Lawn Tennis," *Sporting Life* 11 (11 July 1888): 11.

[23] *Atlanta Constitution*, April 8, 1902, 7, February 15, 1903, 2, March 20, 1904, B8, May 26, 1904, A3, March 20, 1908, 13, April 8, 1909, 11, July 8, 1909, 4, April 28, 1912, 16, June 22, 1913, 13, March 24, 1914, 9; *New York Tribune*, March 10, 1905, 6; *Christian Science Monitor*, June 10, 1912, 3, June 22, 1920, 10; New York *Herald Tribune*, June 13, 1947, 27; *Chicago Tribune*, March 12, 1905, A2; *New York Times*, March 16, 1901, 10, March 15, 1903, 10, March 10, 1905, 7, March 11, 1906, 11, May 2, 1920, 21; *Boston Globe*, February 15, 1903, 2; and *Los Angeles Times*, June 5, 1925, B1.

where everyone was white and everyone had basically equal pocketbooks, winning became the arbiter of prestige, a way to find the first among equals. Even the athletic contest itself, then, became part of the social contest outside of its fault lines.[24]

The club's place as a venue for the Southern Championship lasted into the 1950s, a tournament that would come to be dominated in the 1930s, 40s, and 50s by the diminutive Bryan "Bitsy" Grant (1909–1986), who won the championship eleven times. Grant was the South's best player, despite being 5′4″ and only 120 pounds. The Atlantan had grown up playing on that city's clay courts and translated that experience into three National Clay Court Championships titles. He defeated Ellsworth Vines (1911–1994) and Don Budge (1915–2000) and played on three Davis Cup teams. Despite the lack of clay, New Orleans was a second home for the southerner, who demonstrated to his fellow players that southern tennis could be a vehicle to global renown in the game.[25]

The success of the club and its tournament would certainly redound to Grant, but it would also have more local beneficiaries, as Tulane's tennis team became a dominant force, winning seventeen SEC championships in the 1940s and 1950s. One of its most prominent stars was two-time NCAA singles champion Hamilton "Ham" Richardson (1933–2006), who would supplant Grant as one the dominant southern players in the 1950s and 60s.[26]

Tulane's success was orchestrated by a different kind of migrant. Emmet Paré (1907–1973) was from Chicago, a professional who had toured with Bill Tilden before coming to New Orleans in 1934 to coach the Tulane tennis team and serve as the teaching pro for the NOLTC. Along with his team's SEC championships, he also led them to the 1959 NCAA national championship. Ham Richardson was not his only singles champion. Under Pare's watch, Tulane also produced Jack Tuero (1926–2004), Jose Aguero (1933–), and Ron Holmberg (1938–), all of whom won NCAA titles and became legends of New Orleans tennis at the NOLTC. The club and the university were near one another, and that proximity combined with the dual influence of Paré kept them in a symbiotic relationship.[27]

So too did the devotion of female players. Interest in tennis had been developing among the city's women since its inception. Though tennis had early been

---

24 Reiss makes this case for both early northern, urban athletic clubs and northern, suburban country clubs. See Reis, *City Games*, 57–59.
25 *Atlanta Constitution*, May 28, 1920, 9, June 21, 1920, 7, June 22, 1920, 11, June 13, 1947, 14, June 7, 1953, 4D, June 12, 1953, 30, June 24, 1956, 7D; *Atlanta Journal-Constitution*, September 10, 2005, A8; and *New York Times*, June 10, 1953, 40.
26 *Atlanta Constitution*, May 7, 1959, 48.; and *Atlanta Daily World*, June 12, 1953, 3.
27 Tignor, "The Survivor," 86–89

pilloried as a "ladies game," and men had pushed back against the accusation, others saw the game more positively as "a game in which the elements of exercise and competition are combined." For a woman, "lawn tennis seems to be her only refuge. It is the one athletic game which women may enjoy without being subjected to sundry insinuations of rompishness." Such sentiments drove female interest in tennis, leading, for example, to the NOLTC's "Ladies' Day" and other opportunities to play, the one cardinal rule for women being "no heeled shoes."[28]

With the game's popularity continuing to grow, the city's Audubon Park installed its own lawn tennis court in 1901, as did City Park, and the following year a group of players formed an early version of the City Park Tennis Club. It didn't last, but the city's interest in tennis did begin growing, and in 1922 City Park expanded to include seventeen public tennis courts for white players. In March 1928, a group of thirteen players formed a new version of the City Park Tennis Club. They were a group of far more modest means, including the park's tennis pro, William Macassin – a white middle class coterie of tennis enthusiasts with no possibility of entering the NOLTC. That did not mean that the group was without means. In the heart of the Depression, the now-larger group offered the park $1000 annual rent for the exclusive use of six courts, and for three additional courts if the city would agree to build more. The city did, building nine more courts at a cost of $9,000 and reserving six of the new additions for the CPTC.[29] There was in the endeavor a clear understanding that while the club could not be as restrictive as that of its betters, it was still seeking validation through exclusivity and was willing to pay a substantial amount of Depression-era money to create it. Unlike the NOLTC, which began as an upper-class endeavor, the CPTC evolved from play at a public park over the course of a generation, demonstrating that even when starting from a relatively democratic base, the arc of tennis bent toward class exclusivity.

To mimic its social betters, the club soon started its own championship tournament, dominated in the 1930s by Paul Goosman. Goosman was not a planter or a banking magnate. He was a lower-middle class man who rented a small house on Annunciation Street in the Fourteenth Ward, a factory clerk who had

---

[28] Henry W. Slocum, Jr., "Lawn Tennis as a Game for Women," *Outing* 14 (1889): 289; and Somers, *The Rise of Sports in New Orleans*, 212.

[29] The original 1902 City Park Tennis Club grew quickly in popularity, open to whomever wanted to play. Forty-five had joined within the first month of its existence. Two courts were reserved for the members. New Orleans *Picayune*, 9 June 1902, 3; and "City Park Tennis Club: A Brief History." Accessed January 13, 2018. http://cityparktennisclub.com/.

only completed his second year of high school. His place on the city's social arc was earned not through his accomplishments but through his play.[30]

The obsession with appearance can be seen in two separate debates in the fall of 1937. The first was the use of shorts, a utilitarian new style that had dominated among many of the city's players, allowing for easier movement and a break from New Orleans's stifling heat. Some, however, were resistant, desiring to preserve the game's respectability over and against ease of play.[31]

The second came in a scandal involving Anna Koll (1905–1998), the city's best female player throughout much of the 1930s. In May, she was ruled ineligible to play in the public parks tournament in June and the city open tournament in September after being charged with professionalism by the USLTA. It was a scandal among the city's tennis players, as amateurism was upheld as the ultimate value in the sport, and Koll was accused only after local testimony essentially outed her as charging for tennis lessons. The reality that Koll had been accused by some of her own only added to the scandal, and she vigorously fought the charges. Her lawyer produced receipts that demonstrated the costs she incurred for balls, court rentals, and trophies for her students exceeded the payments she received. Koll, a school teacher by trade, produced a litany of witnesses to testify on her behalf, including the superintendent of athletics for New Orleans public schools. Even after the legal push, Koll's reinstatement in November happened not because the city open tennis committee or the USLTA admitted mistakes in judgment, but instead because the national body ruled that her suspension through the full run of the summer season was a substantial enough punishment. It was the kind of ruling that ended the controversy but kept the scarlet letter upon Koll who never regained her championship form. And so, whether through the more trivial collision between traditional fashion and improved performance or the more substantive clash between amateurism and professionalization, New Orleans tennis courts became a discursive theater for the politics of respectability.[32]

Making the controversy even more illustrative of the evident crosscurrents in national tennis and New Orleans society, earlier that year, the city's newfound passion for the game brought the biggest names in professional tennis to town. American Ellsworth Vines and Englishman Fred Perry (1909–1995) played an exhibition at the Tulane gym. The two major champions played each other on both

---
30 New Orleans *Times-Picayune*, September 23, 1935, 12; and Sixteenth Census of the United States, 1940, Population Schedule, New Orleans City, Louisiana, Sheet No. 8A.
31 It is no coincidence that the city's *Picayune* newspaper's first mention of lawn tennis in 1879 was in a fashion column suggesting outfits for the outing. New Orleans *Picayune*, July 13, 1879, 11; and New Orleans *Times-Picayune*, November 7, 1937, 4–3
32 New Orleans *Times-Picayune*, November 7, 1937, 4–3, November 14, 1937, 4–6.

American and British tours, finally making it to New Orleans, where Vines defeated an ailing Perry in straight sets. It was a contest attended by all of the city's tennis fans, the two players celebrated on their professional tour, just months before Koll was barred from city play after a false reading of a technicality branded her a professional with much different connotations than those of Vines and Perry.[33]

In a February 1938 exhibition, Vines played Perry in an repeat of the pair's earlier contest at the Tulane gym, part of another national professional tour. A decade later, on March 22, 1948, Bobby Riggs (1918–1995), Jack Kramer (1921–2009), Pancho Segura (1921–2017), and Dinny Pails (1921–1986) played exhibition matches at the Tulane gym. At the end of March, Charles E. Hart (1900–1991), former British Davis Cup captain, conducted a weekend clinic at City Park, Audubon Park, and the NOLTC. The event was a temporary postwar stay of the NOLTC's exclusivity, as the event was free and open to the public, putting many on the grounds who would not normally have a chance to do so.[34]

To provide a sense of ownership to those who were normally left out of such events, the city had created a public parks tournament – the same tournament from which Koll was originally barred – to build a measure of exclusivity going the other way. Established in 1923, the tournament, taking place at Audubon Park and City Park, barred those belonging to any club that had its own courts. It charged a twenty-five cent entry fee and required the loser of the match to pay for the balls. It was the people's tournament, and to demonstrate its popularity, the 1938 event had almost two hundred entrants.[35]

Over the first half of the 20th century, there were plenty of other clubs that began their own tennis programs, all with varying degrees of exclusivity. After the NOLTC, the West End Tennis Club organized in 1890, then the New Orleans Country Club, the Aurora Country Club, the Timberlane Country Club, the Audubon Tennis Club, the Lakewood Country Club, the Orleans Women's Tennis Club, and the Metairie Country Club all fielded players in the city's various tournaments. The New Orleans Bicycle Club and the Metropolitan Athletic Club drew court boundaries on croquet lawns to allow their members to play. Even more social organizations like the Elks and Linwood clubs began playing in the 1890s, all demonstrating that even those unable to join a club were interested in the game. Several more wealthy citizens built their own private courts. One local commentator suggested approvingly that "the laying out of the 'garden district'" in the city "makes possible many

---

33 New Orleans *Times-Picayune*, February 20, 1938, 4–6.
34 New Orleans *Times-Picayune*, February 13, 1938, 4–3, March 10, 1948, 18.
35 New Orleans *Times-Picayune*, June 15, 1923, 18, May 22, 1938, 4–2.

more private courts than in most large cities." Some tennis clubs, like Timberlane and Audubon, maintained teams in a Metropolitan New Orleans League pitting clubs against one another in the years following World War II. The rivalries between the groups were friendly ones. In 1930, for example, when rain slowed play at the New Orleans Country Club's annual men's invitational tournament, the NOLTC offered use of its courts to speed up play. In January 1967, when rain slowed the annual Sugar Bowl tournament, the championship match was moved to the NOLTC because the club had artificial light that facilitated nighttime play.[36]

City Park and Audubon Park remained the most influential early venues, though the grass of "lawn tennis" would prove too costly and labor-intensive to maintain. Audubon switched to clay and asphalt courts and City Park to clay, but clay too, had its problems, particularly for an area as water-logged as New Orleans. Clay retained water, keeping players off the courts long after a rain. In 1937, Audubon resurfaced its asphalt courts with concrete and its clay courts with brickdust, followed shortly by City Park, as brickdust was just as easy as clay to maintain but drained water far more rapidly.[37]

The new courts were part of a democratizing trend for white tennis in New Orleans, with players passionate about playing creating opportunities for themselves. Those opportunities would then generate greater expansion. From the early 1930s until World War II, Howard Jacobs's "Men in White" column in the New Orleans *Times-Picayune*, the city's largest daily newspaper, became the public voice of New Orleans tennis, reporting on local tournaments and players and showing citizens otherwise barred from the city's various clubs how and where they could participate. From the 1940s to the 1960s, the *Times-Picayune*'s Jimmie Powers served much the same purpose with his long-running "Over the Net" column.[38] The opportunities of new courts and columns in white newspapers, however, were not available to the white players' black counterparts.

African American tennis was almost as old as American tennis itself. The first black tennis clubs on the east coast began in the 1890s, the Chautauqua Club in Philadelphia in 1890, the Monumental City Tennis Club in Baltimore in 1895, and

---

36 New Orleans *Times-Picayune*, July 1, 1901, 11, December 9, 1901, 7, July 18, 1937, 4–6, September 10, 1964, 2–14; *New York Herald Tribune*, April 3, 1930, 28; Jackson, *New Orleans in the Gilded Age*, 266; Dale Somers, *The Rise of Sports in New Orleans, 1850–1900* (Baton Rouge: Louisiana State University Press, 1972), 211; *Spirit of the South*, February 2, 1889, 1; and *New York Times*, January 2, 1967, 27. Further, when major national conferences like the American Legion's annual gathering in 1922 occurred in New Orleans, the NOLTC allowed the conventioneers to hold their tennis tournament on the property. *New York Tribune*, September 10, 1922, B10.
37 New Orleans *Times-Picayune*, July 18, 1937, 4–6.
38 See, for example, New Orleans *Times-Picayune*, June 28, 1934, 16, May 22, 1938, 49, December 3, 1944, 28, October 30, 1949, 88, September 2, 1956, 58.

others forming during the decade in New York and Washington. Black tennis in the South also had its beginnings in the 1890s when Tuskegee built faculty courts on campus. Such foundings occurred in the era of Jim Crow retrenchment. They were necessary because early private tennis clubs like the NOLTC "were not just for the elites," notes historian Sundiata Djata, "but for white elites."[39] The black clubs that rose in response to that segregation began organizing tournaments as early as 1898, and at one such tournament in 1916, the idea for the American Tennis Association was conceived. The ATA was founded later that year to be the chief organizing body of black tennis, led for its first twelve years by Dr. H. Stanton McCard of Baltimore's Monumental City club. The organization held national championships and supported the game throughout metropolitan areas, particularly on the east coast.[40]

Of course, New Orleans had a prosperous black community even prior to the outbreak of the Civil War, and in the two decades after the conflict, that prosperity – or that prosperity's proximity to its white counterpart – continued to grow. Along with it grew the cultural life that accompanied privilege. "Negro social life in New Orleans was varied, rich, and in many ways a reflection of activities in the white community," explains John Blassingame. "This social life united the black community while at the same time accentuating class divisions." As the NOLTC was being formed, black New Orleans had its own symphony orchestra. It engaged in crew contests at the Saratoga Rowing Association and the Antoine Rowing Club. Upper-class endeavors like rifle matches or horse races also dominated, though tennis, as a game comparatively new compared to equestrian events, crew, and shooting, took longer to make an imprint.[41]

Such is not to say a nascent black interest did not exist. As early as 1881, five years after the founding of the NOLTC, the black *Weekly Louisianian* mentioned tennis as a distinctly British game. "*Nous connsiasons deja le cricket, le croquet, le lawn tennis, le polo et antres jeux d'importation anglaise,*" the *Louisianian* explained, lumping it with other games that black New Orleans did not play, like polo and cricket. Still, while the paper grouped the games together as English

---

39 Sundiata Djata, *Blacks at the Net: Black Achievement in the History of Tennis*, vol. 1 (Syracuse: Syracuse University Press, 2006), 2–4.
40 Gerald F. Norman, "National American Tennis Association Championships," *Opportunity* 6 (October 1928): 306–307; and Bertram Barker, "A Black Tennis Association: Active since 1916," in *American Tennis Association National Rankings, 1983–1984* (Philadelphia: American Tennis Association, 1984), 60.
41 John W. Blassingame, *Black New Orleans: 1860–1880* (Chicago: University of Chicago Press, 1973). 139–143.

imports, they were also games that served as signposts of social advancement and institutional wealth. They were foreign games, but they were also goals.⁴²

In December 1886, the *Weekly Pelican*, a later Gilded Age New Orleans black newspaper, ran a *New York Tribune* advertisement for *The Tribune Book of Open Air Sports*, a volume "especially for the young men of the United States" that would include chapters on both "Court Tennis" and "Lawn Tennis." The *Tribune* assured black New Orleans readers that "no book of this character has ever been put into print in America."⁴³ The same edition of the *Pelican* featured a story, "A Fir Pillow," about a relationship on a summer retreat between a man in his twenties and a woman in her fifties. The man, Jack, was "an active young fellow so devoted to tennis and baseball," which made the woman all the more curious as to why he would sit and sew with her, or as to "what tender, loving thoughts he was working into those great clumsy arms when I saw that peculiar far off look come into his beautiful brown eyes."⁴⁴

The *Pelican* was devoted to creating a cultured black middle class, reprinting articles from white papers throughout the country and world designed to aid such an end. Tennis was a symbol of social respectability, and so made it into the paper, despite a lack of any real play from black New Orleanians. In January 1887, for example, an article about the frustration of Parisians about the dress of Englishmen at French opera houses reported that one French newspaper suggested that "the unmannerly English will shortly look on at the play in their flannels 'du lawn tennis,' leaving their racquets in the cloak room."⁴⁵ Later that year, the *Pelican* reproduced an *American Magazine* article about "care in taking exercise." Mountain climbing "is to be avoided," as was most rowing and swimming, which could be "dangerous to any one whose heart is weak." It was, the article reasoned, an unnecessary risk. But "tennis is different. Although it requires agility and considerable exertion, there are intervals of rest that make it one of the safest of games. It is only necessary to slip on a light coat or shawl when a set is finished to avoid sudden chill."⁴⁶

An 1889 *Pelican* reprint, told in the voice of a rural upstate New York farmer who had seen his life transformed by cosmopolitans from the city vacationing on his farm, described experiencing the game for the first time. "Lucy's feller and the college dudes was playin' what they call lawn tennis out in the cow pastur

---

42 *Weekly Louisianian*, October 22, 1881, 1.
43 *Weekly Pelican*, December 25, 1886, 3, January 8, 1887, 3.
44 Another such upper-middle class genteel tale used tennis as another respectability signpost in 1889. *Weekly Pelican*, December 25, 1886, 4, January 15, 1887, 4, October 19, 1889, 1.
45 *Weekly Pelican*, January 8, 1887, 1.
46 *Weekly Pelican*, October 22, 1887, 4.

one day," explained the narrator. "The boys was waltzin' around the pastur' with their white coats and panties on." He had never seen a game that "looked more thrillin'. Me and the hired man just stood there and watched." Tennis, the article implied, was a cosmopolitan, elite game. Those who didn't play it were rubes. Black New Orleans residents were not yet playing the game in any sustained way, but they were receiving messages equating the game with Victorian respectability standards from an aspirational newspaper devoted to touting those standards.[47]

The *Louisiana Weekly*, founded in September 1925, first mentioned tennis in an Associated Negro Press article about the American Tennis Association 1926 national tournament in St. Louis. While the president of the St. Louis Tennis Association's statement that tennis fans in the city had "organized to secure the backing of the tournament by the entire Colored population" surely rankled the black upper class of New Orleans, forever in a rivalry with their Mississippi River neighbor to the north, tennis was only a developing interest of the city's black social set in the early 1920s.[48] The African-American clubs of New Orleans focused their early attention on dinners, dancing, and whist, a 17th century trick-taking card game popular in New Orleans and throughout south Louisiana. The Phyllis Wheatley Club, the Twentieth Century Whist Club, the Entre Nous Club, the Autocrat Club, the Marble Heart Whist Club, the Marechal Neil Aid and Pleasure Club, the Young Men Twenty Club, the Housewives Industrial Sewing Club, and dozens of other organized secular groups held meetings, parties, dances, teas, suppers, and "whists," but did not early entertain tennis as part of the social hierarchy.[49] Neither did the Iroquois Club, the oldest and most prominent black social club in the city.[50]

Though it wasn't as accessible as dancing, dinners, and whist, however, there was a small but prominent early black tennis presence in New Orleans. The St. Katherine Tennis Club served as the early home of the game's enthusiasts. Unlike

---

[47] *Weekly Pelican*, October 26, 1889, 3. There were other black weeklies in the city during this period, but what issues of those papers survive do not mention tennis. One of them, the Southern Republican, did, in 1900, demonstrate an interest in bicycling, but never expanded its coverage to any ball games. *Southern Republican*, April 14, 1900, 1, 3; *The Crusader*, July 19, 1890; *Black Republican*, April 15, 1865, April 22, 1865, April 29, 1865, May 13, 1865, May 20, 1865; and *Republican Courier*, December 2, 1899, January 20, 1900.
[48] *Louisiana Weekly*, January 9, 1926, 7.
[49] For further examples of some of these clubs, see the society page of the *Louisiana Weekly*. The listed entities, some of the most popular and continuous, appear in several of many mentions on January 16, 1926, 8; October 9, 1926, 5.
[50] Such is not to say that black New Orleans did not participate in the athletic fads of the era. Bicycling was popular. One black student even planned a bicycling excursion from New Orleans to New York. *Louisiana Weekly*, May 29, 1926, 1.

the NOLTC, membership was not based on social exclusivity but instead on a passion to play. In August 1926, the club announced that Edna Cordier, a local school teacher, and William Mitchell, the executive director of the Dryades Street YMCA, would represent the club at the ATA's St. Louis event. "Much interest is being manifested in tennis in New Orleans," St. Katherine's announced confidently, "with the result that there are several exceptional players." So much so that the group was helping to organize a Gulf States' Tennis Association that would have its headquarters in New Orleans.[51]

The Dryades Street YMCA was an important hub for such activity. In 1927, it sponsored the Colored Public School Athletic League to give boys and girls access to sports that school budgets couldn't give them. The Y's Young Men's Division paid particular attention to developing male youth. Other programs targeted boys and girls of various ages and interests. Such programs were necessary in 1920s New Orleans, when the Jim Crow line was starker than ever. The Amateur Athletic Union had scheduled its annual track meet for New Orleans in July 1927, for example, but pulled the event in April of that year after city officials and local leadership refused to include black athletes in an integrated meet. A city willing to sacrifice that much revenue and reputation to uphold the racial line in athletics made the mission of the Y that much more substantial. One of its chief projects was an annual summer camp in nearby Waveland, Mississippi at the Gulfside Chautauqua and Camp Meeting Grounds, a resort of more than six-hundred acres maintained entirely by black leaders for the recreation of the black population. The boys who made the trip camped in tents, they swam, hiked, did craft projects, and played tennis on the facility's new courts.[52]

In July 1927, Xavier University installed three tennis courts and began forming a tennis club. Xavier was a relatively new institution, founded in 1914, the same year that Southern University, originally a New Orleans school founded in 1880, moved to Scotlandville, just outside of Baton Rouge. Straight College was much older, established as Straight University in 1868 by the American Missionary Association. As such, it had already installed tennis courts and hosted an annual tournament in July for the city's black players. There were also courts for black players on the playground of the Thomy Lafon School, a public primary and secondary school associated with Straight, founded in honor of one of its principal donors, the Creole abolitionist and philanthropist Thomy Lafon (1810–1893). The school had been around since 1897, though the first iteration of the institution

---

51 *Louisiana Weekly*, August 26, 1929, 1.
52 *Louisiana Weekly*, April 2, 1927, 1, April 14, 1927, 1, 2, April 23, 1927, 2, April 30, 1927, 8, May 28, 1927, 8, August 13, 1927, 1, August 27, 1927, 1, September 3, 1927, 1.

destroyed in the New Orleans Race Riot of 1900. Its tennis courts did not appear until the 1920s. Additionally, black players could find a place to play on the Willow St. courts of the relatively new Lusher Elementary School, founded in 1917, where the YMCA would sometimes hold boys tournaments, or the John W. Hoffman Junior High School on South Prieur Street, where tennis courts were also part of the playground facilities. There were also courts at Daniel Hand School, a black preparatory school funded by the American Missionary Association and aligned with Straight.[53] Finally, there were courts available to black players at Gaudet House on Gentilly Road, the former rehabilitation compound of black social worker Frances Joseph-Gaudet (1861–1934), who used the several buildings on what became a wide campus for a school and orphanage before donating it to the Episcopal Diocese of Louisiana. The tennis courts on the property, then, became open to interested black Episcopalians who wanted to play.[54]

Late in July, the city's black newspaper, the *Louisiana Weekly*, began publishing a tennis column. "Yes, sir, tennis is here to stay," began the column's opening effort, devoted to celebrating Xavier's new courts. They would "become among the finest in the city if the plans for developing and maintaining them do not miscarry." The courts were clay and would drain well. "There is one thing sure and that is organization can do things. Xavier is organized. Tennis there will go." Everyone was invited, and yearly dues were one dollar. "This is a splendid opportunity for beginners to get a chance to play," the column encouraged. And they could even play on Sundays, "as tennis is considered as pure, wholesome recreation."[55]

The author of that and future efforts was E. Belfield Spriggins (unknown-1973), a teacher at McDonogh #35 High and Normal School who also wrote for the *Weekly* about his other passion, jazz. In his second tennis column, Spriggins lamented that "tennis is a great game and deserves to be played and studied by more of our group, both young and old." To that end, the column began in the proceeding weeks explaining how to choose a racket, where to buy supplies, the

---

53 *Louisiana Weekly*, July 23, 1927, 1, 8, August 20, 1927, 8, June 16, 1928, 8, July 7, 1928, 8; and William Ivy Hair, *Carnival of Fury: Robert Charles and the New Orleans Race Riot of 1900* (Baton Rouge: Louisiana State University Press, 1986), 177–178. For more on the influence of Thomy Lafon, see Frederick D. Smith, "Thomy Lafon," in *Encyclopedia of African American Business*, vol. 2, ed. Jessie Carney Smith (Westport, CT: Greenwood, 2006), 447–449.

54 The growth in availability of such courts benefited from a national boom in the production of places to play, particularly in urban areas. Between 1924 and 1931, the number of tennis courts in the United States increased by 81 percent. Reiss, *City Games*, 141–142; and *Louisiana Weekly*, August 11, 1828, 8. For more on Frances Joseph-Gaudet, see her autobiography, *He Leadeth Me* (New Orleans: Louisiana Printing Co., 1913).

55 *Louisiana Weekly*, July 30, 1927, 5.

rules and various methods for play.⁵⁶ It was a demonstration in microcosm of the differences between the sporting tendencies of white and black New Orleans. White players began immediately by coding the game with exclusivity, while black players pushed for democracy. Courts at the private Catholic college would be open to everyone with a small membership fee. Columns in the newspaper encouraged people to play and gave them advice for making that possible. It was a democratization of the game from those in power, from the top down, those with access instinctively opening the door to those who otherwise would not have access. Meanwhile, though a measure of democracy came to white tennis in New Orleans, it developed from the bottom up, players seeking access outside the cloister of the NOLTC making new opportunities to play the game.

That year, 1927, the ATA held its annual national tournament in Hampton, Virginia, on the campus of Hampton Institute. Spriggins was disheartened to note that no one from New Orleans would be representing the city at the event, but hoped that continued development of the game would grow national success and participation. At the national tournament, Ted Thompson of Washington defeated Everest Saitch of New York, Thompson avenging a finals loss to Saitch from the previous year. The women's final was also a return engagement, Lulu Ballard defeating Isadora Channels for the second year in a row. Thompson and Saitch, Ballard and Channels, along with Ora Washington (1898–1971), Edgar Brown (1898–1954), and Reginald Weir (1911–1987) were the powerhouses of black tennis, the precipice of where columnists like Spriggins wanted New Orleans to be.⁵⁷

In an effort to get there, Xavier held its now-annual tournament in September. Thirty-six entries marked a record for a black New Orleans event. The men's winner, Olando Moss, "the diminutive but explosive tennis flash, finally settled all disputes as to his local tennis supremacy by blazing his way from the first round to the undisputed local championship." The women's winner was Jeanne Victor, "little school girl southpaw from Xavier College," who "duplicated the feat of Mr. Moss and went him one better by winning all of her matches in straight sets."⁵⁸

Tennis was growing steadily among black New Orleanians. The following June, the Xavier Athletic Club and the Dryades Street YMCA both held tournaments

---

56 *Louisiana Weekly*, August 6, 1927, 5, August 20, 1927, 5, August 27, 1927, 5, September 10, 1927, 5, June 16, 1928, 5; Vic Hobson, *Creating Jazz Counterpoint: New Orleans, Barbershop Harmony, and the Blues* (Jackson: University Press of Mississippi, 2014), 7–31; and Donald M. Marquis, *In Search of Buddy Bolden: First Man of Jazz* (Baton Rouge: Louisiana State University Press, 2005), 2, 109.
57 *Louisiana Weekly*, August 13, 1927, 5; and Sundiata A. Djata, *Blacks at the Net: Black Achievement in the History of Tennis*, vol. 1 (Syracuse: Syracuse University Press, 2006), 221.
58 *Louisiana Weekly*, September 17, 1927, 8.

for their respective members, the Y staging its tournament at Hoffman School. At the same time, the Sylvania F. Williams Community Center, connected to the Thomy Lafon School, held its own junior tennis tournament at the Lafon School courts. At the end of the month, a dance and celebration was hosted for the city's tennis champions at Piron's House of Joy, a dance hall established in 1927 in the Pythian Temple at the corner of Loyola and Gravier Streets. Two local players even played an exhibition match during the party on a court marked off on Piron's dance floor.[59]

One of the city's premiere early black players was Woody I. McCann, an elementary school teacher who won several tournaments, most of them in the doubles division with his partner, Henry Jones. Spriggins himself was an accomplished player, as was Castro Haroldson, Carle E. Smith, and mail carrier Edward Dejoie Burbridge.[60] The best male singles player of the period was Moss, a local barber who dominated much of the early competition. His female counterpart was Victor, a young mulatto college student.[61] Jeanne Victor's sister Lydia was an accomplished player as well, as were Pearl Cahn, Maude Johnson, and Edna M. Cordier, all public school teachers.[62]

Despite this apparent democracy of tennis access, however, historian Lee Sartain has produced a more problematic analysis. Thomy Lafon was "situated in one of the rougher neighborhoods of New Orleans." The Williams Community Center was incredibly active in creating outreach projects for youth and for adults, "yet such projects were often restricted within the confines of dominant middle-class gender expectations." Sartain noted handicraft clubs and calisthenics classes for girls, athletic clubs and the Boy Scouts for boys. That imposition of middle class values and expectations, however, was not limited to restrictive

---

59 *Louisiana Weekly*, June 23, 1928, 5, July 14, 1928, 8.
60 Burbridge would go on to become a sportswriter at the *Louisiana Weekly*, owned as it was by the Dejoie family. Fifteenth Census of the United States, 1930, Population Schedule, New Orleans City, Louisiana, Sheet No. 3A, 11A; Sixteenth Census of the United States, 1940, Population Schedule, New Orleans City, Louisiana, Sheet No. 16B; and *Louisiana Weekly*, July 16, 1927, 5, July 23, 1927, 8.
61 Victor would not finish school, leaving after meeting and marrying her husband, Victor Hayes Labat, in 1931. *Soards' New Orleans City Directory, 1929* (New Orleans: Soards Directory Co., 1929), 1034; Fourteenth Census of the United States, 1920, Population Schedule, New Orleans City, Louisiana, Sheet No. 13A; Sixteenth Census of the United States, 1940, Population Schedule, New Orleans City, Louisiana, Sheet No. 7B; and *Louisiana Weekly*, July 23, 1927, 8, September 3, 1927, 8.
62 Fifteenth Census of the United States, 1930, Population Schedule, New Orleans City, Louisiana, Sheet No. 14B; 16B, 4A; and *Louisiana Weekly*, July 23, 1927, 1, September 3, 1927, 8, July 7, 1928, 8.

gendered norms. Tennis was open to both boy and girls in the community center's junior tournament, but the effort was clearly designed to expose black children of the working poor to a more upscale game as a paternalistic civilizing force. Tennis offered the juniors amazing competition and did valuable things for those playing, but such lessons could be taught with myriad sports. Tennis was different precisely because of its class-based reputation.[63]

Such efforts, whatever their intent, did grow the game. In the summer of 1928, a new club formed, the Northside Tennis Club, associated with the American Tennis Association, and built its own courts near Canal Street. Leaders promised that the club would be "one of the classiest and most up-to-date tennis clubs seen in this neck of the woods," a club that would "send representatives to the national tournament every year." Edward Dejoie Burbridge was president of the new group; Straight athlete James Cherault (1855–1914) was vice president. Earl M. Wright, *Louisiana Weekly* sports editor, was named secretary, along with assistant secretary Agnes Adams and treasurer Ezell Farrell, also a student at Straight. Until their private courts were complete, the new club would play at Straight's Daniel Hand School. The new group quickly realized, however, the costs involved with building its own courts, and thus subsumed a ladies' club, the St. James AME Church Usherettes, in an effort to secure space on the church grounds to build and equip a court. Another group, the Optimo Tennis Club, which played at the Gaudet Home on Gentilly Road, had been languishing, leading many to assume they too would be combining with Northside. The Northside group was now a larger and wealthier aggregation, but in an effort to stay young, it capped membership to those 25 years old and younger, angering many who tried to join. This was a different kind of exclusivity, an ageist exclusivity, only adding to the nexus of cultural codes and limits associated with the game in New Orleans.[64]

A 1928 *Louisiana Weekly* editorial was pleased with the growth of new clubs and interest in tennis, but lamented the various restrictive exclusivities that placed a ceiling on that growth. In particular, the paper argued that "many more people would be converted into the various clubs if the officials and learned players would devote more time to the novice." It was the kind of exclusivity that was inherent in all sports, but had particularly dire repercussions for those

---

63 Lee Sartain, *Invisible Activists: Women of the Louisiana NAACP and the Struggle for Civil Rights, 1915–1945* (Baton Rouge: Louisiana State University Press, 2007), 85–88; and Harriet Elsa Weidman, "The Sylvania F. Williams Community Center" (MA Thesis: Tulane University, 1933), 2–10.

64 *Louisiana Weekly*, June 30, 1928, 8, July 7, 1928, 8, July 21, 1828, 8, July 28, 1928, 8, August 11, 1928, 8.

playing a game that measured respectability. "Most of our clubs fail to exercise the slogan 'Join and Learn.' If they did, their membership would be much larger, the number of class 'A' performers greater." The respectability that redounded to the race, the paper seemed to argue, was not measured by a handful of quality players, but instead by the broad spread of competence and interest in exclusive sports like tennis. Experience restrictions only diminished the broader communal benefits of the game.[65]

Another substantial hindrance to tennis's growth among the black population was the Great Depression, followed by the upheaval of World War II. After those conflagrations, however, black tennis in New Orleans was led into the civil rights era by one man, Nehemiah Atkinson (1918–2003).

In 1945, Atkinson founded the Crescent City Hard Court Tennis Club to teach tennis and garner interest in the sport among black students in New Orleans. He and the club used the two courts at the Dryades Street YMCA and the two cement courts at Xavier, charging eight dollars an hour for lessons. "We helped to develop many young black tennis players when there was little interest in the schools," he later remembered, adding that "many went on and won scholarships at Southern and Grambling Universities." While in the city, the Crescent City club held its annual tournament at Xavier and the Dryades Y. Atkinson was originally from Biloxi, but had moved to New Orleans as a child, growing up on Saratoga Street in the neighborhood of the New Orleans Lawn Tennis Club. He later described himself as the only one of his friends who followed tennis, which was not popular among black residents of the city. When he returned to the city in 1945 after service in World War II and created the Crescent City Club, however, he attempted to change that with the help of the NOLTC, which, while clearly observing the restrictions of the racial line, did sell Atkinson tennis balls three for a dollar. "They always tried to look out for me there," remembered Atkinson, contextualizing "looking out" through the prism of the restrictive Jim Crow standard of the day. (Still, while such talk seems to romanticize a wholly unequal situation, his access was legitimately rare, and it is hard to imagine leadership of the NOLTC opening its doors to sell balls to poor white players without the contacts Atkinson had at the club.)[66]

The Crescent City Hard Court Tennis Club, like its forerunners, was affiliated with the American Tennis Association. The group would organize tournaments and national championships every year. Because of the South's Jim Crow restrictions, the ATA held its national events at HBCUs, which provided not only the

---

65 *Louisiana Weekly*, August 18, 1928, 8.
66 New Orleans *Times-Picayune*, January 20, 1974, 6–7.

courts but also residential space to accommodate players who would not be welcomed at most southern hotels. School administrators, for their parts, welcomed the events, hungry to make the acquaintance of the black upper class, who they saw as potential donors to their schools. The group would also be a part of ending the segregated state of tennis. In 1940, grand slam champion Don Budge played at the ATA-affiliated Cosmopolitan Tennis Club in New York. Eight years later, Dr. Reginald Weir played in the formerly all-white US Indoor Lawn Tennis Championship, also in New York. Two years after that, in 1950, Althea Gibson became the first black athlete to compete at the United States Lawn Tennis Association's national championship at Forest Hills, beginning what would become her dominance of women's tennis through much of the 1950s. In 1952, Weir would become the first black male to compete at Forest Hills.[67]

The one thing such milestones had in common was that they all came in New York, far from the Gulf Coast and Atkinson's Crescent City club. For years after Gibson's pioneering efforts, New Orleans tennis kept its race bar as sternly fixed as its class bar. From 1956 to 1958, however, Gibson won five major titles, demonstrating that quality tennis required the best players, not the wealthiest or most socially acceptable. And so in 1960, Atkinson played in the state closed tennis tournament, an annual event held only for residents of the state. He was only the second black player to participate in the event, ultimately losing to Paul DeCamp (1915–2012), a surgeon at Ochsner Medical Center in New Orleans and a member of the NOLTC. Again the restricted club was on the fringe of positive racial contact. The tournament was held at the City Park courts, not at the NOLTC, but members played against those in their draw.[68]

That year, however, was known less for bridging the color line in local tennis and more for bridging it in New Orleans public schools, and the resulting desegregation crisis would become international news, cripple the city, and provide a new intensity for seemingly smaller acts like participating in a formerly white tennis tournament. New Orleans's public school desegregation was more controversial. The case had been instigated by the NAACP's Legal Defense Fund and headed by Louisiana lawyer and civil rights activist Alexander Pierre Tureaud (1899–1972). Largely because of his effort, the US District Court ordered the Orleans Parish

---

67 Djata, *Blacks at the Net*, 2–4; and Barker, "A Black Tennis Association," 60.
68 New Orleans *Times-Picayune*, August 13, 1960, 22, September 2, 1960, 3–2, January 20, 1974, 6–7, August 7, 2012, B2.

School Board to come up with a desegregation plan, but they stalled, leading to controversy that enveloped the population throughout much of 1960.[69]

In November 1960, two New Orleans public schools desegregated. By the end of the week, white parents had pulled their children from the schools and enrolled them in private schools (or kept them out all together). On November 15, the White Citizens Council held a massive rally, with infamous Plaquemines Parish race-baiter Leander Perez (1891–1969) and others whipping the crowd into such a frenzy that the next day a white mob began marching to the school board. The police turned the water hoses on the protesters, which kept them from the school board, but only made them angrier. They turned their attention to black bystanders, injuring almost twenty. After New Orleans mayor DeLesseps Morrison (1912–1964) tried to calm the white rebels by assuring them that the police department was not going to enforce the integration order, an angry black population took to the streets, too. Though no one died in the protests, there were more than one hundred casualties and more than 250 arrests, and almost all of those arrested were black. Two years later, the Archdiocese of New Orleans desegregated the city's 153 Catholic elementary and high schools to much less violence and national fanfare.[70]

Just like the efforts of the city's black children attempting to desegregate local public education, Atkinson's early endeavors in integrated tennis were not easy, despite his success, winning tournaments in Baton Rouge, Lafayette, and elsewhere. He suffered indignities at tournaments outside of New Orleans that ran the gamut from urine-filled tennis balls from a taunting crowd to racist umpires calling rogue foot faults against him. As the 1960s progressed, however, relations – particularly in the city – began to improve. "Although there are savage segregationists who have caused trouble from time to time, many New Orleans whites seem to live amicably alongside New Orleans Negroes, in closer proximity than in any other southern or northern city," explained *Sports Illustrated* in 1966. "Golf courses, tennis courts and baseball fields are fully integrated with no resulting difficulty." The magazine explained that the New Orleans Recreation Department had integrated programs for boys and girls in a variety of sports, save swimming, and the organization was hopeful that even its swimming pools would soon be open and

---

[69] Alan Wieder, "The New Orleans School Crisis of 1960: Causes and Consequences," *Phylon* 48 (1987): 122–131; and Adam Fairclough, *Race & Democracy: The Civil Rights Struggle in Louisiana, 1915–1972* (Athens: University of Georgia Press, 1995), 234–264.

[70] Wieder, "The New Orleans School Crisis of 1960," 122–131; Juliette Landphair, "Sewerage, Sidewalks, and Schools: The New Orleans Ninth Ward and Public School Desegregation," *Louisiana History* 40 (1999): 35–62; Diane T. Manning and Perry Rogers, "Desegregation of the New Orleans Parochial Schools," *Journal of Negro Education* 71 (2002): 31–42; and *Bush v. Orleans Parish School Board*, 138 F. Supp. 337 (1956).

integrated. As if to validate the optimism of *Sports Illustrated* and NORD, one of Atkinson's students, Sharon Pettis, became the first black competitor at the national junior Sugar Bowl tournament, originally founded in 1934, at Tulane. Atkinson became a member of the formerly all-white City Park Tennis Club. He was sponsored for membership by a Jewish geologist for Esso, Harry Anisgard (1917–2014), who was temporarily expelled for his effort. When he returned in a few months, Atkinson actually sponsored his membership. He also wrote a column, "Hard Court Tennis Notes," for the *Louisiana Weekly*, doing for the city's black population of the 1950s and 1960s what Spriggins had done in the 1920s.[71]

The standard for New Orleans tennis, however, would always be the New Orleans Lawn Tennis Club, which did not integrate its membership until approximately 1986. The NOLTC was the oldest tennis club in the nation. The New Orleans Fair Grounds, founded in 1872, was the nation's third oldest racetrack, and the Southern Yacht Club, founded in 1849, was the country's second oldest yacht club. Such milestones were celebrated by the city's white elite, as they not only demonstrated wealth and prestige, but a currency even more valuable in southern social standing – longevity.[72]

And social standing was the thing. Tennis in New Orleans used restrictive exclusivity to define the contours of race and class in the Crescent City. White players went first, beginning with the most exclusive NOLTC. Then other players had to draw new boundaries and create new clubs to carve a place for themselves in that hierarchy from the bottom up to create the landscape of white tennis. Black players began differently, developing early exclusivity as markers of class distinction within the community, but, partially because there was a racial ceiling on the heights such markers could reach, the black tennis community shared its knowledge and access to generate a more democratic game from the top-down. When the sport's standard-bearer would not desegregate until the mid-1980s, there was little other opportunity.

In December 1970, Vice President Spiro Agnew (1918–1996), in town for a fundraising dinner at the Jung Hotel, managed to make time to venture over to the

---

[71] Tim Lyman, "Jumping the Net," *Gambit*, 10 December 2002, n.p. (article available online at https://www.bestofneworleans.com/gambit/jumping-the-net/Content?oid=1240979. Accessed January 13, 2018); and M.R. Werner, "Footloose: New Orleans – A Mixture Of the Old and the New and All That Dixie Jazz," *Sports Illustrated*, March 21, 1966, E1–E2.

[72] Lee Stall, General Manager of the NOLTC, said that the club desegregated "sometime before 1987" but was unable to recall an exact date for the first black membership. Interview with Lee Stall, conducted by Kelley Clark, February 15, 2018; and *Atlanta Constitution*, October 22, 1968, 40. Boston's Longwood Cricket Club began playing tennis in 1878. Merion Cricket Club outside of Philadelphia, founded in 1873, began playing tennis in 1879. *Boston Globe*, August 21, 1977, K8.

NOLTC to play a private game of tennis. Reporters seeking a glimpse of the vice president's play, however, discovered that the club's exclusivity applied to the press, as well. His visit, however, was not celebrated by club members who were incredulous and visibly frustrated when Secret Service agents, for example, forced them to park in different spaces because of Agnew's pending arrival. It was a frustration borne of the class intersections tied to tennis since its American birth. If Rhode Island's Casino Club was not good enough for Chester Arthur in the 1880s, members of the NOLTC felt that their club was not good enough for the vice president if it meant disrupting their normal routine.[73]

One can only imagine that LaGrande McGruder from Gilchrist's land of dreamy dreams would have been one of those most perturbed by Agnew's imposition on the pace of club life. For those who loved it, tennis was a passion, an outlet, an obsession. But it was also a symbol – a signpost of social, economic, or athletic achievement that built its meaning depending on where a given player found himself or herself in the nexus of those forces. For those like McGruder, sitting comfortably at the top of each of tennis's myriad semiotic hierarchies, Agnew would have been just another new money interloper who probably didn't belong in tennis, and certainly didn't belong in New Orleans.

Works Cited

Newspapers

Atlanta Constitution
Atlanta Daily World
Atlanta Journal-Constitution
Black Republican
Boston Globe
Chicago Tribune
Christian Science Monitor
The Crusader
Harvard Crimson
Los Angeles Times
Louisiana Weekly
New Orleans *Picayune*
New Orleans *Times-Picayune*
New York *Herald Tribune*
New York Times
New York Tribune

---

73 New Orleans *Times-Picayune*, December 3, 1970, 1–22.

Republican Courier
Southern Republican
Spirit of the South
Weekly Louisianian
Weekly Pelican

Additional Primary Sources

Biographical and Historical Memoirs of Louisiana, vol. 2. Chicago: Goodspeed Publishing Co., 1892.
Bush v. Orleans Parish School Board, 138 F.Supp. 337 (1956).
Fifteenth Census of the United States, 1930.
Fourteenth Census of the United States, 1920.
Interview with Lee Stall, conducted by Kelley Clark, February 15, 2018.
Joseph-Gaudet, Frances. *He Leadeth Me*. New Orleans: Louisiana Printing Co., 1913.
Koehl, et al. v. Schoenhausen, 47 La. An. 1316, 17 So. 809 (1895).
"Lawn Tennis," *Sporting Life* 11 (11 July 1888): 11.
Missouri Pacific Railroad Co. v. International Marine Insurance Co., 84 Texas 149. In *The American and English Railroad Cases*, vol. 55, ed. William M. McKinney, 549. Northport, Long Island: Edward Thompson Co., 1893.
Morrison, Andrew. *New Orleans and the New South*. New Orleans: Metropolitan Publishing Co., 1888.
Norman, Gerald F. "National American Tennis Association Championships." *Opportunity* 6 (October 1928): 306–307.
Sixteenth Census of the United States, 1940.
Slocum, Henry W. "Lawn Tennis as a Game for Women," *Outing* 14 (1889): 289.
Slocum, Henry W. "Lawn Tennis in the South," *Outing* 13 (March 1889): 496.
Soards' New Orleans City Directory, 1929. New Orleans: Soards Directory Co., 1929.
"Stenographic Report of the Discussion at the Meeting of the Louisiana Sugar Planters' Association," *Louisiana Planter and Sugar Manufacturer* 56 (17 June 1916): 394–395.
Thompson, T.P. "Early Financing in New Orleans, Being the Story of Canal Bank, 1831–1915." In *Publications of the Louisiana Historical Society*, vol. 7, 1913–1914. New Orleans: Louisiana Historical Society, 1915.

Secondary Sources

Arnesen, Eric. *Waterfront Workers of New Orleans: Race, Class, and Politics, 1863–1923*. New York: Oxford University Press, 1991.
Barker, Bertram. "A Black Tennis Association: Active since 1916." In *American Tennis Association National Rankings, 1983–1984*. Philadelphia: American Tennis Association, 1984.

Blassingame, John W. *Black New Orleans: 1860–1880*. Chicago: University of Chicago Press, 1973.

Bloom, Khaled J. *The Mississippi Valley's Great Yellow Fever Epidemic of 1878*. Baton Rouge: Louisiana State University Press, 1993.

Danhoff, Eric. "The Struggle for Control of Amateur Track and Field in the United States." *Canadian Journal of History of Sport and physical Education* 6, no. 1 (1975): 43–85.

Deford, Frank. *Big Bill Tilden: The Triumphs and the Tragedy*. New York: Simon and Schuster, 1976.

Djata, Sundiata. *Blacks at the Net: Black Achievement in the History of Tennis*, vol. 1. Syracuse: Syracuse University Press, 2006.

Engelmann, Larry. *The Goddess and the American Girl: The Story of Suzanne Lenglen and Helen Wills*. New York: Oxford University Press, 1988.

Fairclough, Adam. *Race & Democracy: The Civil Rights Struggle in Louisiana, 1915–1972*. Athens: University of Georgia Press, 1995.

Fisher, Marshall Jon. *A Terrible Splendor: Three Extraordinary Men, a World Poised for War, and the Greatest Tennis Match Ever Played*. New York: Broadway Books, 2010.

Gilchrist, Ellen. "In the Land of Dreamy Dreams." In *In the Land of Dreamy Dreams: Short Fiction*, 60–71. Fayetteville: University of Arkansas Press, 1981.

Gorn, Elliott J. *The Manly Art: Bare-Knuckle Prize Fighting in America*. Ithaca: Cornell University Press, 1986.

Hair, William Ivy. *Carnival of Fury: Robert Charles and the New Orleans Race Riot of 1900*. Baton Rouge: Louisiana State University Press, 1986.

Hobson, Vic. *Creating Jazz Counterpoint: New Orleans, Barbershop Harmony, and the Blues*. Jackson: University Press of Mississippi, 2014.

Hollandsworth, James G. *An Absolute Massacre: The New Orleans Race Riot of July 30, 1866*. Baton Rouge: Louisiana State University Press, 2004.

Jackson, Joy J. *New Orleans in the Gilded Age: Politics and Urban Progress, 1880–1896*. Baton Rouge: Louisiana State University Press, 1969.

Kolb, Carolyn. "For the Love of Tennis." *New Orleans Magazine* 44 (December 2009): 54–55.

Landphair, Juliette. "Sewerage, Sidewalks, and Schools: The New Orleans Ninth Ward and Public School Desegregation." *Louisiana History* 40 (1999): 35–62.

Long, Alecia P. *The Great Southern Babylon: Sex, Race, and Respectability in New Orleans, 1865–1920*. Baton Rouge: Louisiana State University Press, 2004.

Lyman, Tim. "Jumping the Net." *Gambit*, 10 December 2002, n.p.

Maden, Ann. "Popular Sports in New Orleans, 1890–1900." MA Thesis: Tulane University, 1956.

Manning, Diane T., and Perry Rogers, "Desegregation of the New Orleans Parochial Schools." *Journal of Negro Education* 71 (2002): 31–42.

Marquis, Donald M. *In Search of Buddy Bolden: First Man of Jazz*. Baton Rouge: Louisiana State University Press, 2005.

Nystrom, Justin. *New Orleans After the Civil War: Race, Politics, and a New Birth of Freedom*. Baltimore: Johns Hopkins University Press, 2010.

Perez, Louis A. *On Becoming Cuban: Identity, Nationality, and Culture*. Chapel Hill: University of North Carolina Press, 1999.

Putney, Clifford. *Muscular Christianity: Manhood and Sports in Protestant America, 1880–1920*. Cambridge: Harvard University Press, 2003.

Rader, Benjamin G. *American Sports, from the Age of Folk Games to the Age of Televised Sports*, Fifth ed. Upper Saddle River, NJ: Prentice Hall, 2004.
Riess, Steven A. *City Games: The Evolution of American Urban Society and the Rise of Sports*. Urbana: University of Illinois Press, 1989.
Sartain, Lee. *Invisible Activists: Women of the Louisiana NAACP and the Struggle for Civil Rights, 1915–1945*. Baton Rouge: Louisiana State University Press, 2007.
Schwartz, Rosalie. *Pleasure Island: Tourism and Temptation in Cuba*. Lincoln: University of Nebraska Press, 1997.
Shugg, Roger W. *Origins of Class Struggle in Louisiana: A Social History of White Farmers and Laborers during Slavery and After, 1840–1875*. Baton Rouge: Louisiana State University Press, 1939.
Smith, Frederick D. "Thomy Lafon." In *Encyclopedia of African American Business*, vol. 2, ed. Jessie Carney Smith, 447–449. Westport, CT: Greenwood, 2006.
Somers, Dale. *The Rise of Sports in New Orleans, 1850–1900*. Baton Rouge: Louisiana State University Press, 1972.
Tignor, Stephen. "The Survivor." *Tennis* 42 (September 2006): 86–89.
Weidman, Harriet Elsa. "The Sylvania F. Williams Community Center." MA Thesis: Tulane University, 1933.
Werner, M.R. "Footloose: New Orleans – A Mixture Of the Old and the New and All That Dixie Jazz." *Sports Illustrated*, March 21, 1966, E1–E2.
Wettan, Richard, and J.D. Willis. "Effect of New York Athletic Clubs on Amateur Athletic Governance, 1870–1915." *Research Quarterly. American Alliance for Health, Physical Education and Recreation* 47, no. 3 (1976): 499–505.
Wieder, Alan. "The New Orleans School Crisis of 1960: Causes and Consequences." *Phylon* 48 (1987): 122–131.
Wilson, Elizabeth. *Love Game: A History of Tennis, from Victorian Pastime to Global Phenomenon*. Chicago: University of Chicago Press, 2014.
Youngs, Larry R. "The Sporting Set Winters in Florida: Fertile Ground for the Leisure Revolution, 1870–1930." *Florida Historical Quarterly* 84 (2005): 57–78.

Nicole Hirschfelder
5 "Change Starts with Us": The Issue of Media Representation of Athletes' Activism for Black Lives

> *"Wouldn't you love to see one of these NFL owners when somebody disrespects our flag, to say, 'Get that son of a bitch off the field right now. Out! He's fired. He's fired!'"*[1]
> Donald Trump, 45th President of the United States, at a campaign rally in Huntsville, Alabama, Friday, September 22, 2017.

Social activism and sports share entangled histories and a long tradition in the United States: From the horse jockey Isaac Murphy (1861–1896),[2] whose mere, highly successful presence in a white dominated discipline and society must be – and was – considered a sign of resistance against the status quo in the 19th century,[3] to Muhammad Ali's (1942–2016) outspoken comments on racial inequality in the 1960s, or to Tommie Smith's and John Carlos' Black Power protest during the medal ceremony at the Olympic Games in Mexico-City in 1968, to contemporary athletes, such as Serena Williams; there are numerous examples of athletes who did (and could) not separate the private from the political or the social from the economic and used their platform to inveigh against racial discrimination.

Whereas continuities certainly exist in athlete activism, it is crucial to pay attention to aspects specific to the time in which the political protest takes place in order to understand the ever-changing challenges of – what remains – the same struggle. Accordingly, although present-day athlete activism is often compared to the 1960s and certainly shares a variety of parallels, paying attention to

---

[1] Bryan Armen Graham, "Donald Trump Blasts NFL Anthem Protesters: 'Get That Son of a Bitch Off the Field,'" *The Guardian*, September 23, 2017. Accessed February 20, 2019. https://www.theguardian.com/sport/2017/sep/22/donald-trump-nfl-national-anthem-protests.
[2] David K. Wiggins, *Glory Bound: Black Athletes in a White America* (New York: Syracuse University Press, 1997), 21.
[3] Describing the situation with which former slaves were faced with regard to sport in the 19th century, Wiggins states: "Freedom from slavery promised to provide African Americans an opportunity to engage in sport on an unlimited basis depending on their talent level and physical skills. The entry into sport, however, would be arduous and fraught with difficulties even for the most gifted black athletes because of the racial realities of American culture." David K. Wiggins, *More Than a Game: A History of the African American Experience in Sport* (Lanham: Rowman & Littlefield, 2018), 2.

https://doi.org/10.1515/9783110679397-005

the peculiarities and new – if seemingly positive – developments in today's athlete activism marks a central step in the process for analyzing and potentially overcoming the abovementioned challenges. Since sports constitutes a highly dynamic industry that brings together body, mind, social practices, capitalism, entertainment and politics in a high-pressure environment with a significant amount of public attention, it both crystallizes and initiates debates about political issues faster and sooner than most other professional fields.

Yet, this 'headstart' does not only imply advantages. One of sports' greatest selling points – that it can move its audience – also marks its Achilles heel: Since sports literally disciplines fights by turning them into – what seems to be – apolitical competition,[4] the industry typically focuses solely on the athletes' *skills*, not their backgrounds or other structural baggage unless it makes for a success story that will further fan the belief in a level playing field for the strongest players.[5] However, once it comes to the re-introduction of those structural forces by the very protest of athletes who are living memorials of those struggles, the fragility of this belief in 'individual skills' and 'mere achievement' is exposed. The confines within which 'personal' achievement finds recognition remain not only clear but also clearly dominated by those in power.[6]

Nevertheless, this does not discourage athletes from engaging in activist efforts, and in times when politics appear increasingly similar to the entertainment industry – as has been the case in recent years – sports and other forms of entertainment become more political and even showcase an increase in athlete activism. In contrast to the 1960s, one can observe a *new* dimension of media attention to political activism in sports that mirrors the polarized views

---

[4] In the Preface to the seminal work, *Quest for Excitement: Sport and Leisure in the Civilizing Process*, that he co-authored with Norbert Elias (1897–1990), sociologist Eric Dunning (1936–2019) poignantly formulates: "Finally, sport can be used as a kind of 'natural laboratory' for the exploration of such properties of social relations as competition and co-operation, conflict and harmony, which seem logically and in terms of current values to be mutually exclusive alternatives, but which, on account of the intrinsic structure of sport, are clearly revealed in that context to be complexly interdependent." Norbert Elias and Eric Dunning, *Quest for Excitement: Sport and Leisure in the Civilizing Process* (Oxford, UK: Basil Blackwell, 1986), 5.
[5] Wiggins, *More Than a Game*, 199.
[6] Colin Kaepernick's confidential settlement with the NFL that he accused of conspiring against hiring him despite his good statistics constitutes an insightful example in this context. The case of the football player Kaepernick and his protest will be explored in detail later in this article. Dan Mangan, "Colin Kaepernick Reaches Settlement in National Anthem Kneeling Collusion Case Against NFL," *CNBC*, February 15, 2019. Accessed February 20, 2019. https://www.cnbc.com/2019/02/15/colin-kaepernick-reaches-settlement-in-collusion-case-against-nfl-lawyer-says.html.

of two political camps. Accordingly, progressive and conservative media adopt clear positions in their reporting, or non-reporting that are likely to affirm their recipients' existing opinions.

In part, this intense media attention is nothing new. Controversy in an environment that is intended to serve the purpose of recreation and leisure as well as entertainment has long been a guarantor for selling stories and has thus attracted journalists' interest for decades. What is perhaps new these days is the impression that *liberal* media outlets today seem to be more openly supportive of the athletes' agenda. This finds expression in the fact that liberal media extensively cover these cases at all and cast a favorable light on these stories.[7] Yet, while the protests by NFL quarterback Colin Kaepernick have indeed received a significant amount of media attention, this 'new dimension' of attention should rather be attributed to larger changes in the media landscape[8] and not be mistaken for the media's 'positive effect' on the cause. In other words, just as any type of intentionality should always be questioned, the unprecedented hypervisibility of this protest resulted in both, immense support *and* backlash and thus worked well within the economic logic of selling news.

The polarized views on sports activism and the negative reactions to black bodies and minds that openly challenge the status quo in the sports and entertainment industry would certainly also deserve attention. I will focus on the side that presently claims to be *supportive* of athletes' activism, however, as this exploration will shed light on both the current challenges of the *black freedom struggle* and potential blind spots of those who consider themselves supportive

---

[7] The following articles may serve as examples here: Sean Gregory, "Colin Kaepernick: The Quarterback Who Upended the NFL Without Taking a Snap," *Time*, n.d. Accessed August 25, 2019. http://www.time.com/time-person-of-the-year-2017-colin-kaepernick-runner-up/; Josh Levin, "Colin Kaepernick Won: In Angering the NFL's White Billionaire Owners, the Quarterback Lost His Job but Started a Movement," *Slate*, August 18, 2017. Accessed August 25, 2017. https://slate.com/sports/2017/08/colin-kaepernicks-protest-cost-him-his-job-but-started-a-movement.html; Zito Madu, "Colin Kaepernick Is Doing What Heroes Do," *Sbnation*, Sep 5, 2016. Accessed May 25, 2017. https://www.sbnation.com/2016/9/5/12795542/colin-kaepernick-heroes-national-anthem-captain-america-nfl.
[8] Due to the limited scope of this paper, the two central changes, increase of speed in news reporting due to the internet and the impact of social media, cannot be elaborated on at length here. The following books provide insightful discussions of larger changes in media landscape and (media) culture as such: Jay David Bolter. *The Digital Plenitude: The Decline of Elite Culture and the Rise of New Media* (Cambridge, MA: The Massachusetts Institute of Technology Press, 2019). Peter Vasterman. *From Media Hype to Twitter Storm: New Explosions and Their Impact on Issues, Crises and Public Opinion* (Amsterdam, NL: Amsterdam University Press, 2018).

of racial equality.[9] I argue that, although well-intended, progressive media outlets indeed still operate on the very same problematic social and political structures, that activist networks, such as the Black Lives Matter movement, with which Kaepernick is affiliated, seek to eradicate. In other words, mis- and underrepresentation – that is, issues certain critics would perhaps be more inclined to expect in conservative coverage, also continue to persist in the *liberal* discourse on Black Lives Matter activism among athletes. This is particularly problematic, because the frequency, as well as the (seemingly) affirmative and probably even well-meaning content of the reports in addition to the framing in liberal outlets do *not* immediately appear to do a disservice to the causes of racism, sexism, capitalism, and social justice but do so – in spite of good intentions.

The prominent case of Colin Kaepernick, who last played for the *San Francisco 49ers*, serves as a clear illustration of this claim. The background of the controversy surrounding Kaepernick unfolded in the following manner: On August 26, 2016, Kaepernick, after having previously been vocal about racism and recurrent cases of injustice due to white supremacy,[10] did not stand during the national anthem and instead remained seated prior to a home preseason game of the *49ers*. Then, on September 1, 2016, Kaepernick – together with his teammate Eric Reid – took the protest a step further by deciding to kneel during the national anthem before a preseason game in San Diego in order to protest recurrent cases of state violence against African Americans. Although he also announced he would donate 1 million dollars for charitable causes, public opinion was soon divided. Some critics claimed Kaepernick did not respect the flag, prioritized his feelings about the current political debates over the country's past, and thus allegedly dismissed its many achievements.[11] Kaepernick's statements, "I'm not going to stand up to show pride in a flag for a country that oppresses black people and people of

---

9 That being said: this article too remains subject to the very criticism it puts forth and might thus also elicit similar points of criticism. While it may seem unusual to some readers, openly addressing and admitting this kind of vulnerability that could be seen to weaken the argumentation of this article at this point, is meant to invite the type of contemplation and debate that race relations need in order to improve.

10 Apart from Kaepernick's gradual development as an activist (John Branch, "The Awakening of Colin Kaepernick," *New York Times*, September 7, 2017. Accessed August 25, 2017. https://www.nytimes.com/2017/09/07/sports/colin-kaepernick-nfl-protests.html), it is also important to understand that his activism fell into a period in which racist incidents saw a stark increase in the field of sports. For a recollection of several cases see Wiggins, *More than a Game*, 195–198.

11 Victor Mather, "A Timeline of Colin Kaepernick vs. the N.F.L.: Key Moments in Kaepernick's Protests during the National Anthem and the League's Response," *New York Times*, February 15, 2019. Accessed August 25, 2019. https://www.nytimes.com/2019/02/15/sports/nfl-colin-kaepernick-protests-timeline.html.

color" and "I love America. I love people. That's why I'm doing this. I want to help make America better"[12] were not favorably received by his critics. Instead, social media and conservative websites scapegoated Kaepernick as a troublemaker and "idiot"[13] rather than as part of a larger group that had been strategically mobilizing to bring about sustainable change.

Yet, 'benign' or 'positive' media coverage of Kaepernick *also* has its flaws and is not free from racial charge. In a variety of depictions on title pages and articles, Kaepernick is typically depicted alone rather than as part of a group, let alone of a larger movement. While in some instances, he is shown with one or more teammates (such as Eric Reid) their names usually do not rise to equal prominence or cause the same level of hostility as Kaepernick's. Even when NFL *players* (plural) make the headline, Kaepernick's role as their leader is immediately established in the caption or, at the latest, in the following article.[14] As a result, Kaepernick's role as the single warrior is highlighted. As the signature image and slogan of the *Nike* campaign ad, for which Kaepernick was contracted after the scandal surrounding his refusal to stand for the anthem, show, he has not only advanced to the 'face of the protest' but is also represented as a role model and man with principles, as the slogan, "Believe in something. Even if it means sacrificing everything"[15] suggests.

---

12 Mather, "A Timeline."
13 Headlines, such as "Kaepernick is an Idiot" may serve as sufficient illustration here. Clay Travis, "Kaepernick is an Idiot," *Outkick the Coverage*, August 27, 2016. Accessed August 25, 2019. https://www.outkickthecoverage.com/colin-kaepernick-is-an-idiot-082716/
14 The following articles provide some examples: Jarrett Bell, "NFL Players Show They Won't Acquiesce to League, President Trump on Protests," *USAToday*, August 10, 2018. Accessed August 25, 2019. https://www.usatoday.com/story/sports/nfl/columnist/bell/2018/08/10/nfl-player-protests-kenny-stills-malcolm-jenkins-anthem/959506002/; Andy McDonald, "Colin Kaepernick Praises NFL Players For Protesting As Trump Fumes: In the League's Opening Week, One Player Sat During the National Anthem and Two Others Have Kneeled," *Huffpost*, September 10, 2018. Accessed August 25, 2019. https://www.huffpost.com/entry/colin-kaepernick-president-trump-kneeling-nfl-national-anthem_n_5b956a23e4b0162f472e58aa; Clark Mindock, "Taking a Knee: Why Are NFL Players Protesting and When Did They Start to Kneel? Critics Say Colin Kaepernick's Gesture is 'Unpatriotic' and that Sport Should be Clear of Politics but Athletes Have Often Used Their Platform to Protest in the Past," *Independent*, 4 February 2019. Accessed August 25, 2019. https://www.independent.co.uk/news/world/americas/us-politics/taking-a-knee-national-anthem-nfl-trump-why-meaning-origins-racism-us-colin-kaepernick-a8521741.html.
15 Eric Risberg, "A Nike Advertisement Featuring Colin Kaepernick on a Billboard in San Francisco," *New York Times*, Credit /Associated Press, Picture, August 26, 2018. Accessed August 25, 2019. https://www.nytimes.com/2018/09/26/sports/nike-colin-kaepernick.html

Declaring and depicting Kaepernick as the poster child of this anti-racist protest in the NFL is not only inaccurate. It is also problematic if not damaging for the cause of this type of activism, especially when the reporting is generally meant to be favorable. While I will later elaborate on the fact that singling out Kaepernick simply rendered a factually wrong image of the situation in sports with regard to protest, it is first important to understand why this type of media representation does not raise questions about factual accuracy, but instead 'immediately makes *sense*'. These images of the lone social justice warrior Kaepernick, along with the tone of the corresponding articles indeed '*feel* more right' than they actually prove right, neglecting – apparently – any sort of factual verification. They thus literally make sense. This is certainly neither mere coincidence nor evidence of their validity. Rather, these media representations likely tend to 'feel right' to many recipients because they are in fact all too familiar. In other words, they do *not* disturb the established order but blend right in. These images smoothly and comfortably latch on to a longstanding (white-dominated) discourse in which narratives like the one of Kaepernick, the single warrior for social justice, are all too common but should be profoundly contested with regard to their underlying, and ultimately racist thinking patterns, that refuse to pay attention to *collective* action by oppressed people and instead overemphasize but also diminish it as individual action.

Catering to the myth of 'the single, individual activist' is a recurrent trope in the distortion and cooptation of activism. This was, for example, the case with Rosa Parks (1913–2005), the allegedly elderly (she was 42 at the time), tired seamstress who refused to give up her seat on a bus in 1955 – a refusal that is frequently credited for having sparked the Civil Rights Movement. Parks' close ties to and involvement with the NAACP, and the fact that she acted deliberately and not impulsively with a dense network of like-minded activists backing her up, do not find reflection in this narrative. Instead, the story of "Rosa the Tired"[16] continues to be perpetuated – either actively or passively because of still insufficient counter-storytelling. Singling out individual activists and making their protests seem more like a spontaneous action on a particular day than a strategic, deliberate step, minimizes and indeed dismisses the radical potential of their personal as well as their networks' agenda. This overemphasis on individual action – even if it appears to be entirely laudatory – diverts the discussions away from structural critique and instead turns conversations about these activist efforts into assessments of individual decisions, isolating them

---

[16] Cynthia Stokes Brown, *Refusing Racism: White Allies and the Struggle for Civil Rights* (New York: Teachers College Press, 2002), 133.

from the activist *context* and *collective* action of which they are part. This is particularly ironic because movements, such as Black Lives Matter do not only highlight systemic racism but also deliberately break with the 'charismatic leader' cult of the Civil Rights Movement by structuring their own network in non-hierarchical ways.[17]

Returning to the example of the single athlete activist, other athletes, by contrast, do not receive a fraction of the media attention that Kaepernick does. The Women's National Basketball Association (WNBA) players of *Indiana Fever*, for example, who were the first to take a *unanimous* stance as a team and collectively knelt and locked arms in September 2016 during the anthem before a game against the *Phoenix Mercury*,[18] did not lend themselves to the protest narrative favored by the majority of news outlets – regardless of their position on the political spectrum. Although they certainly received a noteworthy degree of attention, most news outlets tended to privilege the story of the single male trailblazer and warrior for social justice. By contrast, stories by women's basketball *teams* did not garner the same amount of media attention.

The reasons for this effect are likely multi-faceted: Perhaps focusing on Kaepernick was in line with the capitalist logic that men's football generates more profit than women's basketball, or the sexist logic in which men's stories generally tend to draw more attention than women's[19] and accordingly generate more money. It might also be the racist logic of the (white) savior narrative. Here, the story of an unemployed, hence isolated Kaepernick who lost lucrative contracts with top NFL teams[20] and then received a generous testimonial offer by capitalist savior *Nike*[21] was privileged over the story of women's teams who

---

[17] For more information on new forms of leadership within the larger network for Black lives, cf.: Keeanga-Yamahtta Taylor, *From #BlackLivesMatter to Black Liberation Chicago* (Chicago: Haymarket Books, 2016), 173–177.

[18] Gregg Doyel, "Entire Indiana Fever roster kneels for national anthem," *IndyStar*, September 22, 2016. Accessed August 25, 2019. https://www.indystar.com/story/sports/basketball/wnba/fever/2016/09/21/entire-fever-roster-kneels-national-anthem/90692648/.

[19] This tendency also finds reflection in activism. Networks, such as Black Lives Matter thus try to counter an overemphasis on black male victims with specific campaigns, such as #SayHerName, that raises awareness for (trans)women by encouraging protesters to say the victims' names out loud, for example (Andrea J. Ritchie, *Invisible No More: Police Violence Against Black Women and Women of Color* (Boston: Beacon Press, 2017), 219–221).

[20] As sportswriter Christine Brennan notes, Kaepernick's unemployment must also be regarded in relation to numerous cases of other athletes who, faced with accusations of rape and violence against women (but no engagement in protest), had no trouble receiving lucrative offers for the next season. (Wiggins, *More Than a Game*, 195).

[21] For an interesting contribution to the discussion on this deal, cf.: Ben Carrington and Jules Boykoff, "Is Colin Kaepernick's Nike Deal Activism – or Just Capitalism?" *The Guardian*,

took a unified stance against racism and state violence and whose fines – if there were any – were later rescinded.[22]

While certainly a commendable act on part of the league, not fining the athlete activists could also be seen as a sign of cooptation in which the league decided to refrain from punishing entire teams out of self-interest to eradicate the truly radical message of collective activism against racist structures and instead 'quiet down' the protesters. Capitalism – which Black Lives Matter would identify as one of the root causes of racism – is thus not fundamentally questioned but ultimately enforced. This is particularly problematic in the context of Black Liberation, as the history of slavery in relation to capitalism shows.[23]

Given the sheer number of women's teams who either unanimously or partially took a clear stance pro Black Lives Matter and were thus also subject to severe backlash (without comparable popularity or financial backing), it may be surprising that their stories did not rise to equal national, let alone international prominence as those about Kaepernick. However, as black women including their accomplishments (not only in sports) have been systematically marginalized throughout American history,[24] liberal media's immense focus on an individual, black male athlete was less progressive and in fact more conservative than it might seem at first glance. In an attention economy, where public interest equates to selling news, media outlets are certainly not the sole culprits to blame for this dynamic. Since they are operating within this framework and frequently are sympathetic to the cause, however, pushing a truly *progressive* agenda would not stop short at reporting favorably on Kaepernick and to gain the expected traction, but would aim to shed (more) light on the existing *links* between his, his teammates' and fellow athletes' and black women's activism, that is, on the *growing network* for black lives.

September 6, 2018. Accessed August 25, 2019. https://www.theguardian.com/commentisfree/2018/sep/06/colin-kaepernick-nike-activism-capitalism-nfl.

22 The *Liberty, Fever* and *Phoenix Mercury* were also first fined $5000 and each player was fined $500 after wearing the t-shirts for multiple games, later the fine was rescinded (Ryan Cortes, "WNBA Players Speak Out After League Rescinds Fines For Supportive Shirts: Players and the League Will Meet Over the Coming Olympics Break to Try and Broker a Resolution," *The Undefeated*, July 25, 2016. Accessed August 25, 2019. http://theundefeated.com/features/wnba-players-speak-out-after-league-rescinds-fines-for-supportive-shirts/.)

23 For an insightful discussion of the entanglements of slavery and American capitalism, cf.: Edward E. Baptist, *The Half Has Never Been Told: Slavery and the Making of American Capitalism* (New York: Basic Books, 2016).

24 The following two books provide insights into historical and more recent material on this issue. See Gerda Lerner, *Black Women in White America: A Documentary History* (New York: Vintage Books, 1992) and Ritchie, *Invisible No More*.

That black people have been increasingly organizing and building structures against racial discrimination and for their liberation is no secret. Yet, publications and recognition of the existence not of single fragments but of a solid structure of activism still remain rare. Reporting on *various* examples of a unified effort would constitute a first crack in the established structure of journalism and possibly work towards providing new perspectives on the issue at stake. Frequently, however, progressive journalists simply observe that male victims of police brutality receive significantly more attention than women. They may run 'a special story' on campaigns like "Say her Name" but then continue with business as usual afterwards, once again focusing mostly on male cases. In this social and medial climate, women's activism easily takes second priority. Yet, publicizing their protest more prominently and commenting on them *in relation* to the issues at stake would, I argue, provide a more nuanced picture of athlete activism and would possibly also remove some public pressure from Kaepernick, who is the main target of the majority of hate-speech at the moment.

Against this background, I will now turn to women's activism and explore some of their protests. The women's basketball team of *New York Liberty*, for example, wore t-shirts that openly supported Black Lives Matter and also honored the Dallas 5, who were five policemen who had been killed by a sniper in 2016. By doing so, the team wanted to send a message of unity and respect for lives. The t-shirt also featured a blank hashtag that probably was meant to symbolize the next victim of state violence implying once more that this was an ongoing, systemic issue that could potentially render *any* black or brown person a victim of frequently unsanctioned, deadly violence.

In June 2016, the *Minnesota Lynx* also opted for t-shirts to promote their activist cause:

> "Change starts with us. Justice and accountability" was printed on the front of the black warm up gear. The names of police brutality victims Castile and Sterling, along with the Dallas Police Department shield and 'Black Lives Matter' were on the back.[25]

At a press conference preceding the game, the Lynx point guard Maya Moore explained the concerted action on behalf of her team members as follows:

> If we take this time to see that this is a human issue and speak out together, we can greatly decrease fear and create change. Tonight we will be wearing shirts to honor and mourn the losses of precious American citizens and to plead for change in all of us.[26]

---

[25] Alex Titus, "Game Security Angered Over Minnesota Lynx Player Shirts," *Ebony*, August 12, 2016. Accessed August 25, 2019. https://www.ebony.com/entertainment/lynx-blm-shirts/.
[26] Titus, "Game Security."

The team – like most other athlete activists – also elaborated upon their intentions and invited conversation about their protest. Considering Moore's thoughts as well as the media's role in paying adequate recognition to *collective* action as mentioned above, the slogan 'Change starts with *us*' – as opposed to with 'you', 'me', 'him' or 'her' – carries more significance than merely referring to each person's *individual* responsibility, which would constitute a rather typical individualist approach to social and political issues. The women's basketball teams' protest, by contrast, highlights the role of the collective and of community for bringing about social change. The slogan, in fact, condenses one of the central messages of Black Lives Matter that highlights the importance of the network and the role of community, as Black Lives Matter also states in an "About" section on their website:

> The Black Lives Matter Global Network is as powerful as it is because of our membership, our partners, our supporters, our staff, and you. Our continued commitment to liberation for all Black people means we are continuing the work of our ancestors and fighting for our collective freedom because it is our duty.
>
> Every day, we recommit to healing ourselves and each other, and to co-creating alongside comrades, allies, and family a culture where each person feels seen, heard, and supported.[27]

In addition, using their own black, female bodies as media by wearing these t-shirts individually, yet as a team, the players conveyed the importance of collective action and simultaneously put this insight into *practice* by standing together and wearing these t-shirts together. This means: although the *Lynx*' and other teams' activism may not strike one as overly militant or radical at first glance, since it does not comply with what has come to be commonly established as such, for instance violence, noise, or aggression, their protest was in fact radical in the truest sense of the word and hence triggered strong reactions in some people. The players indeed exposed one of the 'root' problems of race relations,[28] which is that standards for the evaluation of blacks' protest are highly dynamic and ultimately subject to those in power. In other words, while a lack of 'civility' is commonly used to discredit protest, its obvious presence, similarly to nonviolent campaigns in the Civil Rights Movements, does not, despite claims that suggest otherwise, lead to (more) acceptance, either. Instead of addressing the pressing issue of state violence (the athletes' reason to protest in the first place),

---

[27] "About: What We Believe," About, Black Lives Matter, accessed April 24, 2019. Accessed August 25, 2019. https://blacklivesmatter.com/about/what-we-believe/.
[28] "Radical," History and Etymology, Merriam-Webster, accessed April 24, 2019. Accessed August 25, 2019. https://www.merriam-webster.com/dictionary/radical.

public debates are often bogged down in discussions about questions, such as if behavior towards the flag was respectful or disrespectful. The fact that those opposing the protest can 'run out' the crucial time in which the short-lived spotlight of public attention is on these events, lays open the discrepancy in power between the two camps.

As already mentioned, all abovementioned protests by athletes could be said to comply with common demands for 'civility' and might even share that as their main characteristic: All campaigns by athletes to this day have been calm, in some cases completely silent, and did not involve destruction, overtly offensive behavior, or profanity. The case of the *New York Liberty* serves as an example to illustrate that athletes even tried to compromise with officials from the WNBA when they encountered first signs of unease from the league:

> After three teams (the New York Liberty, Indiana Fever and the Phoenix Mercury) donned shirts that included the phrases "Black Lives Matter" and "Dallas 5," the WNBA sent a letter out reminding teams of its uniform policy but not fining them. Multiple players on the New York Liberty gathered and decided on a compromise that they hoped would please everyone involved. Instead of shirts with writing, they would wear plain, all-black shirts with only the Adidas logo (the WNBA's primary sponsor), sticking true to the causes they wanted to advocate for, but also respecting the wishes of the league and its uniform policy. The players wore the shirts for four games with no objection from the WNBA, according to Swin Cash of the New York Liberty.[29]

These examples show that the athletes themselves opted for compromise. They honored black civilian victims *and* – with the 'Dallas 5' – white police officers, and also catered to requests of wearing shirts with their sponsor. Moreover, they used de-escalating language, chose to protest in complete silence, but offered, like the *Minnesota Lynx*, for example, explanations during press conferences and interviews.

The fact that peaceful protests tend to resonate 'better' with addressees than radical campaigns is by no means a recent insight. The former usually have a higher chance of reactions that could be (mis)understood as receptive to the activists' message. Yet, as mentioned above, activists' campaigns should not be mistaken for docile attempts to seek approval by the established. Rather, they try to reveal the true agenda behind those polite reactions. With regard to this issue, Scott and Smith already observed in their article "The Rhetoric of Confrontation" in 1969 that

> [a] rhetorical theory suitable to . . . [their] age must take into account the charge that civility and decorum serve as masks for the preservation of injustice, that they condemn

---

[29] Cortes, "WNBA Players."

the dispossessed to non-being . . . [and that] they become the instrumentalities of power for those who 'have'.[30]

They thus warn against falling for a polished façade by the bourgeois that exploits yet disables retaliation.

This aspect evokes memories of the Civil Rights Movement when Dr. Martin Luther King Jr. (1929–1968) spoke about so-called 'riots' in the context of racial inequality, which were frequently met with a lack of understanding by the majority of whites. After famously noting that "a riot is the language of the unheard,"[31] King continues with a passage that is cited less frequently, but proves critical both then, and now, when it comes to the persisting conditions that the current protests address. With regard to the present, his words possibly also foreshadow a plausible radicalization of protests. This could be the case if the current peaceful protests that comply with demands for civility are further scandalized in a way that equates their violation of a social norm with violence and then – nevertheless – dismisses and ignores them, while many of the same unacceptable conditions persist. With regard to the late 1960s King states:

> And what is it that America's failed to hear? It's failed to hear that the plight of the Negro poor has worsened over the last few years. It has failed to hear that the promises of justice and freedom have not been met. It has failed to hear that large segments of white society are more concerned about tranquility and the status quo than about justice, humanity, and equality, and it is still true. It is still true that these things are being ignored. Now, every year here about this time our newspapers and our television, and people generally . . . begin to talk about the long hot summer ahead. And what always bothers me about this is that the long hot summer has always been preceded by a long cold winter. And the tragedy is that the nation has failed to use its winters creatively, compassionately . . . and our nation's summers of riots are still caused by our nation's winters of delay. And as long as justice is postponed, as long as there are those in power who fail to address themselves to the problem, we're going to find outselves sinking into darker nights of social disruption.[32]

Although riot prevention may be one of the main goals of those in power today, the issue remains complex – even when that goal seems to be met. Kneeling and arm-locking athletes certainly constitute pretty ideal examples of those very '*peaceful* protesters' that bourgeois society frequently calls for as a prerequisite for receiving the protesters' message in the first place. It is important to

---

30 Robert L. Scott and Donald K. Smith, "The Rhetoric of Confrontation," *Quarterly Journal of Speech 56* (1969): 8.
31 Martin Luther King, Jr. "The Other America," in *The Radical King (King Legacy)*, ed. Cornel West (Boston: Beacon Press, 2016), 235–244.
32 239.

understand, however, that 'non-violence' has never meant a complete absence of violence. Rather, non-violent protesters seek to expose and make visible to everybody, the violence they routinely experience in their everyday lives. The mirror they hold up to the addressees of the protest hence presents them with a shocking, unsettling picture of themselves. The two alternative reactions to this self-realization are either to reflect and reform, or to lash out. While the latter is certainly unpleasant for everyone involved, it still serves the cause of non-violent protests. The fact that the absence of aggression on the protesters' side ignites such profanity, hate-speech or even (threats of) physical violence in response to something – as seemingly trivial – as breaking with a ritual and social convention, lays open the presence of tension and aggression that is otherwise not recognized by those in power.

It is interesting then that the President of the United States felt compelled to refer to the athlete activists who chose to kneel or sit during the anthem with the following words, quoted as an epigraph for this article: "Wouldn't you love to see one of these NFL owners when somebody disrespects our flag, to say, 'Get that son of a bitch off the field right now. Out! He's fired. He's fired!'"[33]

Against the previously established context, Trump's apparently spontaneous, casual remarks are actually surprisingly in line with many of the above-mentioned points that are both relevant and at stake in this debate: By using emotionally charged language, such as the strong and positive verb "love" and the exclamation "Out!" before repeating the sentence "He's fired," evoking allusions to his time as a judge in the show, *The Apprentice*, which made both him and his tough leadership style popular and ingrained the catchphrase into popular culture, Trump perfectly caters to the "affective canon"[34] of his audience. The issue he addresses is indeed not about facts, but about affect and emotions. This is also precisely why honoring the flag by standing up and placing one's hand on the heart, i.e. involving (physical) practices, marks such a crucial stumbling block in the context of creating and regularly performing the afore-mentioned affective canon, which makes reactions not only foreseeable but also susceptible to manipulation. As Leanne Munroe contends: "routine ways of acting and thinking are bound together with certain emotional regimes that can constrain how we act, feel and think in the present and future."[35] In other

---

[33] Bryan Armen Graham, "Donald Trump blasts NFL anthem protesters."
[34] Margaret Wetherell, *Affect and Emotion: A New Social Science Understanding*. (London: Sage Publications, 2012), 116.
[35] Leanne Munroe, "Constructing Affective Narratives in Transatlantic Slavery Museums in the UK," in *Heritage, Affect and Emotion: Politics, Practices and Infrastructures*, eds. Divya Tolia-Kelly, et al. (London: Routledge, 2017), 128.

words, routines performed without ever being questioned create not only moments of elation and a team spirit but also *similar* feelings and thoughts about many other issues, which can surface as merely affective responses to situations where the perceived unity and equality of everybody in the stadium is even farer from a given than it ever was in the first place. Since everybody is made aware of the affective canon through countless daily interactions and observations, the consequence of this problematic effect is what Margaret Wetherell refers to when she observes that "[a]ffect can function ... to construct and mark boundaries and to reject the 'other'. It can work to keep people in line as their anxiety and fear, for instance, push them to conform."[36] Thus, it becomes clear that when public figures – like Kaepernick – that are meant to function as multipliers of the affective canon refuse to conform but are *not* fearful, they indeed fundamentally question the order of things.

Returning to Trump's quote, the facts that he only refers to a male protester erases not only collective activist efforts, but also women's presence and agency as activists altogether. Moreover, Trump's choice of the particular derogatory expression, "son of a bitch," casually adds this – by now all too common – sexist insult to his rhetorical question with which he captures and entertains his audience while further normalizing this slur. The profanity, he uses, that is received with nods and approving cheers by his audience shows that Trump – and the people he represents – are not subject to the standards of 'civility' to which black athlete activists are held. Furthermore, the sentence in which he employs the image of one of many (white, strong, male) NFL *owners* that would have the power to simply throw unpleasant (mostly black) workers off the *field*, also evokes an eerily parallel history in the US. As scholar Billy Hawkins points out when explaining the provocative title of his book, *The New Plantation*, in which he delineates the imbalance of power between black athletes and predominantly white institutions:

> The title may be alarming for most, because the term plantation conjures up images of brutality, deprivation, and exploitation. Despite these images, the slave plantation demonstrated a relationship of power white slave owners had over black slaves' labor. This relationship quintessentially represented the complete ownership of the black body and the labor it produced. The title, though provocative, seeks capture the relationship where Black males are dispossessed of their athletic labor.[37]

It is crucial to emphasize at this point that the intentionality or implications on Trump's part are secondary with regard to the affective and emotional effects

---

36 Margaret Wetherell, *Affect and Emotion*, 114.
37 Billy Hawkins, *The New Plantation: Black Athletes, College Sports, and Predominantly White NCAA Institutions* (London: Palgrave Macmillan, 2010), xi.

his words cause in both, his followers and the athlete activists. What is perhaps more decisive to note is that the sensibilities pertaining to his comment are completely divided. One group might not think much of it but agrees with Trump's overall message, the other group might not dissect the comment in the fashion done above, but most likely *feels* the sting it entails for them and certainly disagrees with his message. This is due to the fact that the past still remains a deeply unsettled terrain. The unity (meant to be) performed during anthems is not substantialized by a unified take on America's history; or, to remain within the imagery of football: America's self-image does not stand the test of being tackled by the present.

It is crucial to emphasize once more that the purpose of this article is not to pit Kaepernick against WNBA teams, or to discredit any *individual* athlete that feels strongly about the struggle for black lives, but to point out how flawed the representation of activism for Black Lives is – that frequently prioritizes the story of a single, male hero and in turn underreports cases of women's teams that equally take a clear stance and are equally subject to harsh criticism. While liberal media discourse on sports activism may not be the most pressing issue when dealing with racial inequality, as there are far more existential problems to address, this article operates on the premise that racism permeates every part of society and therefore seeks to shed light on those parts that tend to receive less public attention but also constitute important touchstones on the path to racial equality. Especially when some realms, such as liberal journalism may have good intentions and consider themselves generally supportive of athletes' agenda, it is crucial to reflect on potential blind spots and the subtle workings of capitalism, sexism, and racism – particularly when these publications are met with unanimous, instant approval by its progressive readers, as this probably means that the story ultimately affirms more than subverts the status quo. Since athlete activism between 2016 and today has mostly met the general public's demands for 'civility' when it came to *how* the protest has been conducted, the furious reactions by various people in positions of power who felt attacked, disturbed, and perhaps also exposed by the athletes' actions, may serve as an indication of the fact that these protests have indeed struck a nerve that potentially lies at the core of debates on racial equality: Despite a rhetoric that suggested otherwise, a *common*, nuanced and unapologetic evaluation of America's past, expressed through daily practices, still has not been achieved.[38]

---

38 The term 'post-racial' in the context of Obama's presidency constitutes an example of this misleading rhetoric. Particularly in the second chapter, "Obama and the Myth of a Post-racial America," of his book, *Racial Realities and Post-Racial Dreams*, Julius Bailey elaborates on the problematic implications of the term 'post-racial.'

Frequently unsanctioned state violence against black and brown people does not constitute 'an example' but only the tip of the iceberg in this context. State violence might be police brutality in one of its most extreme scenarios, but on a daily basis, state and structural violence might be a subtle, or, as scholar Pierre Bourdieu (1930–2002) would call it, 'symbolic violence'[39] that is not tangible but omnipresent.

Against this background, paying 'respect for the flag' may be such a controversial issue, because it is meant to serve an important function in society. Unlike colleges and the workplace, sporting events still *voluntarily* attract a diverse audience and thus bring together a great variety of people and allow them to share positive and negative emotions as supporters of their teams or athletes. Just like many other examples of what Robert Bellah (1927–2013) referred to as expressions of *civil religion*,[40] honoring the flag *together* may have appeared to work as a tentative clog to fill a void left by the lack of a commonly shared version of the past. Now that athletes' protest has publicly laid open this void, paying tribute to the flag in the stadium and elsewhere cannot remain a non-negotiable duty for some and absolute joy for others while America claims to be a country of equality and freedom for all. Engaging in the uneasy and uncomfortable discussions (not tweets) that these difficult topics require, adopting a more critical perspective on America's past, and evidencing that understanding in the present will be paramount to living up to the following excerpt from the pledge of allegiance, the recital of which frequently accompanies paying respect to flag. It reads: "one nation indivisible – with liberty and justice for all."[41]

(Julius Bailey. *Racial Realities and Post-Racial Dreams: The Age of Obama and Beyond* (Peterborough, Ontario, Canada: Broadview Press, 2016)).

39 Since *symbolic violence* is precisely so impactful, because it is defined as "violence which is exercised upon a social agent with his or her complicity", for it operates with imaginative investments and thus does not necessitate physical coercion, 'forsaking' this consent that is usually given subconsciously and never needs to be actively sought by those in power by protesting against oppression, constitutes a major violation of the unwritten rules of symbolic violence that only can become visible when those oppressed become aware of the power dynamics in society and as a consequence actively withdraw their 'consent'. (Pierre Bourdieu and Loïc J. D. Wacquant, *An Invitation to Reflexive Sociology* (Chicago: University of Chicago Press, 1992), 167).

40 Robert Bellah, "Civil Religion in America," *Daedalus* 96, no. 1 (1967), *Religion in America*: 1–21 (Winter, 1967).

41 Francis Bellamy. *The Pledge of Allegiance* (Art Evans Productions, 1971).

Works Cited

Bailey, Julius. *Racial Realities and Post-Racial Dreams: The Age of Obama and Beyond.* Peterborough, Ontario, Canada: Broadview Press, 2016.

Baptist, Edward E. *The Half Has Never Been Told: Slavery and the Making of American Capitalism.* New York: Basic Books, 2016.

Bell, Jarrett. "NFL players show they won't acquiesce to league, President Trump on protests." *USAToday*, August 10, 2018. https://www.usatoday.com/story/sports/nfl/columnist/bell/2018/08/10/nfl-player-protests-kenny-stills-malcolm-jenkins-anthem/959506002/.

Bellah, Robert. "Civil Religion in America." *Daedalus*, Vol. 96, No. 1, *Religion in America* (Winter, 1967): 1–21.

Bellamy, Francis. *The Pledge of Allegiance.* Art Evans Productions, 1971.

Black Lives Matter. "About: What We Believe." Accessed April 24, 2019. https://blacklivesmatter.com/about/what-we-believe/.

Bolter, Jay David. *The Digital Plenitude: The Decline of Elite Culture and the Rise of New Media.* Cambridge, MA: The Massachusetts Institute of Technology Press, 2019.

Bourdieu, Pierre, and Loïc J. D. Wacquant. *An Invitation to Reflexive Sociology.* Chicago: University of Chicago Press, 1992.

Branch, John. "The Awakening of Colin Kaepernick." *New York Times*, September 7, 2017. https://www.nytimes.com/2017/09/07/sports/colin-kaepernick-nfl-protests.html

Brown, Cynthia Stokes. *Refusing Racism: White Allies and the Struggle for Civil Rights.* New York: Teachers College Press, 2002.

Cortes, Ryan. "WNBA Players Speak Out After League Rescinds Fines For Supportive Shirts: Players and the league will meet over the coming Olympics break to try and broker a resolution." *The Undefeated*, July 25, 2016. http://theundefeated.com/features/wnba-players-speak-out-after-league-rescinds-fines-for-supportive-shirts/.

Doyel, Gregg. "Entire Indiana Fever roster kneels for national anthem," *IndyStar*, September 22, 2016. https://www.indystar.com/story/sports/basketball/wnba/fever/2016/09/21/entire-fever-roster-kneels-national-anthem/90692648/.

Elias, Norbert and Eric Dunning. *Quest for Excitement: Sport and Leisure in the Civilizing Process.* Oxford, UK: Basil Blackwell, 1986.

Graham, Bryan Armen. "Donald Trump blasts NFL anthem protesters: 'Get that son of a bitch off the field.'" *The Guardian*, September 23, 2017. https://www.theguardian.com/sport/2017/sep/22/donald-trump-nfl-national-anthem-protests.

Gregory, Sean. "Colin Kaepernick: The quarterback who upended the NFL without taking a snap," *Time*, n.d. http://time.com/time-person-of-the-year-2017-colin-kaepernick-runner-up/.

Hawkins, Billy. *The New Plantation: Black Athletes, College Sports, and Predominantly White NCAA Institutions.* London: Palgrave Macmillan, 2010.

King Jr., Martin Luther. "The Other America," in *The Radical King (King Legacy)*, edited by Cornel West, 235–44. Boston: Beacon Press, 2016.

Lerner, Gerda. *Black Women in White America: A Documentary History.* New York: Vintage Books, 1992.

Levin, Josh. "Colin Kaepernick Won: In angering the NFL's white billionaire owners, the quarterback lost his job but started a movement," *Slate*, August 18, 2017. https://slate.com/sports/2017/08/colin-kaepernicks-protest-cost-him-his-job-but-started-a-movement.html.

McDonald, Andy. "Colin Kaepernick Praises NFL Players For Protesting As Trump Fumes: In the league's opening week, one player sat during the national anthem and two others have kneeled," *Huffpost*, September 10, 2018. https://www.huffpost.com/entry/colin-kaepernick-president-trump-kneeling-nfl-national-anthem_n_5b956a23e4b0162f472e58aa.

Madu, Zito. "Colin Kaepernick is doing what heroes do," *Sbnation*, Sep 5, 2016. https://www.sbnation.com/2016/9/5/12795542/colin-kaepernick-heroes-national-anthem-captain-america-nfl

Mangan, Dan. "Colin Kaepernick reaches settlement in national anthem kneeling collusion case against NFL." *CNBC*, February 15, 2019. https://www.cnbc.com/2019/02/15/colin-kaepernick-reaches-settlement-in-collusion-case-against-nfl-lawyer-says.html.

Mather, Victor. "A Timeline of Colin Kaepernick vs. the N.F.L.: Key moments in Kaepernick's protests during the national anthem and the league's response." *New York Times*, February 15, 2019. https://www.nytimes.com/2019/02/15/sports/nfl-colin-kaepernick-protests-timeline.html.

Merriam-Webster. "History and Etymology: Radical." Accessed April 24, 2019. https://www.merriam-webster.com/dictionary/radical.

Mindock, Clark. "Taking a knee: Why are NFL players protesting and when did they start to kneel? Critics say Colin Kaepernick's gesture is 'unpatriotic' and that sport should be clear of politics but athletes have often used their platform to protest in the past," *Independent*, 4 February 2019. https://www.independent.co.uk/news/world/americas/us-politics/taking-a-knee-national-anthem-nfl-trump-why-meaning-origins-racism-us-colin-kaepernick-a8521741.html.

Munroe, Leanne. "Constructing Affective Narratives in Transatlantic Slavery Museums in the UK," in *Heritage, Affect and Emotion: Politics, Practices and Infrastructures*, edited by Divya Tolia-Kelly, et al., 114–132. London: Routledge, 2017.

Risberg, Eric. "A Nike advertisement featuring Colin Kaepernick on a billboard in San Francisco," New York Times, Credit /Associated Press, Picture, August 26, 2018. https://www.nytimes.com/2018/09/26/sports/nike-colin-kaepernick.html.

Ritchie, Andrea J. *Invisible No More: Police Violence Against Black Women and Women of Color*. Boston: Beacon Press, 2017.

Scott, Robert L., and Donald K. Smith. "The Rhetoric of Confrontation." *Quarterly Journal of Speech 56* (1969): 8.

Taylor, Keeanga-Yamahtta. *From #BlackLivesMatter to Black Liberation Chicago*. Chicago: Haymarket Books, 2016.

Titus, Alex. "Game Security Angered Over Minnesota Lynx Player Shirts." *Ebony*, August 12, 2016. https://www.ebony.com/entertainment/lynx-blm-shirts/.

Travis, Clay. "Kaepernick is an Idiot." *Outkick the Coverage*, August 27, 2016. https://www.outkickthecoverage.com/colin-kaepernick-is-an-idiot-082716/.

Vasterman, Peter. *From Media Hype to Twitter Storm: New Explosions and Their Impact on Issues, Crises and Public Opinion*. Amsterdam, NL: Amsterdam University Press, 2018.

Wetherell, Margaret. *Affect and Emotion: A New Social Science Understanding*. London: Sage Publications, 2012.

Wiggins, David K. *Glory Bound: Black Athletes in a White America*. New York: Syracuse University Press, 1997.

Wiggins, David K. *More Than a Game: A History of the African American Experience in Sport*. Lanham: Rowman & Littlefield, 2018.

Steve Marston

6 The Revival of Athlete Activism(s): Divergent Black Politics in the 2016 Presidential Election Engagements of LeBron James and Colin Kaepernick

On the morning of November 9, 2016, in the aftermath of the U.S. Presidential election, LeBron James posted a decree to his Instagram social media page. The high-profile National Basketball Association (NBA) player had publicly endorsed Democratic candidate Hillary Clinton, and he now responded to her defeat to celebrity executive Donald Trump. Next to an embedded music video for Kendrick Lamar's hip-hop anthem "Alright," James offered an optimistic vision:

> As I woke up today looking and searching for answers on what has happened this song hit it right on the head! . . . Yes we all wanna lace up the boots, put on the hard hats and strike but that's not the answer . . . Love, genuine LOVE and FAITH will be the only thing that can get us through this . . . The man above will never put something in our paths that we can [not] handle no matter how difficult it may feel/be! To all the youth out there I PROMISE I'll continue to lead u guys every single day without no hesitation!! Time to educate and even more mold my children into being the greatest model citizens they can become in life! They will continue the legacy beyond life![1]

The post's expressed faith in higher power, embodied by "the man above," displaces the need to "strike" against the incoming administration. James's emphasis on American youth, and his leadership of them, indirectly positions *himself* as the "man above" who will guide his followers into a better future. His declaration received over 1.5 million views and 175,000 "likes," indicating a broad resonance.

One day later, National Football League (NFL) player Colin Kaepernick, who had vaulted himself into the public eye through a protest during pregame renditions of "The Star-Spangled Banner," delivered his own Instagram response. Kaepernick posted a pair of video recordings of Malcolm X being interviewed

---

[1] LeBron James (@KingJames), "As I woke up today looking and searching for answers on what has happened this song hit it right on the head! . . .," Instagram post, November 9, 2016. Accessed August 20, 2019. https://www.instagram.com/p/BMmHGr0B0C-/.

Note: This article was first published under the same title in *Fair Play: Journal of Philosophy, Ethics and Sports Law* 10 (Fall 2017): 45–68. Republished with the permission of the journal.

https://doi.org/10.1515/9783110679397-006

prior to the 1964 Presidential election.[2] When asked by the White interviewer, "Who would you suggest that Negroes vote for in the coming election?", X responded, "I wouldn't suggest that they vote for *any* party or *any*body." He expressed his desire for "so-called 'Negroes' to become politically mature, and realize the power they hold in the field of politics," which would generate more attention and respect from political leaders; at the moment, in his view, "most of the Negro leaders sell out to the political, to the White politicians for crumbs." In the second video clip, X mused that a victory by Republican candidate Barry Goldwater would force Black Americans to "face up to the facts":

> This in itself is *good*, in that Goldwater is a man who's not capable of hiding his racist tendencies. And at the same time he's not capable of even pretending, to Negroes, that he's their friend, so this will have a tendency to make the Negro, probably for the first time, do something to stand on his *own* feet and solve his *own* problem instead of putting himself in a position to be misled, misused, exploited by the Whites who pose as liberals only for the purpose of getting the support of the Negroes.

Kaepernick offered no additional commentary to the videos, instead implying a consonance between his present-day views and those of Malcolm X a half-century earlier.

Placed side by side, James's and Kaepernick's social media posts feature overlap and discrepancy. Both affirm Black political optimism despite the election of Trump, a candidate who had brazenly appealed to White Christian nativism and earned the endorsement of White supremacist groups. However, they present divergent paths toward a progressive future. James favors "faith" over "strike," advocating a process in which he will act as a benevolent leader in guiding others through adversity. By contrast, Kaepernick downplays his role as a social leader, instead deferring to the words of Malcolm X, who promotes political consciousness and the doing of "*whatever* is necessary" to gain political equality. X's radical call for confrontation clearly departs from the faith-based invocation of James; furthermore, his wariness of alliance between Black Americans and White leaders reverberates in James's endorsement of Clinton.

These digital texts reflected broader differences between James and Kaepernick, two of the highest-profile activist athletes during the fall 2016 Presidential campaign spectacle. While James gestured toward radicalism through "Alright," which had emerged as the anthem of the Black Lives Matter (BLM) movement, his advocacy of faith over radical "strike" echoed the Black liberalism embedded in his general

---

2 Colin Kaepernick (@kaepernick7), [Malcolm X responds to interviewer's question about his recommended candidate for Black voters in the 1964 Presidential election], Instagram video, November 10, 2016. Accessed August 20, 2019. https://www.instagram.com/p/BMolji0jg9H/.

politics. He was a leading figure in the revival of Leftist athlete activism in the 2010s, which was intertwined with BLM in protest against police violence in Black communities. James had also aligned himself closely with Barack Obama and Hillary Clinton, both representatives of corporate-capitalist "New Democrat" identity. Kaepernick joined the athlete-activist movement in August 2016 through his protest during the national anthem, eventually expanding into a broader set of actions from press conference commentaries to financial donations for community development organizations. In the process, he largely embodied the antiestablishment, self-help ethos of Malcolm X and other Black radicals of the past and present. Thus while they are both key figures in the contemporary revival of athlete activism, James's and Kaepernick's particular expressions, or "activisms," differ in significant ways.

Approaching the intersection of athlete activism(s) and Presidential politics, this article addresses LeBron James's and Colin Kaepernick's engagements with the 2016 election. Hermeneutical analysis reveals that two distinct strains of Black liberation politics, deeply embedded in history, are resonant in their actions. James tended toward Black liberalism, most evidently through his association with the Clinton campaign, while Kaepernick favored Black radicalism in rejecting establishment politics as fundamentally oppressive. However, this is not to simplify James as "purely" liberal or Kaepernick as "purely" radical, just as it would be erroneous to characterize liberalism and radicalism as mutually exclusive ideologies. This is, instead, an examination of political currents' overlapping iterations within the rhetoric of two major athlete-activists. Such a study reveals that, rather than as a homogenous movement, the recent revival of Leftist sport activism is better understood through attention to its nuance.

"Liberalism" is an opaque concept in contemporary American political discourse. As noted by cultural historian Nikhil Singh, the interchangeable use of the terms "liberal" and "Left" obscures the deeply embedded liberalism within which major political parties offer competing interpretations.[3] Stuart Hall defined liberalism, which emerged in 18th century Euro-American context, as an ideology emphasizing "individualism in politics, civil and political rights, parliamentary government, moderate reform, limited state intervention, and a private enterprise economy."[4] This system, predicated on the individual "rational

---

[3] Nikhil Pal Singh, "Liberalism," in *Keywords for American Cultural Studies*, eds. Bruce Burgett and Glenn Hendler, second edition (New York: NYU Press, 2014), 153–154.
[4] Stuart Hall, "Variants of Liberalism," in *Politics and Ideology: A Reader*, eds. James Donald and Stuart Hall (Philadelphia, PA: Open University Press, 1986), 34–35.

agent" who thrives when "free from coercive and/or arbitrary political authority," is promoted as an engine of human progress.[5] Liberalism has persisted as a foundational ideology in American politics; as succinctly stated by Michael C. Dawson, "Liberalism is hegemonic."[6]

However, this is not to say that liberalism is uniformly inflected. Political scientists Beth A. Simmons, Frank Dobbin, and Geoffrey Garrett identified two strains of liberalism with distinct emphases: economic ("free market" activity with minimal state interference) and political (state protection of "rights to political participation").[7] These strains developed in tandem, particularly as the rise of liberalism coincided with that of capitalism. Singh noted, "Central to every version of liberalism is an insistent, quasi-naturalistic link between human and market 'freedom.'"[8] In the past half century, economic liberalism has been incarnate in the form of neoliberalism, an orientation based on the premise that "free markets automatically generate civic order and economic prosperity," in turn prioritizing economic over civic participation.[9] Liberalism (of both the economic and political varieties) has spread globally, resulting in increased resources and structural instability at the aggregate level.[10]

Liberal ideology has also been inflected through Black liberation movements, particularly since the turn of the 20th century. In comparing this iteration with "traditional American liberalism," Dawson points to the stronger Black demand for political equality through the "belief that liberal egalitarianism should encompass the economic as well as the social and political realms." Black distrust of economic liberalism, given the historical meshing of racism and capitalist logic (slavery onward), has facilitated an emphasis on political liberalism through state protection of rights.[11] This demand is accompanied by a willingness to work with White liberal leaders to discover shared interests, mirroring the general promotion of racial integration as a progressive process.

---

5 Luigi Esposito and John W. Murphy, "Post Civil Rights Racism and the Need to Challenge Racial/Ethnic Inequality beyond the Limits of Liberalism," *Theory In Action* 3, no. 2 (2010): 41; Norberto Bobbio, *Liberalism and Democracy* (London: Verso, 2005); John Gray, *Liberalism* (Minneapolis: University of Minnesota Press, 1986).
6 Michael C. Dawson, *Black Visions: The Roots of Contemporary African-American Political Ideologies* (Chicago, IL: University of Chicago Press, 2001), 241.
7 Beth A. Simmons, Frank Dobbin, and Geoffrey Garrett, "Introduction: The International Diffusion of Liberalism," in *Key Concepts in the New Global Economy. Volume 1*, ed. David A. Baldwin (Cheltenham, U.K./Northampton, MA: Elgar, 2012), 782–783.
8 Singh, "Liberalism," 154; see also Hall, "Variants of Liberalism," 39.
9 Singh, "Liberalism," 157.
10 Simmons, Dobbin, and Garrett, "Introduction," 781.
11 Dawson, *Black Visions*, 240, 243–244.

However, throughout its history, support for Black liberalism has been accompanied by criticism. Black nationalists, Marxists, and feminists have expressed particularly strong suspicion of liberalism as an idealistic ideology whose promise goes unfilled. Furthermore, such prominent leaders as W.E.B. Dubois (1868–1963), James Baldwin (1924–1987), and Martin Luther King, Jr. (1929–1968) became disenchanted with liberalism late in life, eventually viewing racism is so entrenched in American society as to impair integrationist paths toward equality.[12] Contemporary scholars have joined these criticisms. Luigi Esposito and John W. Murphy argued that racism is "inherent to liberalism itself," pointing toward the capitalist-liberalist assumption that all humans are wealth-seeking. Furthermore, despite framings of neoliberalism as apolitical in the promotion of the "free market," deregulation allows for embedded racism to persist in private spaces.[13] Critics have also focused on the assimilationist emphasis within liberalism, arguing that the process prioritizes White over Black cultural norms, resulting in the loss of the latter.[14]

Such counterpoints emanate from Black Left-radicalism, which has existed in various forms in the U.S. since acts of slave resistance. Robin Kelley noted the "freedom dreams" that have driven such radicalism, particularly Black visions of a future in which the liberal notion of "freedom" was reimagined through alternatives to capitalism. Such narratives have been informed by the transnational flow of anticolonialist ideology between the U.S. and abroad, including post-colonial Africa.[15] In the 1960s, Malcolm X (1925–1965) emerged as the "ideological father" of the student Left, promoting Black nationalism and inspiring plots to overthrow the U.S. capitalist system.[16] The rise of the Black Power movement in this decade also drew in a number of high-profile athletes, including Muhammad Ali (1942–2016), Bill Russell (1934–), and sprinters Tommie Smith (1944–) and John Carlos (1945–), who famously raised their fists in a "power to the people" salute at the 1968 Olympics. Though each figure varied in their expressive activisms,

---

12 Ibid., 86–87, 238–239, 273–280; Bill Lyne, "God's Black Revolutionary Mouth: James Baldwin's Black Radicalism," *Science & Society* 74, no. 1 (2010): 15–18.
13 Esposito and Murphy, "Post Civil Rights Racism," 50–53; see also Vikash Singh, "Race, the Condition of Neo-liberalism," *Social Sciences* 6, no. 84 (2017). In "Thinking with Flint: Racial Liberalism and the Roots of an American Water Tragedy," *Capitalism Nature Socialism*, July 19, 2016, Malini Ranganathan applies this argument to the recent Flint, Michigan water crisis, remarking that liberalism was critical in obscuring "the racial foundations of capitalist exploitation" (3).
14 Esposito and Murphy, "Post Civil Rights Racism."
15 Robin D.G. Kelley, *Freedom Dreams: The Black Radical Imagination* (Boston, MA: Beacon Press, 2002); see also Lyne, "God's Black Revolutionary Mouth," 28.
16 Ibram H. Rogers, "'People All Over the World Are Supporting You': Malcolm X, Ideological Formations, and Black Student Activism, 1960–1972," *Journal Of African American History* 96, no. 1 (2011): 16.

they collectively named and confronted systemic racism in a more direct manner, staging what became known as "the revolt of the Black athlete."[17]

By the late 20th century, Black Americans (particularly in the lower socioeconomic tier) were largely abandoned in regards to social welfare, while targeted in regards to law enforcement, and Black leaders generally favored the liberal themes of "personality responsibility" and "self help" as solutions to racial inequality. In response, the Black Radical Congress was formed in the late 1990s, representing a Leftist alliance focused on intersectional oppression.[18] Such activist emphases were eventually renewed by the Black Lives Matter movement of the 2010s, further discussed below.

When viewing these radical movements in sum, it should be acknowledged that while they represent challenges to liberal ideology, they are also infused with elements of liberalism. Black radical critiques of the oppression inherent in "racial capitalism" have also been informed by the liberal tenets of individual human rights and equality, at times targeting the ineffectiveness of liberal strategies toward realizing such conditions.[19] Thus liberalism and radicalism are distinct but intersecting ideologies; the present study is an effort to capture such complexity within contemporary athlete activism.

LeBron James, Colin Kaepernick, and the 2016 Presidential Election

In March 2012, American media discourse was heavily focused on the shooting and killing of Trayvon Martin by "neighborhood watch" person George Zimmerman in Sanford, Florida. The event set off a national conversation about race, particularly violence against Black men. Amid this discourse, the Miami Heat basketball team, led by LeBron James, posed for a photograph that he posted to his Twitter account.[20] In the image, thirteen Miami players are dressed in their dark-gray hooded

---

[17] Harry Edwards, *The Revolt of the Black Athlete* (New York: Free Press, 1969); Douglas Hartmann, *Race, Culture and the Revolt of the Black Athlete: The 1968 Olympics Protests and Their Aftermath* (Chicago: University of Chicago Press, 2003).
[18] Jennifer Hamer and Clarence Lang, "Black Radicalism, Reinvented," in *Race & Resistance: African Americans In the Twenty-First Century*, ed. Herb Boyd (Cambridge, MA: South End Press, 2002), 109–136.
[19] Cedric J. Robinson, *Black Marxism: The making of the Black radical tradition* (Chapel Hill: University of North Carolina Press, 2000), 2.
[20] Lebron James (@KingJames), "#WeAreTrayvonMartin #Hoodies #Stereotyped #WeWantJustice," Twitter post, March 23, 2012. Accessed August 20, 2019. https://twitter.com/kingjames/status/183243305428058112?lang=en.

team sweatshirts, their faces partially obscured as they look to the ground. It is a pose of mourning, but the image also connotes, through covered faces, a generalized and shared identity between each subject and Martin. The caption clarified the post's political intent: "#WeAreTrayvonMartin #Hoodies #Stereotyped #WeWantJustice." Mimi Thi Nguyen has noted the hoodie's operation as a racialized signifier of threat, and James's engagement with the politics of this symbol signaled his, and other athletes', arrival in the political arena.[21]

The Martin-Zimmerman event ignited a general reinvigoration of Black politics, most visibly in the form of the Black Lives Matter (BLM) movement. After Zimmerman was acquitted of all charges in 2013, Oakland resident Alicia Garza wrote a "love letter to black people" on Facebook, which concluded with the phrase "Our lives matter."[22] Her post helped launch a movement that truly expanded in 2014 after the police killings of Eric Garner and Michael Brown.[23] The movement is radical in its attention to the inequalities of "racial capitalism," and poses a deeper challenge to institutional devaluation of Black health and wellbeing.[24] Though sharing the occupation technique with past Black liberal movements, BLM is a rejection of the "politics of respectability"; in the words of Juliet Hooker, it entails a "radical critique of the carceral state that rejects the distinction between law-abiding middle-class black citizens and always-already criminalized black 'thugs' in urban ghettos."[25] In a departure from some past iterations of Black radicalism, BLM is led by women and is highly intersectional and inclusive, as indicated by its focus on police targeting of transgender people.[26]

---

21 Mimi Thi Nguyen, "The Hoodie as Sign, Screen, Expectation, and Force," *Signs: Journal of Women in Culture and Society* 40, no. 4 (2015): 793.
22 Ruth Milkman, "A New Political Generation: Millennials and the Post-2008 Wave of Protest," *American Sociological Review* 82, no. 1 (2017): 24; Martha Biondi, "The Radicalism of Black Lives Matter," *In These Times* 40, no. 9 (2016): 16–19; Russell Rickford, "Black Lives Matter: Toward a Modern Practice of Mass Struggle," *New Labor Forum* 25, no. 1 (2016): 35.
23 BLM reflected the broadly heightened political consciousness among "millennials," which emerged from the 2008 economic recession and was partially enabled by social-media mobilization. See: Nikita Carney, "All Lives Matter, but so Does Race: Black Lives Matter and the Evolving Role of Social Media," *Humanity & Society* 40, no. 2 (2016): 180–198; Milkman, "A New Political Generation."
24 Barbara Ransby, "The Class Politics of Black Lives Matter," *Dissent* 62, no. 4 (2015): 31–34; Alondra Nelson, "The Longue Durée of Black Lives Matter," *American Journal Of Public Health* 106, no. 10 (2016): 1734–1737.
25 Juliet Hooker, "Black Lives Matter and the Paradoxes of U.S. Black Politics," *Political Theory* 44, no. 4 (2016), 465; Biondi, "The Radicalism of Black Lives Matter," 16–17; Rickford, "Black Lives Matter," 36.
26 Ransby, "The Class Politics of Black Lives Matter," 32; Biondi, "The Radicalism of Black Lives Matter," 19.

James's #WeAreTrayvonMartin post predated Garza's "love letter" by one year, indicating that the athlete-activist revival was not a product of BLM so much as intertwined with it. It also previewed the blend of radicalism and liberalism in James's political rhetoric. His very expression of resistance might be considered "radical" in the context of muted major-athlete political advocacy since the 1970s; furthermore, James leaned toward radicalism when addressing violence against Black men. In December 2014, he and other National Basketball Association players took the court in t-shirts emblazoned with the phrase "I Can't Breathe," echoing Eric Garner's final words; in July 2016, after the police killings of Alton Sterling and Philando Castile, he Tweeted a *Time* story with this comment: "This article says it all man! Sickens me and I shed multiple tears about it all. #ItNeedsToStop #BlackLivesMatter."[27] On the other hand, James carried on a close public association with President Obama, who had ridden a wave of multiculturalist liberal optimism to the White House.[28] James led a 2008 get-out-the vote rally for Obama in Ohio, publicly joined Michelle Obama in support of her "Let's Move" initiative, and promoted the Affordable Care Act.[29]

Liberalism was particularly embedded in James's politics in 2016, as evidenced by his rhetoric at that summer's Excellence in Sports Performance Yearly (ESPY) awards show. In an indication of amplified Black activism inside and outside of sport, James joined fellow NBA players Carmelo Anthony, Chris Paul, and Dwayne Wade as they opened the show, solemnly standing in suits, with a commentary on the outbreak of documented police attacks on Black Americans. After Anthony began by declaring, "The system is broken . . . the urgency to create change is at an all-time high," Paul and Wade followed with forceful criticisms of the police system, though also highlighting the ongoing gun violence in Chicago and elsewhere that, in Wade's refrain, "has to stop." James then offered his closing statement:

> We all feel helpless and frustrated by the violence. We do. But that's not acceptable. It's time to look in the mirror and ask ourselves, what are *we* doing to create change? It's not about

---

[27] "LeBron James, Kyrie Irving, more wear 'I Can't Breathe' shirts," *Sports Illustrated*, December 9, 2014. Accessed August 20, 2019. https://www.si.com/nba/2014/12/08/LeBron-james-kyrie-irving-i-cant-breathe-eric-garner; Lebron James (@KingJames), "This article says it all man! Sickens me and I shed multiple tears about it all. http://time.com/4397086/minnesota-shooting-philando-castile-role-model-school/?xid=tcoshare . . . #ItNeedsToStop #BlackLivesMatter," Twitter post, July 7, 2016. Accessed August 20, 2019. https://twitter.com/kingjames/status/751234227836841989.

[28] Stephen Campagna-Pinto, "Barack Obama and the Habit of Hope," *Anglican Theological Review* 97, no. 3 (2016): 519–536; Kenneth Fuchsman, "Barack Obama and the Cycle of American Liberalism," *The Journal of Psychohistory* 37, no. 2 (2009): 145–159.

[29] Alexander Wolff, *The Audacity of Hoop: Basketball and the Age of Obama* (Philadelphia, PA: Temple University Press, 2016).

being a role model, it's not about our responsibility to a condition of activism. I know tonight, we're honoring Muhammad Ali, the G.O.A.T. [Greatest Of All Time]. But to do his legacy any justice [audience applause], let's use this moment as a call to action for all professional athletes to educate ourselves. Explore these issues, speak up, use our influence, and renounce all violence. And most importantly, go back to our communities, invest our time, our resources, help rebuild them, help strengthen them, help change them. We *all* have to do better. Thank you.

James's speech drew on conservative iterations of Black liberalism through an emphasis on self-accountability ("what are *we* doing to create change?", "educate ourselves," "We *all* have to do better") and the call to "renounce all violence."[30] It would also preview the politics of his engagement with the Presidential election that fall.

Within one month of the ESPYs, Colin Kaepernick initiated his own protest. He began by sitting, unnoticed, during the national anthem before two preseason games. Once spotted and questioned about the gesture, Kaepernick offered comment to the National Football League's official media outlet: "I am not going to stand up to show pride in a flag for a country that oppresses black people and people of color." He followed with direct criticism of US institutions of power for not fulfilling liberal promises: "I'm going to continue to stand with the people that are being oppressed. To me, this is something that has to change . . . People are dying in vain because this country isn't holding their end of the bargain up, as far as giving freedom and justice, liberty to everybody."[31] Over the course of the season, Kaepernick's protest led to a wave of others around the NFL, though the intended messages (through sitting, kneeling, raising a fist, or locking arms) were not always clear. His own practices shifted as well: after being accused of disrespect for military personnel, Kaepernick switched from sitting to kneeling in order to "get the message back on track . . . [and] show more respect to the men and women who fight for this country."[32] This might be characterized as a moderation of radicalism, given the symbolic deference of kneeling. Thus like James, his activist performance mixed elements of radicalism and liberalism, at times adaptively shifting the mode of protest.

---

[30] Dawson outlines this conservatism in *Black Visions*, 19–20.
[31] Steve Wyche, "Colin Kaepernick Explains Why He Sat during National Anthem," *NFL Media*, August 27, 2016. Accessed August 20, 2019. http://www.nfl.com/news/story/0ap3000000691077/article/colin-kaepernick-explains-protest-of-national-anthem.
[32] David Fucillo, "Colin Kaepernick, Nate Boyer Meet in San Diego, Discuss National Anthem Controversy," *SBNation Niners Nation*, September 1, 2016. Accessed August 20, 2019. http://www.ninersnation.com/2016/9/1/12761112/colin-kaepernick-nate-boyer-meet-in-san-diego-national-anthem-controversy/in/12463381.

These practices took place within differing league-political contexts. The NBA, in regards to image management, has recently projected a multiculturalist (neo)liberalism that might be termed "corporate leftism." This orientation has been particularly evident during the tenure, beginning in 2014, of Commissioner Adam Silver. Within months of his new role, Silver expelled Los Angeles Clippers owner Donald Sterling for audio-recorded comments in favor of excluding Black spectators from his games; Sterling's ownership had not been jeopardized by a deep history of racist practices, including housing discrimination, but this overtly anti-Black discourse offered Silver an opportunity to affirm his commitment to racial liberalism.[33] He also followed previous commissioner David Stern in openly facilitating a relationship with President Obama, whose public embrace of basketball was accompanied by his own liberal orientation.[34] By contrast, the NFL has tended toward a more conservative politics and less overt embrace of multiculturalism. The league's nationalism, distinct from the NBA's globalist identity, is reinforced by its militaristic ethos, both in regards to game aesthetics and close relations with the U.S. military, particularly since the September 11 attacks and subsequent "War on Terror."[35] Thus, as will be demonstrated below, James's predominant liberalism largely aligned not only with Obama (and later Clinton) but also his own league's ideological orientation. By contrast, Kaepernick's radicalism more sharply diverged from NFL politics, particularly in his protest during a militaristic ritual, and likely shaped his future inclusion in the league.

James and Kaepernick would be drawn into a contest, between Hillary Clinton and Donald Trump, that featured starkly disparate tones, if not equally disparate ideologies. Exceptional as the first female Presidential candidate in a U.S. general election, Clinton had long engaged in a gendered struggle to appear "authentic," particularly given notions of womanhood that emphasize warmth, kindness and "likeability."[36] As a candidate, she promoted the "American nationalist thesis"

---

[33] Mark Berman, "Why the World Finally Noticed Donald Sterling's Appalling History," *The Washington Post*, April 28, 2014. Accessed August 20, 2019. http://wapo.st/1iuSiTT?tid=ss_mail&utm_term=.4d8161174228.

[34] Wolff, *The Audacity of Hoop*.

[35] Michael Butterworth, "Fox Sports, Super Bowl XLII, and the Affirmation of American Civil Religion," *Journal of Sport and Social Issues* 32, no. 3 (2008): 318–323; Michael Butterworth, "NFL Films and the Militarization of Professional Football," 205–225 and Samantha King, "Offensive Lines: Sport-State Synergy in an Era of Perpetual War," 191–204, in *The NFL: Critical and Cultural Perspectives*, eds. Thomas Oates and Zack Furness (Philadelphia, PA: Temple University Press, 2014); Adam Rugg, "America's Game: The NFL's 'Salute to Service' Campaign, the Diffused Military Presence, and Corporate Social Responsibility," *Popular Communication* 14, no. 1 (2016): 21–29.

[36] Shawn J. Parry-Giles, *Hillary Clinton in the News: Gender and Authenticity in American Politics* (Urbana: University of Illinois Press, 2014).

that posited a common "social ethos, a political creed" across a culturally diverse citizenry, and shared with Barack Obama an optimistic vision of the American past, present, and future.[37] In the midst of a fracturing Democratic Party, itself split between liberal and radical factions, she exuded (neo)liberalism through a "New Democrat" faith in corporate capitalism's facilitation of social wellbeing.[38] In contrast with Clinton's establishment ethos, Trump offered anti-establishment populist rhetoric. He was a longtime celebrity executive and "master of media spectacle" whose ascent was enabled by the hegemony of corporate capitalism.[39] Trump had paved the way for his candidacy through a White-nativist campaign of doubt that Obama was, in fact, born in the U.S. and thus qualified to serve as President.[40] As a candidate, Trump tapped into widespread disenchantment with economic opportunity, arguing that the "American Dream" was in danger of extinction, while also contrasting with Clinton through his "sincere"-seeming, somewhat unpredictable oratory that frequently had little basis in evidence.[41] Drawing on Adam Harmes, I join Sasha Bush in describing Trump's projected ideology as *nationalist neoliberalism*, an iteration of neoliberal economics that emphasizes national rather than global circulation.[42] His slogan "America First"

---

[37] Anatol Lieven, "Clinton and Trump: Two Faces of American Nationalism," *Survival* 58, no. 5 (2016): 7–22; hari stephen kumar, "'I Was Born . . . ' (No You Were Not!): Birtherism and Political Challenges to Personal Self-Authorizations," *Qualitative Inquiry* 19, no. 8 (2013): 621–633.

[38] Kathleen Geier, "Who's Ready for Hillary?," *Nation* 299, no. 24/25 (2014): 22–25.

[39] Douglas Kellner, *American Nightmare: Donald Trump, Media Spectacle, and Authoritarian Populism* (Rotterdam/ Boston, MA: Sense Publishers, 2016), 1; Henry A. Giroux, "Feature Article: Political Frauds, Donald Trump, and the Ghost of Totalitarianism," *Knowledge Cultures* 4, no. 5 (2016): 95–108.

[40] kumar, "'I Was Born . . . ' (No You Were Not!)," 628–630.

[41] Jeff Taylor, "Historical and Ideological Context of Donald Trump," *Faculty Work: Comprehensive List*, Paper 575, 2016: 7–8. Accessed August 20, 2019. http://digitalcollections.dordt.edu/faculty_work/575/?utm_source=digitalcollections.dordt.edu%2Ffaculty_work%2F575&utm_medium=PDF&utm_campaign=PDFCoverPages; John Kenneth White, "Donald Trump and the Scourge of Populism," *Forum (2194–6183)*, 14, no. 3 (2016): 272.

[42] Sasha Breger Bush, "Trump and National Neoliberalism," *Dollars & Sense*, December 16, 2016. Accessed August 20, 2019. http://dollarsandsense.org/archives/2016/1216bregerbush.html; Adam Harmes, "The Rise of National Neoliberalism," *Review of International Political Economy* 19, no. 1 (2011): 59–86. See also Christian Fuchs, "Donald Trump: A Critical Theory-Perspective on Authoritarian Capitalism," *Triplec (Cognition, Communication, Co-Operation): Open Access Journal For A Global Sustainable Information Society* 15, no. 1 (2017): 40–41, and John Shattuck, "The Rise of Populist Nationalism in Europe and the United States," *American Prospect* 28, no. 1 (2017): 40–44. I favor the term "nationalist" over Harmes's "national" due to the former's more direct hailing of nationalism, which undergirds this iteration of neoliberalism.

called for an invigoration of nationalism through protectionist economics and militaristic hard power, accompanied by the repression of dissent.

Such starkly different candidate identities seemed to augment interest in the Presidential campaign, which at times intersected with the ever-present American sport spectacle. Kaepernick's protest neatly coincided with the launching of the general election campaign, resulting in their nearly inevitable collision. In the wake of his initial anthem protest, on August 28, Kaepernick was asked about his views on the Presidential candidates, and responded bluntly:

> You have Hillary who's called Black teens super-predators. You have Trump who's openly racist. I mean, we have a Presidential candidate who's deleted and done things illegally and is a Presidential candidate. That doesn't make sense to me. 'Cause if that was any other person, you'd be in prison. So, what is this country really standing for?[43]

While sharing liberal criticism of the "openly racist" candidate Trump, Kaepernick's radicalism is evident in his accompanying criticism of the liberal-establishment alternative. And while addressing Clinton's record, he expresses cynicism regarding liberal notions of opportunity, touching on the privilege and protection of the political elite. In a strange moment of alliance, his comment that Clinton should "be in prison" mirrored Trump supporters' "lock her up" chants.

However, Kaepernick's indirect public clashes with Trump would be more prominent. The candidate was asked by a Seattle-area radio host about Kaepernick's comments and replied, "I think it's a terrible thing. And uh, you know, he'll uh – maybe he should find a country that works better for him. Let him try, it won't happen."[44] In late October, at a rally in Colorado, Trump attributed the NFL's declining ratings to the national anthem protest; he uttered "Kaepernick" twice with a frown, eliciting boos from the audience.[45] It appears, then, that Kaepernick emerged as a useful foil (the unpatriotic, unappreciative Black dissident) against which Trump effectively constructed his own brand of White nationalism. Kaepernick responded by critiquing Trump's nationalist-nostalgic slogan, "Make America Great Again," remarking: "Well, America's

---

43 Steven Ruiz, "Colin Kaepernick Says He'll Continue to Sit during Anthem, Calls Donald Trump 'Openly Racist,'" *USA Today Sports*, August 28, 2016. Accessed August 20, 2019. http://ftw.usatoday.com/2016/08/colin-kaepernick-national-anthem-donald-trump.

44 Charlotte Wilder, "Donald Trump Says Colin Kaepernick Should Find a New Country," *USA Today Sports*, August 30, 2016. Accessed August 20, 2019. http://ftw.usatoday.com/2016/08/donald-trump-colin-kaepernick-new-country-national-anthem-protest-response.

45 "Donald Trump: NFL's Ratings Are Down Because of Colin Kaepernick," *Sports Illustrated*, October 30, 2016. Accessed August 20, 2019. https://www.si.com/nfl/2016/10/30/donald-trump-nfl-ratings-down-colin-kaepernick.

never been great for people of color. And that's something that needs to be addressed. Let's make America great for the first time." When asked about the first Clinton-Trump debate, he replied that "it was embarrassing to watch that these are our two candidates," describing them both as "liars" and concluding that "you have to pick the lesser of two evils, but in the end it's still evil."[46] Thus while most explicitly critiquing Trump, he still refused to endorse Clinton, mirroring Black Lives Matter leaders' own rejection of the Democratic Party's statement of support.[47] For both Kaepernick and BLM, a radical agenda was incompatible with the party of establishment liberalism.

By contrast, James embraced the tenets of Black liberalism, most evidently in his direct alignment with Clinton. On October 2, *Business Insider* published his letter of endorsement, which opens with a nod to self-accountability through reference to the LeBron James Family Foundation's activities in his hometown. Black (political) liberalism is also reflected by his emphasis on State assistance: "Opportunities, a support system, and a safety net for kids in poverty or kids in single-parent households shouldn't be limited to those lucky enough to be blessed with athletic talent." After a reference to "my good friend, President Barack Obama," the following passage renders his liberalism most apparent: "[W]e need a president who brings us together and keeps us unified. Policies and ideas that divide us more are not the solution. We must all stand together – no matter where we are from or the color of our skin."[48] In consonance with Clinton, James's faith in the existing liberal order, through which he favors integration, precludes a call for radical resistance to it.

The letter's themes were reiterated in James's introduction of Clinton, on the Sunday before Election Day, at a Cleveland rally. Standing in front of her signature "STRONGER TOGETHER" podium logo, James remarked that he "grew up in the inner city," a coding of his own Black, working-class identity, and noted that fellow residents may believe that "our vote doesn't matter. But it really does. It really, really does." He then discussed his foundation and its goal of "giving my kids an opportunity to feel like they're important," as well as convincing children that people "care about them." These comments point to an emergent theme in his politics: as indicated by the naming of his "Family Foundation," James

---

[46] Matt Maiocco, "Kaepernick: 'Let's Make America Great For The First Time,'" *CSN Bay Area*, September 27, 2016. Accessed August 20, 2019. http://www.csnbayarea.com/49ers/kaepernick-lets-make-america-great-first-time.

[47] Rickford, "Black Lives Matter," 39.

[48] LeBron James, "LeBron James: Why I'm Endorsing Hillary Clinton," *Business Insider*, October 2, 2016. Accessed August 20, 2019. http://www.businessinsider.com/LeBron-james-why-endorsing-hillary-clinton-for-president-2016-9.

framed himself as an embodiment of social fatherhood, consistently focused on the wellbeing of children inside and outside of his biological family. Speaking next, Clinton herself lauded James's representation of fatherhood: "What he does off the court is to care for every child as if that child were his own."[49] Of course, fatherhood is a central element in American-national mythology, traced back to the "founding fathers." The political-parental model taps into the liberal notion of benevolent leadership which Clinton now sought to reconfigure as social motherhood.[50]

However, she was unable to garner sufficient public support; despite Clinton's victory in the popular vote, Trump won the Electoral College and the Presidency. It was a blow to establishment liberalism, indicating a broad current of disenchantment with the current American political system. In the face of this setback, as documented in the present study's opening, James's Instagram response reaffirmed optimism and faith in liberal progress. He again foregrounded social fatherhood in declaring, "To all the youth out there I PROMISE I'll continue to lead u guys every single day without no hesitation!!" Furthermore, his trust in "the man above" over a "strike" indicated opposition to radical intervention into institutions of power. At the same time, his inclusion of Kendrick Lamar's "Alright" carried complex connotations. While James's faith was echoed in the optimistic refrain, particularly "if God got us, then we gon' be alright," the song and video were also a scathing indictment of police and general institutional oppression of Black Americans. James had previously affirmed alliance with Black Lives Matter, and now posted a protest song closely associated with the movement. Colin Kaepernick's own posted videos, the following day, were more explicitly radical through the words of Malcolm X. The lamentation that "most of the Negro leaders sell out to the political, to the White politicians for crumbs" operates as a repudiation of James's endorsement of candidate Clinton. On the other hand, Kaepernick also included X's characterization of a Goldwater victory as potentially "good," in forcing Black American to "face up to facts" of an overtly racist leadership. Thus he joined James in expressing optimism about the implications of a Trump Presidency, though Kaepernick offered a decidedly more radical vision of Black self-preservation.

---

[49] "LeBron James Campaigns for Hillary Clinton in Ohio [FULL SPEECH]," *ABC News* video, 25:56, November 6, 2016. Accessed August 20, 2019. https://www.youtube.com/watch?v=isbW5RLIeDY.

[50] Karen Ferguson, *Top Down: The Ford Foundation, Black Power, and the Reinvention of Racial Liberalism* (Philadelphia: University of Pennsylvania Press, 2013), 26–29.

Kaepernick had been asked on Election Day if he would vote, and responded in the negative.[51] On the Sunday afterward, he offered the following rationalization:

> I think it would be hypocritical of me to vote. I'd said from the beginning I was against oppression, I was against a system of oppression. I'm not going to show support for that system. And, to me, the oppressor isn't going to allow you to vote your way out of your oppression.[52]

The comments reinforced his past rejection of the "system of oppression" within which Kaepernick had grouped both Presidential candidates. The revelation elicited a strong response from commentators: for example, ESPN's Stephen A. Smith declared Kaepernick to be "absolutely irrelevant" as a result, while Leftist sportswriter Dave Zirin dismissed Smith's "political wheeze" and defended Kaepernick's ideological sincerity.[53] That week's Zirin podcast interview with Harry Edwards, a leading figure in the original "revolt of the Black athlete" who had attempted to organize a boycott of the 1968 Olympics, reiterated the ideological complexity of athlete activism. Edwards acted as a mentor to Kaepernick, and despite his history of radicalism, he now expressed disappointment in the public rejection of the ballot box. In arguing for Black Americans' "obligation to vote," Edwards remarked, "We must utilize every arrow that we have in our quiver, no matter how small or how short distance," and highlighted "what the impact of his not voting is upon all of those other millennials and young people who look to him for courage, direction, guidance, insight, and so forth."[54] Through these

---

51 "Kaepernick Declined to Vote on Election Day: Report," *NBC Bay Area*, November 8, 2016. Accessed August 20, 2019. http://www.nbcbayarea.com/news/local/Kaepernick-Election-Day-400458701.html.
52 Matt Maiocco, "Kaepernick: 'It Would Be Hypocritical of Me to Vote,'" *NBC Bay Area*, November 13, 2016. Accessed August 20, 2019. http://www.nbcbayarea.com/news/sports/csn/49ers/Kaepernick__It_would_be_hypocritical_of_me_to_vote-401040155.html?_osource=SocialFlowTwt_BAYBrand.
53 First Take (@FirstTake), "'For him not to vote . . . as far as I'm concerned, everything he said meant absolutely nothing!' – @stephenasmith on Colin Kaepernick," Twitter post, November 9, 2016. Accessed August 20, 2019. https://twitter.com/FirstTake/status/796387727793131520; Dave Zirin, "On Colin Kaepernick's Decision Not to Vote," *The Nation*, November 14, 2016. Accessed August 20, 2019. https://www.thenation.com/article/on-colin-kaepernicks-decision-not-to-vote/.
54 Dave Zirin, interview with Harry Edwards, *Edge of Sports*, podcast audio, November 16, 2016. Accessed August 20, 2019. http://www.edgeofsportspodcast.com/post/153277948375/dr-harry-edwards-on-the-athlete-activist-under.

words, a major figure in Black athletic radicalism now criticized the rejection of establishment politics.

While Kaepernick offered his political expression through social media and press conferences, James occupied a very different space in the election's aftermath. On the following Thursday, he attended the White House as part of a culturally dissonant set of events. First, Barack Obama and Donald Trump, who had openly clashed since Trump's launching of the "birther" movement, met in private before making a joint appearance on camera.[55] It was a striking visual pairing: the leader of the liberal establishment and the man who had predicated his campaign on its deconstruction, a bust of Martin Luther King, Jr. peering over the latter's shoulder. Hours later, Obama welcomed the NBA champion Cleveland Cavaliers, led by James, and they collectively stood behind the President as he gave a lighthearted, comfortable speech of congratulations.[56] Later, the team staged a "Mannequin Challenge" video, and James's close relationship with the First Family was reflected by his smiling pose with Michelle Obama.[57] The next day, when asked about Trump's election, James reiterated his own role in "giving back to the community, giving back to the youth," and finished on an exceptionalist note: "This is the best country in the world, so we all have to do our part."[58] Even in the face of voter repudiation, James refused to express doubt on the promise of American liberal progress.

Conclusion/Epilogue

An examination of the revival of athlete activism reveals that, reflective of history, Black progress politics are constituted by distinct but intertwined ideological strands. This acknowledgment is key to understanding the complexities, sometimes present within a single figure's expression, at the intersection of sport

---

55 David Nakamura and Juliet Eilperin, "Trump Meets with Obama at the White House as Whirlwind Transition Starts," *Washington Post*, November 10, 2016. Accessed August 20, 2019. https://www.washingtonpost.com/news/post-politics/wp/2016/11/10/obama-to-welcome-trump-to-white-house-for-first-meeting-since-election/?utm_term=.c5d43ef6e0b7.
56 "Obama Honors Cleveland Cavaliers at White House," *ABC News* video, 19:17, November 10, 2016. Accessed August 20, 2019. https://www.youtube.com/watch?v=zJn-CxN29Hg&t=555s.
57 "LeBron James and Cleveland Cavaliers Mannequin Challenge with First Lady Michelle Obama!", NBA video, 0:30, November 10, 2016. Accessed August 20, 2019. https://www.youtube.com/watch?v=5ZzklOEGW0w.
58 Dave McMenamin, "LeBron James on election fallout: 'Nation has never been built on one guy,'" *ESPN*, November 11, 2016. Accessed August 20, 2019. http://www.espn.com/nba/story/_/id/18023858/LeBron-james-cleveland-cavaliers-donald-trump-victory-guy.

and politics. LeBron James may be considered radicalist through his alignment with Black Lives Matter, as well as his general leadership in the Leftist sport revival; on the other hand, in the context of the 2016 election, he largely projected Black liberalism through association with Clinton and the corollary promotion of community self-help, Black paternal responsibility, and faith in institutions of power. Colin Kaepernick also expressed faith in the realization of "freedom dreams," as well as promotion of community-based, grassroots work to provide uplift in Black communities. Furthermore, he joined James in opposing candidate Trump, who had so explicitly violated multiculturalist principles as to mobilize Leftist opposition. However, Kaepernick adopted a more radical orientation, framing both Presidential candidates as representative of the systematically oppressive institutions in which racism was embedded. Neither James nor Kaepernick rejected the basic liberal tenets of individual human equality and rights, but differed in their proposed paths towards those ideals. These paths reveal the persistence of ideologies of resistance through cultural memory, whether directly (see James's references to Ali, Kaepernick's references to Malcolm X) or through more opaque means. Whatever the means, they persist.

In the months after the election, both figures remained publicly linked to the incoming President. In December, it was revealed that James and some Cleveland teammates no longer resided at Trump's New York City hotel when playing the Knicks. Asked about the change, James was coy:

> I'm not trying to make a statement. It's just my personal preference. At the end of the day, I hope he's one of the best presidents ever for all of our sake – my family, for all of us. But it's just my personal preference. It would be the same if I went to a restaurant and decided to eat chicken and not steak.[59]

While a somewhat strange denial of the political implications of his action, the comments echoed James's tendency toward positive endorsement of candidates in the place of negatively opposing others, while also reinforcing his resilient optimism. That week, he was named *Sports Illustrated*'s 2016 Sportsperson of the Year; in the cover photo, James wears a safety pin, the emergent symbol of support for marginalized groups. The feature article includes no mention of the gesture, but the writer does note that "his form of engagement differs from Kaepernick's," supported by this quote from James:

> I understand protests, but I think protests can feel almost riotous sometimes, and I don't want that. I want it to be more about what I can do to help my community, what we can

---

[59] Dave McMenamin, "LeBron James: Just Preference to Not Stay at Trump Hotel," *ESPN*, December 7, 2016. Accessed August 20, 2019. http://www.espn.com/nba/story/_/id/18227393/no-statement-not-staying-donald-trump-new-york-hotel.

do so kids feel like they're important to the growth of America, and not like: "These people don't care about us." I'm not here to stomp on Trump. We're here to do our part, which starts in the place we grew up, street by street, brick by brick, person by person.[60]

Even in the impending era of a Trump Presidency, James favored positivity and offered no indication that a more radical politics of resistance was in his own future. His ideological alignment with the liberalism of powerful institutions (the Obama White House, Clinton candidacy, and NBA) facilitated the ongoing amplification of his voice in the public sphere.

Following the 2016 season, Kaepernick was released by the San Francisco 49ers and, as of the summer of 2020, has not been signed by another NFL team. At a March 2017 rally in Louisville, Trump claimed credit for Kaepernick's lack of a contract, drawing cheers when he declared that "NFL owners don't wanna pick him up because they don't wanna get a nasty Tweet from Donald Trump!" He added that his own followers "like it when people actually stand for the American flag, right?"[61] Once again, Trump deployed Kaepernick as a symbolic foil against which to demonstrate his own nationalism, while also exuding authoritarianism through the attack on dissent. The next day, it was reported that Kaepernick donated $50,000 to Meals on Wheels, a federal program targeted for cuts under Trump's proposed budget.[62] Despite the safe politics of this donation, Kaepernick's general radicalism positioned him in stronger opposition, compared with James, to institutions of power. While James continues to enjoy an embrace and voice in the NBA (if not the current White House), Kaepernick likely jeopardized his access to the NFL's highly visible, mass-mediated space. Racial politics do not solely determine such inclusions, but they do play a part.

In the years since the election, the discursive meeting points of James, Kaepernick, and Trump have generated more high-profile events (deserving of their own studies), most notably Trump's September 2017 "Get that son of a bitch off the field" comment in relation to NFL player protests. Whatever follows in the remainder of his Presidency, it seems likely that Trump(ism), the President and associated ideology, will fortify the reinvigorated athlete activism

---

60 Lee Jenkins, "Crowning The King: LeBron James is Sports Illustrated's 2016 Sportsperson of the Year," *Sports Illustrated*, December 1, 2016. Accessed August 20, 2019. https://www.si.com/sportsperson/2016/12/01/LeBron-james-sportsperson-of-the-year-sports-illustrated.
61 Andrew Joseph, "Donald Trump Is Taking Credit for Colin Kaepernick Still Being a Free Agent," *USA Today Sports*, March 20, 2017. Accessed August 20, 2019. http://ftw.usatoday.com/2017/03/donald-trump-credit-colin-kaepernick-free-agency-louisville-nfl-owners-tweet-anthem-protest.
62 Mahita Gajanan, "Colin Kaepernick donates $50,000 to Meals on Wheels," *Time*, March 22, 2017. Accessed August 20, 2019. http://time.com/4708728/colin-kaepernick-meals-on-wheels-donald-trump-nfl/.

of this decade. Given that sport is a well-documented "microcosm of society," broader political fractures have been, and will continue to be, refracted through this mass-mediated cultural apparatus. Sport discourses carry power in establishing the fault lines along which spectators engage in political issues, including the often-crossed line between liberal and radical modes of Black politics. It should be clarified that the present study is not offered as an endorsement of either liberalism or radicalism as a more effective engine of democratic progress. However, in the face of an authoritarian executive administration, the sustenance of democracy demands that high-profile athletes continue to demonstrate political engagement as a model for the rest of the nation.

Works Cited

Berman, Mark. "Why the world finally noticed Donald Sterling's appalling history." *The Washington Post*, April 28, 2014. http://wapo.st/1iuSiTT?tid=ss_mail&utm_term=.4d8161174228.
Biondi, Martha. "The Radicalism of Black Lives Matter." *In These Times* 40, no. 9 (2016): 16–19.
Bobbio, Norberto. *Liberalism and Democracy*. London: Verso, 2005.
Bush, Sasha Breger. "Trump and National Neoliberalism." *Dollars & Sense*, December 16, 2016. http://dollarsandsense.org/archives/2016/1216bregerbush.html.
Butterworth, Michael. "Fox Sports, Super Bowl XLII, and the Affirmation of American Civil Religion." *Journal of Sport and Social Issues* 32, no. 3 (2008): 318–323.
Butterworth, Michael. "NFL Films and the Militarization of Professional Football." In *The NFL: Critical and Cultural Perspectives*, edited by Thomas Oates and Zack Furness, 205–225. Philadelphia, PA: Temple University Press, 2014.
Campagna-Pinto, Stephen. "Barack Obama and the Habit of Hope." *Anglican Theological Review* 97, no. 3 (2016): 519–536.
Carney, Nikita. "All Lives Matter, but so Does Race: Black Lives Matter and the Evolving Role of Social Media." *Humanity & Society* 40, no. 2 (2016): 180–199.
Dawson, Michael C. *Black Visions: The Roots of Contemporary African-American Political Ideologies*. Chicago, IL: University of Chicago Press, 2001.
"Donald Trump: NFL's ratings are down because of Colin Kaepernick." *Sports Illustrated*, October 30, 2016. https://www.si.com/nfl/2016/10/30/donald-trump-nfl-ratings-down-colin-kaepernick.
Edwards, Harry. *The Revolt of the Black Athlete*. New York, NY: Free Press, 1969.
Esposito, Luigi and John W. Murphy. "Post Civil Rights Racism and the Need to Challenge Racial/Ethnic Inequality beyond the Limits of Liberalism." *Theory In Action* 3, no. 2, (2010): 38–63.
Ferguson, Karen. *Top Down: The Ford Foundation, Black Power, and the Reinvention of Racial Liberalism*. Philadelphia: University of Pennsylvania Press, 2013.
First Take (@FirstTake). "'For him not to vote . . . as far as I'm concerned, everything he said meant absolutely nothing!' – @stephenasmith on Colin Kaepernick." Twitter post, November 9, 2016. https://twitter.com/FirstTake/status/796387727793131520.
Fuchs, Christian. "Donald Trump: A Critical Theory-Perspective on Authoritarian Capitalism." *Triplec (Cognition, Communication, Co-Operation): Open Access Journal For A Global Sustainable Information Society* 15, no. 1 (2017): 1–72.

Fuchsman, Kenneth. "Barack Obama and the Cycle of American Liberalism." *The Journal of Psychohistory* 37, no. 2 (2009): 145–159.

Fucillo, David. "Colin Kaepernick, Nate Boyer meet in San Diego, discuss National Anthem controversy." *SBNation Niners Nation*, September 1, 2016. http://www.ninersnation.com/2016/9/1/12761112/colin-kaepernick-nate-boyer-meet-in-san-diego-national-anthem-controversy/in/12463381

Gajanan, Mahita. "Colin Kaepernick donates $50,000 to Meals on Wheels." *Time*, March 22, 2017. http://time.com/4708728/colin-kaepernick-meals-on-wheels-donald-trump-nfl/.

Geier, Kathleen. "Who's Ready for Hillary?" *The Nation* 299, no. 24/25 (2014): 22–25.

Giroux, Henry A. "Feature Article: Political Frauds, Donald Trump, and the Ghost of Totalitarianism." *Knowledge Cultures* 4, no. 5 (2016): 95–108.

Gray, John. *Liberalism*. Minneapolis: University of Minnesota Press, 1986.

Hall, Stuart. "Variants of Liberalism." In *Politics and ideology: a reader*, edited by James Donald and Stuart Hall, 34–69. Philadelphia, PA: Open University Press, 1986.

Hamer, Jennifer and Clarence Lang. "Black Radicalism, Reinvented." In *Race & Resistance: African Americans In The Twenty-First Century*, edited by Herb Boyd, 109–136. Cambridge, MA: South End Press, 2002.

Harmes, Adam. "The Rise of National Neoliberalism." *Review of International Political Economy* 19, no. 1 (2011): 59–86.

Hartmann, Douglas. *Race, Culture and the Revolt of the Black Athlete: the 1968 Olympics Protests and Their Aftermath*. Chicago: University of Chicago Press, 2003.

Hooker, Juliet. "Black Lives Matter and the Paradoxes of U.S. Black Politics." *Political Theory* 44, no. 4 (2016): 448–469.

James, LeBron. "LeBron James: Why I'm endorsing Hillary Clinton." *Business Insider*, October 2, 2016. http://www.businessinsider.com/LeBron-james-why-endorsing-hillary-clinton-for-president-2016-9.

James, Lebron (@KingJames). "#WeAreTrayvonMartin #Hoodies #Stereotyped #WeWantJustice." Twitter post, March 23, 2012. https://twitter.com/kingjames/status/183243305428058112?lang=en.

James, LeBron (@KingJames). "As I woke up today looking and searching for answers on what has happened this song hit it right on the head! . . . " Instagram post, November 9. 2016. https://www.instagram.com/p/BMmHGr0B0C-/.

James, Lebron (@KingJames). "This article says it all man! Sickens me and I shed multiple tears about it all. http://time.com/4397086/minnesota-shooting-philando-castile-role-model-school/=tcoshare ... #ItNeedsToStop #BlackLivesMatter." Twitter post, July 7, 2016.https://twitter.com/kingjames/status/751234227836841989.

Jenkins, Lee. "Crowning The King: LeBron James is Sports Illustrated's 2016 Sportsperson of the Year." *Sports Illustrated*, December 1, 2016. https://www.si.com/sportsperson/2016/12/01/LeBron-james-sportsperson-of-the-year-sports-illustrated.

Joseph, Andrew. "Donald Trump is taking credit for Colin Kaepernick still being a free agent." *USA Today Sports*, March 20, 2017. http://ftw.usatoday.com/2017/03/donald-trump-credit-colin-kaepernick-free-agency-louisville-nfl-owners-tweet-anthem-protest.

Kaepernick, Colin (@kaepernick7). [Malcolm X responds to interviewer's question about his recommended candidate for Black voters in the 1964 Presidential election]. Instagram video, November 10, 2016. https://www.instagram.com/p/BMolji0jg9H/.

"Kaepernick Declined to Vote on Election Day: Report." *NBC Bay Area*, November 8, 2016. http://www.nbcbayarea.com/news/local/Kaepernick-Election-Day-400458701.html.

Kelley, Robin D.G. *Freedom Dreams: The Black Radical Imagination*. Boston, MA: Beacon Press, 2002.

Kellner, Douglas. *American Nightmare: Donald Trump, Media Spectacle, and Authoritarian Populism*. Rotterdam; Boston, MA: Sense Publishers, 2016.

King, Samantha. "Offensive Lines: Sport-State Synergy in an Era of Perpetual War." In *The NFL: Critical and Cultural Perspectives*, edited by Thomas Oates and Zack Furness, 191–204. Philadelphia, PA: Temple University Press, 2014.

Kumar, hari stephen. "'I Was Born . . . ' (No You Were Not!): Birtherism and Political Challenges to Personal Self-Authorizations." *Qualitative Inquiry* 19, no. 8 (2013): 621–633.

"LeBron James, Kyrie Irving, more wear 'I Can't Breathe' shirts." *Sports Illustrated*, December 9, 2014. https://www.si.com/nba/2014/12/08/LeBron-james-kyrie-irving-i-cant-breathe-eric-garner.

"LeBron James and Cleveland Cavaliers Mannequin Challenge with First Lady Michelle Obama!" NBA video, 0: 30. November 10, 2016. https://www.youtube.com/watch?v=5ZzklOEGW0w.

"LeBron James Campaigns for Hillary Clinton in Ohio [FULL SPEECH]." *ABC News* video, 25: 56. November 6, 2016. https://www.youtube.com/watch?v=isbW5RLIeDY.

Lieven, Anatol. "Clinton and Trump: Two Faces of American Nationalism." *Survival* 58, no. 5 (2016): 7–22.

Lyne, Bill. "God's Black Revolutionary Mouth: James Baldwin's Black Radicalism." *Science & Society* 74, no. 1 (2010): 12–36.

Nelson, Alondra. "The Longue Durée of Black Lives Matter." *American Journal Of Public Health* 106, no. 10 (2016): 1734–1737.

Maiocco, Matt. "Kaepernick: 'It Would Be Hypocritical of Me to Vote.'" *NBC Bay Area*, November 13, 2016. http://www.nbcbayarea.com/news/sports/csn/49ers/Kaepernick__It_would_be_hypocritical_of_me_to_vote-401040155.html?_osource=SocialFlowTwt_BAYBrand.

Maiocco, Matt. "Kaepernick: 'Let's Make America Great For The First Time.'" *CSN Bay Area*, September 27, 2016. http://www.csnbayarea.com/49ers/kaepernick-lets-make-america-great-first-time.

McMenamin, Dave. "LeBron James: Just preference to not stay at Trump hotel." *ESPN*, December 7, 2016. http://www.espn.com/nba/story/_/id/18227393/no-statement-not-staying-donald-trump-new-york-hotel.

McMenamin, Dave. "LeBron James on election fallout: 'Nation has never been built on one guy.'" *ESPN*, November 11, 2016. http://www.espn.com/nba/story/_/id/18023858/LeBron-james-cleveland-cavaliers-donald-trump-victory-guy.

Milkman, Ruth. "A New Political Generation: Millennials and the Post-2008 Wave of Protest." *American Sociological Review* 82, no. 1 (2017): 1–31.

Nakamura, David and Juliet Eilperin. "Trump meets with Obama at the White House as whirlwind transition starts." *Washington Post*, November 10, 2016. https://www.washingtonpost.com/news/post-politics/wp/2016/11/10/obama-to-welcome-trump-to-white-house-for-first-meeting-since-election/?utm_term=.c5d43ef6e0b7.

Nguyen, Mimi Thi. "The Hoodie as Sign, Screen, Expectation, and Force." *Signs: Journal of Women in Culture and Society* 40, no. 4 (2015): 791–816.

"Obama Honors Cleveland Cavaliers at White House." *ABC News* video, 19: 17. November 10, 2016. https://www.youtube.com/watch?v=zJn-CxN29Hg&t=555s.

Parry-Giles, Shawn J. *Hillary Clinton in the News: Gender and Authenticity in American Politics.* Urbana: University of Illinois Press, 2014.

Ranganathan, Malini. "Thinking with Flint: Racial Liberalism and the Roots of an American Water Tragedy." *Capitalism Nature Socialism*, July 19, 2016.

Ransby, Barbara. "The Class Politics of Black Lives Matter." *Dissent* 62, no. 4 (2015): 31–34.

Rickford, Russell. "Black Lives Matter: Toward a Modern Practice of Mass Struggle." *New Labor Forum* 25, no. 1 (2016): 34–42.

Robinson, Cedric J. *Black Marxism: The making of the Black radical tradition.* Chapel Hill: University of North Carolina Press, 2000.

Rogers, Ibram H. "'People All Over the World Are Supporting You': Malcolm X, Ideological Formations, and Black Student Activism, 1960–1972." *Journal Of African American History* 96, no. 1 (2011): 14–38.

Rugg, Adam. "America's game: The NFL's 'Salute to Service' campaign, the diffused military presence, and corporate social responsibility." *Popular Communication* 14, no. 1 (2016): 21–29.

Ruiz, Steven. "Colin Kaepernick says he'll continue to sit during anthem, calls Donald Trump 'openly racist.'" *USA Today Sports*, August 28, 2016. http://ftw.usatoday.com/2016/08/colin-kaepernick-national-anthem-donald-trump.

Shattuck, John. "The Rise of Populist Nationalism in Europe and the United States." *American Prospect* 28, no. 1 (2017): 40–44.

Simmons, Beth A., Frank Dobbin, and Geoffrey Garrett. "Introduction: The International Diffusion of Liberalism." In *Key Concepts in the New Global Economy. Volume 1*, edited by David A. Baldwin, 133–162. Cheltenham, U.K. and Northampton, MA: Elgar, 2012.

Singh, Nikhil Pal. "Liberalism." In *Keywords for American Cultural Studies*, 2nd Edition, edited by Bruce Burgett and Glenn Hendler, 153–158. New York: NYU Press, 2014.

Singh, Vikash. "Race, the Condition of Neo-liberalism." *Social Sciences* 6, 84 (2017): 1–16.

Taylor, Jeff. "Historical and Ideological Context of Donald Trump." *Faculty Work: Comprehensive List*, Paper 575, 2016: 7–8. http://digitalcollections.dordt.edu/faculty_work/575/?utm_source=digitalcollections.dordt.edu%2Ffaculty_work%2F575&utm_medium=PDF&utm_campaign=PDFCoverPages

White, John Kenneth. "Donald Trump and the Scourge of Populism." *Forum (2194–6183)*, 14, no. 3 (2016): 265–279.

Wilder, Charlotte. "Donald Trump says Colin Kaepernick should find a new country." *USA Today Sports*, August 30, 2016. http://ftw.usatoday.com/2016/08/donald-trump-colin-kaepernick-new-country-national-anthem-protest-response.

Wolff, Alexander. *The Audacity of Hoop: Basketball and the Age of Obama.* Philadelphia, PA: Temple University Press, 2016.

Wyche, Steve. "Colin Kaepernick explains why he sat during national anthem." *NFL Media*, August 27, 2016. http://www.nfl.com/news/story/0ap3000000691077/article/colin-kaepernick-explains-protest-of-national-anthem.

Zirin, Dave. Interview with Harry Edwards. *Edge of Sports*. Podcast audio. November 16, 2016. http://www.edgeofsportspodcast.com/post/153277948375/dr-harry-edwards-on-the-athlete-activist-under.

Zirin, Dave. "On Colin Kaepernick's Decision Not to Vote." *The Nation*, November 14, 2016. https://www.thenation.com/article/on-colin-kaepernicks-decision-not-to-vote/.

Section III: **Sports, Politics, Sexual Abuse and Homophobia**

Kathleen Bachynski
7 #MeToo, Larry Nassar, and Sexual Abuse in Youth Sports

The #MeToo movement emerged as one of the most important stories in American sports and politics during the late 2010s. Intended to highlight the breadth and impact of sexual violence and harassment, this social movement gained momentum in fall 2017 in the wake of sexual assault allegations against film producer Harvey Weinstein.[1] Women and men promoted the hashtag #MeToo on social media to focus attention on the prevalence of sexual assault and harassment. An increasing willingness to talk publicly about the issue quickly encompassed not just Hollywood but a wide range of other settings, such as politics, higher education, and sports. In the realm of politics, U.S. Supreme Court nomination hearings in fall 2018 saw psychology professor Dr. Christine Blasey Ford testify that nominee Brett Kavanaugh assaulted her when they were in high school. Following the Senate Judiciary hearings, in October 2018 Kavanaugh was sworn in as the 114th Justice of the Supreme Court. And within the world of sports, the trial of Larry Nassar, a doctor accused of abusing hundreds of young gymnasts for decades, became one of the largest sex abuse scandals in American sports history.

These major storylines of sexual violence in sports and politics collided remarkably in December 2018, when Dr. Blasey Ford presented *Sports Illustrated*'s Inspiration of the Year Award to lawyer and former gymnast Rachael Denhollander, the first woman to publicly accuse Larry Nassar of sexual assault.[2] The choice of a national sports magazine to honor an athlete survivor indicated how prominently the issue of sexual abuse had come to feature in national sports conversations. And the connection between women talking about their experiences of abuse on the national stage in the realm of both sports and politics demonstrated the scope of an ongoing social movement.

This essay explores the relationship between #MeToo as a broader political movement and its effects on conversations about athlete welfare and sexual

---

1 "History & Vision," Me Too Movement. Accessed March 5, 2019. https://metoomvmt.org/about/#history.
2 Alaa Abdeldaiem, "Christine Blasey Ford Introduces Rachael Denhollander as SI's Inspiration of the Year," *Sports Illustrated*, December 12, 2018. AccessedOctober 9, 2019. https://www.si.com/sportsperson/2018/12/12/christine-blasey-ford-introduces-rachael-denhollander-sports-illustrated-inspiration-year.

https://doi.org/10.1515/9783110679397-007

abuse in sports. First, a brief timeline of several developments leading up to the recent #MeToo movement indicates some of the factors that facilitated its emergence. Second, an examination of the Larry Nassar case reveals its mutually influential relationship with the #MeToo movement. In particular, national media coverage of the Nassar trial shaped discussions both within and beyond sports regarding sexual violence. Finally, this essay concludes with a comment on what the #MeToo movement reveals about the relationship between sports and politics.

The Origins of #MeToo

Although the expansion of the #MeToo movement in the wake of the Harvey Weinstein accusations might have seemed very sudden, several events in the preceding decades helped to lay the groundwork. Factors that made an acceleration in public conversation about sexual violence possible in 2017 include a history of investigative reporting on sexual assault in other institutional contexts as well as in sports, previous activism to address sexual abuse, and the election of Donald Trump.

In the early 2000s, investigative reporting on sexual abuse in contexts outside of sports, particularly in the Catholic Church, helped shaped public conversation about the issue. Notably, the *Boston Globe* Spotlight team reported on child abuse in the church not as the result of a bad apple or the occasional bad priest, but instead as the outcome of broad institutional failures. In 2003, the editor of the National Catholic Reporter described the church as coming to grips with the fact that "this is corruption and it is, in fact, systemic."[3] Subsequent protests, news reports, and legal cases emphasized that abuse was global and widespread, and highlighted the particular vulnerability of children to abuse in powerful, hierarchal institutions with little oversight.

Several years later, the Jerry Sandusky sexual abuse case at Penn State became what *Sports Illustrated* dubbed "the most explosive scandal in the history of college sports."[4] In June 2012, Sandusky was found guilty of 45 charges, including raping young boys whom he groomed and repeatedly abused while an

---

[3] Mark Jurkowitz, "Globe's Articles on Priests Spurred Scrutiny Worldwide," *Boston Globe*, April 8, 2003. Accessed December 10, 2018. http://archive.boston.com/globe/spotlight/abuse/extras/pulitzers2.htm.
[4] John L. Wertheim and David Epstein, "This is Penn State," *Sports Illustrated* 115, no. 20 (2011): 40–53.

assistant football coach at Penn State.⁵ That Jerry Sandusky was a revered coach at an esteemed college football program, one of the most prominent sports in the United States, drew extraordinary public attention and outrage. Louis Freeh, a former director of the FBI, led a months-long investigation into the Sandusky case which found widespread institutional failures at Penn State. These findings revealed not just individual shortcomings, but "weaknesses of the university's culture, governance, administration, compliance policies and procedures for protecting children."⁶ Numerous commentators highlighted the similarities between the Catholic Church's and Penn State's responses to child sexual abuse, such as failing to report cases to law enforcement and prioritizing the reputation of large, hierarchical institutions over the protection of children.⁷

Media coverage has typically focused on the most notorious and egregious cases of abuse, such as the Sandusky story, which represented about half of news stories pertaining to child sexual abuse in 2011–2012. Nonetheless, an analysis of newspaper and television coverage of child sexual abuse from 2002 to 2012 found a discernible shift toward more frequent mentions of societal-level causes for child sex abuse. Although much reporting continues to focus on appalling individual crimes and individual level solutions, such as locking up specific perpetrators, this finding suggests that news coverage has contributed to growing awareness of the role of institutions in fostering environments conducive to sexual abuse.⁸

In addition to investigative reporting increasingly characterizing child abuse as a systemic problem, the mid-2000s also saw greater attention to the connections between gender bias and sexual violence. In 2006, using MySpace, activist Tarana Burke first coined the phrase "Me Too," as a way to support black girls

---

5 Joe Drape, "Sandusky Guilty of Sexual Abuse of 10 Young Boys," *New York Times*, June 22, 2012. Accessed October 2, 2019. https://www.nytimes.com/2012/06/23/sports/ncaafootball/jerry-sandusky-convicted-of-sexually-abusing-boys.html.
6 Richard Pérez-Peña, "In Report, Failures Throughout Penn State," *New York Times*, July 12, 2012. Accessed October 2, 2019. https://www.nytimes.com/2012/07/13/sports/ncaafootball/in-freeh-report-on-sandusky-failures-throughout-penn-state.html.
7 See, for example, Patrick Hruby, "What the Catholic Church Can Teach Us About the Penn State Scandal," *Atlantic*, November 16, 2011. Accessed October 2, 2019. https://www.theatlantic.com/entertainment/archive/2011/11/what-the-catholic-church-can-teach-us-about-the-penn-state-scandal/248588/. See also Dan Gilgoff, "Seeming Parallels Abound in Penn State, Catholic Church Abuse Scandals," *CNN Belief Blog*, November 10, 2011. Accessed October 2, 2019.http://religion.blogs.cnn.com/2011/11/10/seeming-parallels-abound-in-penn-state-catholic-church-abuse-scandals/.
8 Jane Long Weatherred, "Framing Child Sexual Abuse: A Longitudinal Content Analysis of Newspaper and Television Coverage, 2002–2012," *Journal of Child Sexual Abuse* 26, no. 1 (2017): 3–22.

and women who had survived sexual violence. Numerous activists such as Burke over the past decade have focused efforts on the intersections of sexual violence and race, class, sexual orientation, and other social factors.[9]

The growth of social media facilitated various forms of activism, such as efforts to address campus sexual violence, by providing survivors and activists a platform to share stories and connect with each other.[10] For example, the 2014 #YesAllWomen social media campaign pertaining to harassment, assault and misogyny emerged after a California man went on a shooting spree. Shortly before killing six people and then himself, he had penned a 140 page misogynistic manifesto declaring his hatred toward women for sexually rejecting him.[11] Feminist writer Rebecca Solnit has argued that the response to these murders, including the #YesAllWomen campaign on social media, shaped public discourse about sexist violence. Notably, Solnit suggests that the phrase "sexual entitlement," referring to the idea that "a man has the right to have sex with a woman regardless of her desires" entered into everyday speech in May 2014, and would "help people identify and discredit manifestations of this phenomenon."[12] Indeed, national newspapers such as the *New York Times*[13] and *Wall Street Journal*[14] would subsequently use the expression in examinations of sexism and sexual assault.

Third, the election of Donald Trump, despite the emergence of a video in which he boasted of his ability to grab women's genitalia because of his celebrity status, not only drew attention to the issue of power and sexual violence, but also spurred activist responses, such as the Women's March, that helped

---

9 Najja Parker, "Who is Tarana Burke? Meet the Woman Who Started the Me Too Movement a Decade Ago," *Atlanta Journal-Constitution*, December 6, 2017. Accessed October 2, 2019. https://www.ajc.com/news/world/who-tarana-burke-meet-the-woman-who-started-the-too-movement-decade-ago/i8NEiuFHKaIvBh9ucukidK/.
10 Chris Linder, Jess S. Myers, Colleen Riggle, and Marvette Lacy. "From Margins to Mainstream: Social Media as a Tool for Campus Sexual Violence Activism," *Journal of Diversity in Higher Education* 9, no. 3 (2016): 231–244.
11 Sasha Weiss, "The power of #YesAllWomen," *New Yorker*, May 26, 2014. Accessed October 2, 2019. https://www.newyorker.com/culture/culture-desk/the-power-of-yesallwomen.
12 Rebecca Solnit, "Our Words Are Our Weapons," *Guernica*, June 2, 2014. Accessed October 2, 2019. https://www.guernicamag.com/rebecca-solnit-our-words-are-our-weapons-2/.
13 Lindy West, "Why is Fixing Sexism Women's Work?" *New York Times*, January 3, 2018, https://www.nytimes.com/2018/01/03/opinion/why-is-fixing-sexism-womens-work.html. Accessed October 9, 2019.
14 Melissa Korn, "Pressure Mounts on Harvard's All-Male Clubs to Admit Women," *Wall Street Journal*, April 14, 2016, https://www.wsj.com/articles/pressure-mounts-on-harvards-all-male-clubs-to-admit-women-1460626203. Accessed October 9, 2019.

further lay the groundwork for the 2017 expansion of the #MeToo movement.[15] In addition, Trump's election helped prompt more women to enter politics and seek elective office at every level. According to the Center for American Women and Politics at Rutgers University, in 2017 more than four times as many women candidates for seats in the U.S. House of Representatives were challenging incumbents as compared to 2015.[16] By 2017, over a decade of reporting on child sexual abuse as a systemic issue, activist efforts linking sexual violence with gender bias, and the increasing involvement of women in politics – at least partly in response to the election of a president who had been accused of sexual misconduct – all contributed to an environment where a movement like #MeToo could gain increased traction.

#MeToo and Larry Nassar

Because Harvey Weinstein had assaulted many actresses, their Hollywood and celebrity status galvanized initial attention to the #MeToo movement. In addition, social media had become much more widely available in the decade since Tarana Burke first coined the phrase, making it easier to quickly amplify the #MeToo message. The movement quickly snowballed, with accusations against Matt Lauer, Bill O'Reilly, Senator Al Franken, and many other prominent figures coming to the fore. In October 2017, Olympic gold-medal gymnast McKayla Maroney stated that she was inspired by the #MeToo movement to come forward about Larry Nassar molesting her, becoming the highest profile gymnast to accuse him of abuse.[17] In December 2017, *Time Magazine* named the women who had told their stories their people of the year, calling them the "silence breakers."[18]

Meanwhile, that same fall, on November 22, 2017, Larry Nassar pleaded guilty in Ingham County Circuit Court to seven counts of first-degree criminal

---

[15] Susan Chira and Yamiche Alcindor, "Defiant Voices Flood U.S. Cities as Women Rally for Rights," *New York Times*, January 21, 2017, https://www.nytimes.com/2017/01/21/us/women-march-protest-president-trump.html. Accessed October 9, 2019.
[16] Michael Tackett, "Women Line Up to Run for Office, Harnessing Their Outrage at Trump," *New York Times*, December 4, 2017, https://www.nytimes.com/2017/12/04/us/politics/women-candidates-office.html. Accessed October 9, 2019.
[17] Tracy Connor, "McKayla Maroney Says Dr. Larry Nassar Molested Her in #MeToo Post," *NBC News*, October 18, 2017, https://www.nbcnews.com/news/us-news/olympic-gymnast-mckayla-maroney-says-dr-larry-nassar-molested-her-n811766. Accessed October 9, 2019.
[18] Stephanie Zacharek, Eliana Dockterman, and Haley Sweetland Edwards, "The Silence Breakers," *Time Magazine*, December 18, 2017, http://time.com/time-person-of-the-year-2017-silence-breakers/. Accessed October 9, 2019.

sexual misconduct with minors under the age of sixteen. Nassar was an osteopathic physician at Michigan State University and a USA Gymnastics national team doctor who had been accused of abusing hundreds of young athletes. Given this timing, as well as the sheer number of Nassar's victims, it is perhaps not surprising that media coverage of the Nassar case increased in the wake of #MeToo, and thus helped bring the world of sports into the broader #MeToo conversation. Table 1 provides a selected timeline of events to offer a sense of the extent to which developments in the Larry Nassar case and the broader #MeToo movement intersected.

Table 1: #MeToo Developments and the Larry Nassar Case in Fall 2017.

Date	Event
October 5, 2017	Actress Ashley Judd accuses media mogul Harvey Weinstein
October 18, 2017	Olympic gymnast McKayla Maroney tweets that she was sexually assaulted by Larry Nassar
November 9, 2017	The *Washington Post* publishes an investigative piece about Alabama Republican Senate nominee Roy Moore's alleged history of preying upon underage girls
December 7, 2017	At the urging of his party, U.S. Sen. Al Franken, D-Minn., says he'll resign from Congress amid sexual misconduct allegations
December 7, 2017	Larry Nassar is sentenced to 60 years in prison on federal child pornography charges
December 11, 2017	Chef Mario Batali goes on leave from his show after sexual harassment allegations
January 16–24, 2018	156 women read Victim Impact Statements during an eight-day sentencing hearing for Nassar

Before the #MeToo movement accelerated, the Nassar case had received relatively little national media coverage, but it was local reporting that led to his sentencing in the first place. On September 12, 2016, the *Indianapolis Star* had first reported on the Larry Nassar case.[19] The newspaper's coverage revealed that exploitation and abuse at USA Gymnastics was widespread and systemic, going far beyond the case of Larry Nassar to encompass gyms across the country.

---

19 Dakota Crawford and Amy Haneline, "Follow IndyStar's Investigation of USA Gymnastics and Larry Nassar From Start to Finish," *Indianapolis Star*, January 24, 2018, https://www.indystar.com/story/sports/2018/01/24/indystar-larry-nassar-usa-gymnastics-investigation/1062120001/. Accessed October 9, 2019.

Previous reporting on abuse in contexts like the Catholic Church helped the *Indianapolis Star* highlight numerous important features of USA Gymnastics abuse cases such as Nassar's. These included a lax system of oversight with predatory coaches allowed to move from gym to gym and no tracking of the coaches who were fired, efforts to keep details of abuse cases secret, and institutional fears of tarnishing the sport's image and detracting from inspirational gymnastics stories.[20]

As the *Indianapolis Star* observed, the use of confidentiality agreements as part of settlements of abuse cases, "which often ban disclosure of payment amounts and details about an organization's handling of sex abuse allegations, can hide incidents that enable abuse to continue."[21] The #MeToo movement began to challenge such commonplace tactics that had often shrouded cases of abuse in silence. In fact, USA Gymnastics' use of a confidentiality agreement with Olympic gymnast McKayla Maroney became a particularly potent example of the intersection between sports, politics and the #MeToo movement. When it was reported that McKayla Maroney potentially faced a $100,000 fine for violating her non-disclosure agreement if she were to speak at Larry Nassar's sentencing, multiple high-profile actresses and models who had supported the #MeToo movement stated that they would be willing to pay that fine for her. Their celebrity involvement produced enough public attention that USA Gymnastics swiftly responded by announcing that it would not fine Maroney should she speak out.[22]

This case illustrates just one of many barriers that historically limited survivors of abuse from talking about their experiences, as well as the potential for political and social pressure from a movement like #MeToo to challenge some of those institutional structures. But perhaps the most important development for drawing public attention to the breadth of Nassar's abuse was his sentencing in January 2018. Judge Rosemarie Aquilina announced that she would permit any survivors who wished to do so to read victim impact statements describing how Nassar's actions had affected them. Prosecutors had originally expected 88 women and girls to participate over four days, but ultimately a

---

[20] Tim Evans, Mark Alesia, and Marisa Kwiatkowski, "A 20-Year Toll: 368 Gymnasts Allege Sexual Exploitation," *Indianapolis Star*, February 8, 2018, https://www.indystar.com/story/news/2016/12/15/20-year-toll-368-gymnasts-allege-sexual-exploitation/95198724/. Accessed October 9, 2019.

[21] Evans, Alesia, and Kwiatkowski, "A 20-Year Toll."

[22] Heather Tucker, "USA Gymnastics Says It Will Not Fine McKayla Maroney If She Speaks Out Against Larry Nassar," *USA Today*, January 16, 2018, https://www.usatoday.com/story/sports/olympics/2018/01/16/usa-gymnastics-mckayla-maroney-larry-nassar/1039025001/. Accessed October 9, 2019.

total of 156 came forward to speak in courtroom proceedings that were widely shared and discussed in the national media.[23] Television networks provided live coverage when Aquilina sentenced Nassar to up to 175 years in prison on January 24, 2018.[24] Law professor Janice Nadler contended that Aquilina's decision to offer all survivors of Nassar's abuse the opportunity to read a victim impact statement was a means of demonstrating "to the victims that they matter, that their lives matter, that the state stands ready to impose the punishment that Nassar deserves."[25]

While the victim impact statements functioned to affirm the individual value of each person harmed by Nassar, they also served to highlight that institutions were crucial in enabling sexual abuse to continue unstopped for decades. The final survivor to testify was Rachael Denhollander, who had been the first to publicly accuse Nassar. Her victim impact statement emphasized the failure of organizations like USA Gymnastics and Michigan State University to protect athletes. Denhollander told Judge Aquilina that while Nassar was abusing her, "USAG was systematically burying reports of sexual assault against member coaches in a file cabinet instead of reporting them, creating a culture where predators like Larry and so many others in the organization up to the highest-level coaches were able to sexually abuse children, including our Olympians, without any fear of being caught." She emphasized the devastation of realizing that not only could she not trust Nassar, but she also could not trust the people surrounding him.[26] The #MeToo movement helped provide a broader context for such survivor testimony, and influenced public reception of such allegations by raising public awareness and attention. As a result, the victim impact statements at Nassar's sentencing amplified the broader message of the #MeToo movement that urged accountability for both individuals and institutions.

---

[23] Matt Mencarini, "Inside the Investigation and Prosecution of Larry Nassar," *Lansing State Journal*, April 7, 2018, https://www.lansingstatejournal.com/story/news/local/2018/04/05/larry-nassar-inside-prosecution-investigation/472506002/. Accessed October 9, 2019.

[24] Callum Borchers, "Judge Rosemarie Aquilina Was a Media Master in the Larry Nassar Case," *Washington Post*, January 24, 2018, https://www.washingtonpost.com/news/the-fix/wp/2018/01/24/judge-rosemarie-aquilina-was-a-media-master-in-the-larry-nassar-case/. Accessed October 9, 2019.

[25] Scott Cacciola, "Victims in Larry Nassar Abuse Case Find a Fierce Advocate: The Judge," *New York Times*, January 23, 2018, https://www.nytimes.com/2018/01/23/sports/larry-nassar-rosemarie-aquilina-judge.html. Accessed October 9, 2019.

[26] "Read Rachael Denhollander's Full Victim Impact Statement About Larry Nassar," *CNN*, January 24, 2018, https://www.cnn.com/2018/01/24/us/rachael-denhollander-full-statement/index.html. Accessed October 9, 2019.

Indeed, following Nassar's sentencing, legal and public attention increasingly turned to other individuals at USAG and MSU who enabled Nassar's abuse. For example, in October 2018 former USAG CEO Steve Penny was arrested after a grand jury in Texas indicted him for tampering with evidence while authorities were investigating Nassar's behavior.[27] Three MSU officials – former MSU gymnastics coach Kathie Klages, former university president Lou Anna Simon, and former dean William Strampel – were charged with crimes related to the Nassar scandal.[28] In September 2018, the Justice Department opened an investigation into whether FBI agents mishandled allegations against Nassar.[29] In December 2018, a 233 page independent investigation into how the U.S. Olympic Committee and USA Gymnastics failed to protect athletes was published. The report found that after then-USA Gymnastics CEO Steve Penny informed two top U.S. Olympic Committee officials about Larry Nassar on July 25, 2015, neither official "engaged with USAG on the reported concerns, shared the information with others at the USOC or took any other action in response to the information from Mr. Penny to ensure that responsible steps were being taken by USAG and the USOC to protect athletes."[30] In March 2019, 51 women and girls sued the USOC in federal court in Colorado, for failing to stop abuse by its coaches and by national team doctor Larry Nassar.[31]

Athletes in other sports contended that the USOC's failures described in the Nassar case were evident across other sports at all levels. Dani Bostick, a former child swimmer who began to be abused by a coach when she joined a team at the local YMCA, emphasized that the culture described in the report "also

---

[27] Juliet Macur, "Steve Penny, Former U.S.A. Gymnastics Chief, Arrested on Evidence Tampering Charge," *New York Times*, October 18, 2018, https://www.nytimes.com/2018/10/18/sports/steve-penny-gymnastics-arrest-tampering.html. Accessed October 9, 2019.

[28] Matt Mencarini, "MSU to Pay for Lou Anna Simon's Defense as Legal Bills for Larry Nassar Scandal Near $20M," *Lansing State Journal*, January 23, 2019, https://www.lansingstatejournal.com/story/news/local/2019/01/23/larry-nassar-lou-anna-simon-msu-michigan-state-bills/2645371002/. Accessed October 9, 2019.

[29] Rebecca Davis O'Brien, "U.S. Investigates F.B.I. Response to Gymnasts' Sex Abuse Claims," *Wall Street Journal*, September 4, 2018, https://www.wsj.com/articles/u-s-investigates-fbi-response-to-gymnasts-sex-abuse-claims-1536103576. Accessed October 9, 2019.

[30] Joan McPhee and James P. Dowden, "Report of the Independent Investigation: The Constellation of Factors Underlying Larry Nassar's Abuse of Athletes," *Ropes & Gray*, accessed March 14, 2019, https://www.ropesgray.com/-/media/Files/USOC/ropes-gray-full-report.pdf. Accessed October 9, 2019.

[31] Saja Hindi, "51 Women, Girls Sue U.S. Olympic Committee in Federal Court in Colorado For Failing to Stop Sexual Abuse by Larry Nassar," *Denver Post*, March 15, 2019, https://www.denverpost.com/2019/03/15/us-olympic-committee-larry-nassar-lawsuit-colorado. Accessed October 9, 2019.

affects children whose involvement in sports is casual."[32] Athletes and sportswriters pointed to the U.S. Olympic Committee's lack of accountability and failure to protect children as a sign of the institution's prioritization of money over child welfare.[33] Bostick warned that until the USOC underwent "a seismic shift," all youth athletes playing under its aegis were at risk.[34]

The investigative report highlighted some embedded cultural norms unique to competitive sports, such as the normalization of intense physical discomfort as integral to the path to success.[35] The hierarchal structure of many competitive sports programs, the cultural prominence of sports authorities including coaches, administrators and doctors, and a broad lack of oversight furthered the potential for a harmful environment. The report noted contributing norms that were also evident in other institutions, such as obedience and deference to authority. The unfolding of the Nassar case in tandem with the #MeToo movement spotlighted many of the factors in evidence across movie sets, religious institutions, political campaigns, locker rooms, sports medicine clinics, and other settings where sexual abuse scandals have come to light.

One MSU leader's response to the Nassar case also demonstrated the types of backlash that survivors of sexual assault frequently encounter. John Engler, a former governor of Michigan, was appointed to serve as an interim president of Michigan State University. In a private email to a top adviser, he stated that Rachael Denhollander was likely receiving kickbacks from trial attorneys involved in lawsuits against Michigan State. Denhollander's husband, Jacob Denhollander, told the *Detroit Free Press* that Engler's comments were "a perfect example of why victims remain silent."[36] Engler later told the *Detroit News* editorial board that survivors who had not been in the spotlight were in some ways able to "deal with this better than the ones who've been in the spotlight

---

32 Dani Bostick, "New Report on USA Gymnastics and Larry Nassar a Reminder That Athletes Across America are at Risk," *NBC News*, December 19, 2018, https://www.nbcnews.com/think/opinion/new-report-usa-gymnastics-larry-nassar-reminder-athletes-across-america-ncna 949811. Accessed October 9, 2019.

33 Sally Jenkins, "The USOC Needs a Leader Who Cares More About Athletes Than Expense Accounts," *Washington Post*, July 5, 2018, https://www.washingtonpost.com/sports/olympics/the-usoc-needs-a-leader-who-cares-about-athletes-more-than-expense-accounts/2018/07/03/9554ded8-7ae5-11e8-80be-6d32e182a3bc_story.html?utm_term=.c36ccc3f7c44. Accessed October 9, 2019.

34 Bostick, "New Report."

35 McPhee and Dowden, "Report of the Independent Investigation."

36 David Jesse, "MSU President Engler: Nassar Survivor May Get Kickbacks From Lawyers," *Detroit Free Press*, June 13, 2018, https://www.freep.com/story/news/local/michigan/2018/06/13/msu-larry-nassar-rachael-denhollander/699307002/. Accessed October 9, 2019.

who are still enjoying that moment at times, you know, the awards and recognition." Six days after those comments, Engler was forced to resign.[37]

Such characterizations of victims as seeking fame and money by making claims of sexual assault played on a long history of undermining survivors' credibility. Particularly in the wake of #MeToo cases that received significant media attention, such as accusations against Larry Nassar and Brett Kavanaugh, the credibility of accusers went under a microscope.[38] At least one YouGov poll of 1,500 respondents suggested that a small but significant backlash to #MeToo was making Americans more skeptical of sexual misconduct allegations. For example, between November 2017 and September 2018, the percent of Americans who believed that false accusations of sexual assault were a bigger problem than cases that went unreported or unpunished increased from 13 percent to 18 percent.[39] According to Juliana Horowitz of the Pew Research Center, the largest split on #MeToo was not based on gender or age, but on political affiliation.[40] According to an October 2018 poll from the nonpartisan Public Religion Research Institute, only 34 percent of Republicans said that they would not consider voting for a candidate who had been accused by multiple people of sexual assault, whereas 81 percent of Democrats who responded said they would not vote for such a candidate. The #MeToo movement may have increased, or at least further revealed, partisan divisions among Americans regarding how they perceived accusations of sexual assault, and what they thought the potential consequences should be in response to multiple accusations.[41]

In the Nassar case, university president John Engler expressed distrust of an accuser's motives despite Nassar pleading guilty and being convicted of abusing multiple girls. On the other hand, his repeated expressions of skepticism ultimately contributed in part to Engler's resignation. The Nassar case thus illustrated

---

37 Kim Kozlowski, "How John Engler's MSU Reign Fell Apart," *Detroit News*, January 29, 2019, https://www.detroitnews.com/story/news/education/2019/01/29/how-john-engler-michigan-state-university-reign-fell-apart/2604186002/. Accessed October 9, 2019.
38 Peter Baker, "Christine Blasey Ford's Credibility Under New Attack by Senate Republicans," *New York Times*, October 3, 2018, https://www.nytimes.com/2018/10/03/us/politics/blasey-ford-republicans-kavanaugh.html. Accessed October 9, 2019.
39 "Measuring the #MeToo Backlash," *The Economist*, October 20, 2018, https://www.economist.com/united-states/2018/10/20/measuring-the-metoo-backlash. Accessed October 9, 2019.
40 "What Group of People is Most Hostile to #MeToo?" *The Economist*, January 10, 2019, https://www.economist.com/united-states/2019/01/12/what-group-of-people-is-most-hostile-to-metoo. Accessed October 9, 2019.
41 Zack Beauchamp, "New Poll Shows That Republicans Have Become the Party of #MeToo Backlash," *Vox*, October 3, 2018, https://www.vox.com/policy-and-politics/2018/10/3/17932324/brett-kavanaugh-news-republicans-poll-sexual-assault. Accessed October 9, 2019.

the influence of longstanding skepticism of people making accusations of assault, but also the potential limits of public and institutional tolerance for characterizations of victims as seeking money, fame, recognition and awards.

Maybe, Maybe, I Can Help Other People Too

While the Nassar case was clearly a sports story with certain elements unique to competitive athletics, it was just as clearly a story about power, sexual violence and institutional corruption that the broader political #MeToo movement spotlighted. Moreover, similar to the broader #MeToo movement, the Nassar case had a snowball effect. Several examples illustrate how the sentencing of Larry Nassar sparked further discussion, legislation, and revelations of sexual assault in sports and politics.

In the wake of revelations of Nassar's crimes, MSU student protesters and community activists adopted the phrase #MeToo and explicitly connected Nassar's abuse to this broader political movement. Jessica Smith, a survivor of Nassar's abuse who had criticized the university's handling of the allegations, founded a social media group for survivors called "Me Too MSU."[42] In April 2018, Tarana Burke, the activist who founded the #MeToo movement, traveled to MSU to address hundreds of students and community members. Burke discussed systemic problems with how institutions handle sexual violence and noted that she had been contacted by survivors of Nassar's abuse.[43] At an April 2018 rally calling for MSU interim president John Engler and the entire board of trustees to resign, attendees chanted "Time is up!"[44] Kat Ebert, an MSU student who was assaulted by Nassar, began an effort to establish a 24/7 sexual assault resource center on campus. She explained that she was motivated both by her own experience trying to find support as well as the broader #MeToo movement.[45]

---

42 Madison O'Connor, "President Simon, Trustees Apologize to Survivors, Say Cover-Up False," *The State News*, December 15, 2017, https://statenews.com/article/2017/12/msu-apology-to-survivors-coverup-allegations-false. Accessed October 9, 2019.
43 R.J. Wolcott, "#MeToo Founder Tarana Burke Speaks at MSU: 'This is a Survivor's Movement,'" *Lansing State Journal*, April 20, 2018, https://www.lansingstatejournal.com/story/news/local/2018/04/19/metoo-msu-burke/534083002/. Accessed October 9, 2019.
44 Kate Wells, "'Time is Up,' Protestors Tell MSU's Leaders at 'Resignation Rally,'" *Michigan Radio*, April 21, 2018, https://www.michiganradio.org/post/time-protestors-tell-msus-leaders-resignation-rally. Accessed October 9, 2019.
45 Julie Compton, "She Testified Against Larry Nassar. Now This Survivor is Fighting for Change," *NBC News*, October 31, 2018, https://www.nbcnews.com/feature/nbc-out/she-testified-against-larry-nassar-now-survivor-fighting-change-n926711. Accessed October 9, 2019.

The effect of the Nassar case on shaping activism and public discussions of sexual assault as a systemic issue was also evident at a February 2018 town hall hosted by an MSU trustee. According to MSU professors Stephanie Nawyn and Amy Bonomi, the town hall's organizers had anticipated several hundred attendees, but campus police ultimately estimated that several thousand people crowded outside the door. The organizers had planned to facilitate small group discussions, but

> in reality, there was too much anger and passion among the campus community to use a controlled format. It was emblematic of how corked people's feelings were about Larry Nassar, sexual assault, and our institutional culture . . . The problematic power structures that plague all of society, including our own institution, were underlying nearly every comment made by the MSU community about how sexual assault survivors had been ignored, how advocates for change had been dismissed, and how a range of injustices permeated the way our university operated.[46]

Comments at the town hall were not primarily directed at individual perpetrators, but at norms and institutional structures that had enabled sexual abuse at a prominent university for decades.[47]

Public outrage at Nassar's crimes also contributed to federal legislation. In February 2018, Congress passed and President Trump signed the Protecting Young Victims from Sexual Abuse and Safe Sport Authorization Act into law. The bill required adults who interact with amateur athletes to report suspected child abuse, including sexual abuse, to local law enforcement within 24 hours if or when such behavior occurs.[48] Several high profile U.S. gymnasts, including Aly Raisman, Jordyn Wieber, and McKayla Maroney delivered statements at House hearings on the bill, which received bipartisan support to become the law of the land. Representative Ted Poe (R-Texas) highlighted the influence of the USA Gymnastics case on the bill when he remarked, "how a serial predator like Nassar could have preyed on so many young girls for a long time in such a

---

46 Stephanie Nawyn and Amy Bonomi, "Inside MSU: Taking Risks to Improve Climate," *Journal of American College Health* (2018) DOI: 10.1080/07448481.2018.1472604.

47 Jack Nissen, "Thousands Head to MSU in Wake of Scandal," *Detroit News*, February 1, 2018, https://www.detroitnews.com/story/news/local/michigan/2018/02/01/msu-trustee-forum-larry-nassar-scandal-kellogg-center-msu-michigan-state-university/110028966/. Accessed October 9, 2019.

48 Maureen Groppe, "Trump Signs Law to Prevent Abuse of Athletes – A Response to USA Gymnastics Scandal," *Indianapolis Star*, February 14, 2018, https://www.indystar.com/story/news/politics/2018/02/14/trump-signs-law-prevent-abuse-athletes-response-usa-gymnastics-scandal/336879002/. Accessed October 9, 2019.

flagrant fashion is appalling."[49] Similarly, in the U.S. Senate, Senator Bill Nelson (D-Florida) emphasized, "The system failed those young women horribly. USA Gymnastics failed them. The USOC failed them. Michigan State failed them." The Safe Sport Authorization Act, he insisted, would implement new safeguards to protect athletes from abuse and send a message "that this cannot and must not happen again."[50]

But some sports writers and advocates contended that the SafeSport center was set up to fail and that the Safe Sport Authorization Act lacked adequate funding and accountability. For example, *Deadspin* editor Diana Moskovitz argued that the very phrase "safe sport" was not only a euphemism for preventing sexual assault and rape, but that the SafeSport center was a "root-and-branch creation of the USOC" dependent on funding from national sports bodies. Lacking the independence it claimed, SafeSport was designed to function more as public relations than to effectively and transparently protect athletes.[51] Public health advocate Lyndon Haviland emphasized that the 2018 bill was "effectively an unfunded mandate" which Congress passed "without dedicating the necessary resources to ensure its success. And it provides no enforceable requirement for youth sports organizers to be trained on how to spot the warning signs of child sexual abuse."[52] Consequently, this act might be seen both as a symbol of the power of public opinion on this topic to prompt legislators to do something, but also a sign of how little regulation or enforcement remains in this area. It is also unclear whether efforts to improve sexual assault awareness and training in elite athletic programs were extended to non-elite youth sports.[53]

---

[49] "Following Larry Nassar Case, Congress Passes Bill Aiming to Protect Amateur Athletes From Abuse," *USA Today*, January 29, 2018, https://www.usatoday.com/story/sports/2018/01/29/congress-bill-aiming-protect-amateur-athletes-abuse/1077273001/. Accessed October 9, 2019.

[50] "Thune and Nelson Statements on Passage of Safe Sport Authorization," U.S. Senate Committee on Commerce, Science and Transportation, (press release), January 30, 2018, https://www.commerce.senate.gov/public/index.cfm/2018/1/thune-and-nelson-statements-on-passage-of-safe-sport-authorization. Accessed October 9, 2019.

[51] Diana Moskovitz, "SafeSport, the USOC's Attempt to Stop Child Abuse, is Set Up to Fail – Just Like it Was Supposed To," *Deadspin*, July 24, 2018, https://deadspin.com/safesport-the-usocs-attempt-to-stop-child-abuse-is-se-1826279217. Accessed October 9, 2019.

[52] Lyndon Haviland, "The Safe Sport Act Won't Prevent Child Sex Abuse in Youth Sports," *The Hill*, November 14, 2018, https://thehill.com/opinion/white-house/416659-the-safe-sport-act-wont-prevent-child-sex-abuse-in-youth-sports. Accessed October 9, 2019.

[53] Kelsey Logan and Steve Cuff, "How to Help Parents Cover Their Bases When Choosing a Sports Program," *AAP News*, February 26, 2019, https://www.aappublications.org/news/2019/02/26/sports022619. Accessed October 9, 2019.

In addition to shaping advocacy and legislation related to sexual abuse in sports, the Nassar case prompted other victims of sexual abuse to come forward both within and outside of sports. Importantly, although Nassar's victims were girls and women, their testimony helped both male and female athletes to speak out about their experiences of abuse. For example, in August 2018 the *New York Times* reported on over 100 men who alleged that they had been molested by Richard Strauss, a team doctor and physician at The Ohio State University. Many of the wrestler survivors specifically highlighted the Nassar story as prompting their own reckoning with the doctor who had abused them. For example, one wrestler told the *New York Times* that prior to following the Nassar trial, he had always believed that because his abuser was a doctor, he surely had a justifiable reason for his actions. But watching the courtroom testimony at Nassar's sentencing, he realized "that was precisely the reasoning that so many female victims of Mr. Nassar had used, and now they were coming forward . . . Michigan State is what got us to say, hey, it can happen to even guys."[54] Another former wrestler similarly told *NBC News* that Nassar's conviction had prompted him and other former athletes to speak out about Strauss.[55] Like Nassar, Strauss had allegedly relied on pseudoscientific explanations and unfounded medical techniques to justify abusing his patients.[56]

The Nassar and Strauss cases also both involved allegations that coaches and other university staff had failed to respond appropriately to alleged sexual misconduct. Notably, several former wrestlers accused U.S. Representative Jim Jordan (R-Ohio), a former Ohio State University wrestling coach, of turning a blind eye to Strauss's abuse and failing to stop it. Jordan repeatedly denied knowing anything about the alleged abuse while he was an assistant coach from 1986 to 1994, but several former Ohio State wrestlers insisted it would have been impossible for Jordan to be unaware. According to former wrestler Mike DiSabato, "I considered Jim Jordan a friend, but at the end of the day, he is absolutely lying if he says he doesn't know what was going on."[57] Similarly,

---

[54] Catie Edmondson and Marc Tracy, "'It Can Happen Even to Guys': Ohio State Wrestlers Detail Abuse, Saying #UsToo," *New York Times*, August 2, 2018, https://www.nytimes.com/2018/08/02/us/politics/ohio-state-wrestlers-abuse-me-too.html. Accessed October 9, 2019.

[55] Corky Siemaszko, "Powerful GOP Rep. Jim Jordan Accused of Turning Blind Eye to Sexual Abuse as Ohio State Wrestling Coach," *NBC News*, July 3, 2018, https://www.nbcnews.com/news/us-news/powerful-gop-rep-jim-jordan-accused-turning-blind-eye-sexual-n888386?cid=sm_npd_nn_tw_ma. Accessed October 9, 2019.

[56] Kathleen Bachynski, "#MeToo and Health Research Ethics," *Hastings Center Bioethics Forum*, March 8, 2019, https://www.thehastingscenter.org/metoo-health-research-ethics/. Accessed October 9, 2019.

[57] Corky Siemaszko, "Powerful GOP Rep."

former wrestler Shawn Dailey recalled that "it was very common knowledge in the locker room that if you went to Dr. Strauss for anything, you would have to pull your pants down . . . So I was surprised to hear Jim [Jordan] say that he knew nothing about it."[58]

Meanwhile, President Trump stated of the allegations against Jordan, "I don't believe them at all."[59] Despite the allegations that he had ignored sexual abuse, Jordan handily won re-election to his congressional seat in November 2018. His political victory prompted sports columnist Christine Brennan to urge greater scrutiny of Jordan's role at Ohio State, asking, "How is this not a bigger story? After the horrifying sex abuse scandals at Penn State, Michigan State and USA Gymnastics, how did Jordan simply sail through this election season?"[60] As Brennan's questions suggest, initial reactions to the case of Richard Strauss in many ways highlighted the limits of the #MeToo movement to hold institutions accountable. Despite over 100 allegations of abuse, with the alleged abuser deceased, an alleged bystander in a position of significant political power, and the president of the United States expressing disbelief of the accusers' credibility, the public and legal response to this scandal appeared relatively limited. Nonetheless, at a minimum the testimony from the Nassar case motivated over one hundred men to speak out about alleged abuse, prompting The Ohio State University to open an investigation into the allegations, to seek to reach mediation with the accusers in federal court, and to cover the cost of professionally certified counseling for any students who had been affected by Strauss's misconduct.[61]

For other athletes seeking to come forward, the Nassar case became a potent emblem of the broader tendency of powerful organizations to dismiss abuse allegations. For example, figure skater Craig Maurizi told the U.S. Senate that the U.S. Figure Skating Association had ignored him when he accused a top coach of sexually abusing him. He explained that he had been treated with

---

58 Corky Siemaszko, "More Ohio State Wrestlers Say Rep. Jim Jordan Knew About Sexual Abuse When He Was Coach," *NBC News*, July 6, 2018, https://www.nbcnews.com/news/us-news/fourth-ohio-state-wrestler-says-rep-jim-jordan-knew-about-n889071. Accessed October 9, 2019.

59 Jeremy Diamond, "Trump Says He Doesn't Believe Allegations Against Jim Jordan," *CNN*, July 6, 2018, https://www.cnn.com/2018/07/05/politics/trump-jim-jordan/index.html. Accessed October 9, 2019.

60 Christine Brennan, "With Jim Jordan's Re-Election, It's Time to Look Deeper Into Ohio State Sex Abuse Scandal," *USA Today*, November 7, 2018, https://www.usatoday.com/story/sports/columnist/brennan/2018/11/07/ohio-state-jim-jordan-scrutiny-sexual-abuse-scandal/1906480002/. Accessed October 9, 2019.

61 Edward Sutelan, "Strauss Investigation 'Nearing its Conclusion' as Mediation Search Continues," *The Lantern*, February 22, 2019, https://www.thelantern.com/2019/02/strauss-investigation-nearing-its-conclusion-as-mediation-search-continues/. Accessed October 9, 2019.

"the same disdain, disrespect and disbelief by the U.S. Figure Skating Association as many of the Larry Nassar victims who tried to report him to USA Gymnastics or Michigan State University."[62] The Larry Nassar case thus became a shorthand that other elite athletes could use to describe the obstacles they faced in reporting abuse, and a symbol of the need for greater oversight of sports governing bodies.

Moreover, the Nassar case further inspired victims of alleged abuse to come forward in realms outside of sports. Notably, in February 2019 Dr. Alexandra Arce von Herold, a psychiatrist and antinuclear activist, accused Óscar Arias Sánchez, the former president of Costa Rica, of sexually assaulting her in 2014. She stated that while seeing accusations against powerful men such as Harvey Weinstein and Bill Cosby had been inspiring, it was watching the victim impact statements against Larry Nassar in January 2019 that confirmed her decision to come forward. "All the other women, that did, that helped me . . . So I thought maybe, maybe, I can help other people too," Dr. Arce told the *New York Times*.[63] Dr. Arce's example reveals both the global reach of the Nassar trial as well as the significant political impact beyond the realm of sports of providing athlete survivors of abuse the opportunity to confront their abuser in court.

Sports, Politics, and Preventing Abuse

The Larry Nassar case represents just one prominent example of a much bigger story in sports and politics challenging how American institutions respond to allegations of sexual abuse against powerful authority figures. In many ways, the Nassar case and #MeToo movement have mutually amplified each other. The broader political context of the #MeToo movement has influenced media coverage and legislative action, lawsuits, and ongoing efforts to hold sports organizations accountable. At the same time, the Larry Nassar story has made clear that sports are very much a part of larger efforts to effectively address sexual violence in American society.

Developments in the Larry Nassar case and the #MeToo movement jointly suggest several reasons that responding to sexual abuse represents such an important intersection of 21st century American sports and politics. First, a

---

[62] Pete Madden and Cho Park, "Figure Skater to Congress: I Reported Sexual Abuse and Was Ignored," *ABC News*, April 18, 2018, https://abcnews.go.com/Sports/figure-skater-congress-reported-sexual-abuse/story?id=54564738. Accessed October 9, 2019.

[63] Frances Robles, "Former President of Costa Rica is Accused of Assault," *New York Times*, February 5, 2019, https://www.nytimes.com/2019/02/05/world/americas/oscar-arias-sanchez-sexual-assault.html. Accessed October 9, 2019.

significant history of reporting, activism, lawsuits and political developments have contributed to framing sexual abuse as a broad, systemic societal issue. This history is profoundly connected to structures of power both within and without the world of sports. In particular, the #MeToo movement has helped reveal key features of many sports organizations that facilitate sexual violence, including sports as a hierarchal institution, pressures placed upon young athletes to excel and expectations that they will endure physical pain in order to do so, a lack of regulation or oversight, and the treatment of adult sports figures such as coaches and trainers as pillars of the community to the extent that their authority often goes unquestioned. The #MeToo movement shows how many of these features are evident across powerful institutions in American society, but sports sexual abuse cases also include some specific factors that contribute to fostering an environment of secrecy and cover-ups.

Second, the extraordinary revelations of 2017–2018 alone have shown how important a shifting political and social environment can be to individuals' willingness to come forward. Creating structures that allow survivors to share their stories, such as the courtroom testimony at Larry Nassar's sentencing, have enormous social implications for how communities think about sexual violence. When just one survivor is taken seriously in a particular context, that can empower others to come forward.

Finally, both the #MeToo movement and efforts to address sexual abuse in youth sports in response to the Nassar case have facilitated powerful questionings of social values and priorities. Lawsuits and efforts to change policies have forced some institutions to think about what truly protecting athletes and other potential victims might look like, as well as what justice might entail when abuse does occur. On the other hand, the limits of some of these new policies, and political developments such as Brett Kavanaugh receiving a lifetime appointment to the Supreme Court in the face of sexual assault allegations, have also shown the limits of this current movement. Sports and politics are both arenas where fundamental formulations and expressions of cultural values take place; they cannot be separated amid ongoing social efforts to grapple with what accountability for sexual violence might look like.

A passage from Rachael Denhollander's victim impact statement represents a particularly moving depiction of the stakes of this social movement. She addressed the court at the sentencing of Larry Nassar by stating,

> I ask that you hand down a sentence that tells us that what was done to us matters, that we are known, we are worth everything, worth the greatest protection the law can offer, the greatest measure of justice available. And to everyone who is watching, I ask that same question, how much is a little girl worth?

The survivors of Larry Nassar's abuse, alongside other participants in the broader #MeToo movement, have demonstrated that this question of values is at the core of an ongoing reckoning with sexual abuse throughout prominent American institutions. Whether victims of abuse – be they young girls or adult male wrestlers – can rely on leagues, academic institutions, employers, politicians, and courtrooms to protect them is a question that must be urgently addressed in both sports and politics.

Works Cited

Abdeldaiem, Alaa. "Christine Blasey Ford Introduces Rachael Denhollander as SI's Inspiration of the Year." *Sports Illustrated*, December 12, 2018. https://www.si.com/sportsperson/2018/12/12/christine-blasey-ford-introduces-rachael-denhollander-sports-illustrated-inspiration-year Accessed October 9, 2019.

Bachynski, Kathleen. "#MeToo and Health Research Ethics." *Hastings Center Bioethics Forum*, March 8, 2019. https://www.thehastingscenter.org/metoo-health-research-ethics/. Accessed October 9, 2019.

Baker, Peter. "Christine Blasey Ford's Credibility Under New Attack by Senate Republicans." *New York Times*, October 3, 2018. https://www.nytimes.com/2018/10/03/us/politics/blasey-ford-republicans-kavanaugh.html. Accessed October 9, 2019.

Beauchamp, Zack. "New Poll Shows That Republicans Have Become the Party of #MeToo Backlash." *Vox*, October 3, 2018. https://www.vox.com/policy-and-politics/2018/10/3/17932324/brett-kavanaugh-news-republicans-poll-sexual-assault. Accessed October 9, 2019.

Borchers, Callum. "Judge Rosemarie Aquilina Was a Media Master in the Larry Nassar Case." *Washington Post*, January 24, 2018. https://www.washingtonpost.com/news/the-fix/wp/2018/01/24/judge-rosemarie-aquilina-was-a-media-master-in-the-larry-nassar-case/. Accessed October 9, 2019.

Bostick, Dani. "New Report on USA Gymnastics and Larry Nassar a Reminder That Athletes Across America are at Risk." *NBC News*, December 19, 2018. https://www.nbcnews.com/think/opinion/new-report-usa-gymnastics-larry-nassar-reminder-athletes-across-america-ncna949811. Accessed October 9, 2019.

Brennan, Christine. "With Jim Jordan's Re-Election, It's Time to Look Deeper Into Ohio State Sex Abuse Scandal." *USA Today*, November 7, 2018. https://www.usatoday.com/story/sports/columnist/brennan/2018/11/07/ohio-state-jim-jordan-scrutiny-sexual-abuse-scandal/1906480002/. Accessed October 9, 2019.

Cacciola, Scott. "Victims in Larry Nassar Abuse Case Find a Fierce Advocate: The Judge." *New York Times*, January 23, 2018. https://www.nytimes.com/2018/01/23/sports/larry-nassar-rosemarie-aquilina-judge.html. Accessed October 9, 2019.

Chira, Susan and Yamiche Alcindor. "Defiant Voices Flood U.S. Cities as Women Rally for Rights." *New York Times*, January 21, 2017. https://www.nytimes.com/2017/01/21/us/women-march-protest-president-trump.html. Accessed October 9, 2019.

CNN. "Read Rachael Denhollander's Full Victim Impact Statement About Larry Nassar." January 24, 2018. https://www.cnn.com/2018/01/24/us/rachael-denhollander-full-statement/index.html. Accessed October 9, 2019.

Compton, Julie. "She Testified Against Larry Nassar. Now This Survivor is Fighting for Change." *NBC News*, October 31, 2018. https://www.nbcnews.com/feature/nbc-out/she-testified-against-larry-nassar-now-survivor-fighting-change-n926711. Accessed October 9, 2019.

Connor, Tracy. "McKayla Maroney Says Dr. Larry Nassar Molested Her in #MeToo Post," *NBC News*, October 18, 2017, https://www.nbcnews.com/news/us-news/olympic-gymnast-mckayla-maroney-says-dr-larry-nassar-molested-her-n811766. Accessed October 9, 2019.

Crawford, Dakota, and Amy Haneline, "Follow IndyStar's Investigation of USA Gymnastics and Larry Nassar From Start to Finish." *Indianapolis Star*, January 24, 2018. https://www.indystar.com/story/sports/2018/01/24/indystar-larry-nassar-usa-gymnastics-investigation/1062120001/. Accessed October 9, 2019.

Diamond, Jeremy. "Trump Says He Doesn't Believe Allegations Against Jim Jordan." *CNN*, July 6, 2018. https://www.cnn.com/2018/07/05/politics/trump-jim-jordan/index.html. Accessed October 9, 2019.

Drape, Joe. "Sandusky Guilty of Sexual Abuse of 10 Young Boys." *New York Times*, June 22, 2012. https://www.nytimes.com/2012/06/23/sports/ncaafootball/jerry-sandusky-convicted-of-sexually-abusing-boys.html. Accessed October 2, 2019.

Edmondson, Catie and Marc Tracy. "'It Can Happen Even to Guys': Ohio State Wrestlers Detail Abuse, Saying #UsToo." *New York Times*, August 2, 2018. https://www.nytimes.com/2018/08/02/us/politics/ohio-state-wrestlers-abuse-me-too.html. Accessed October 9, 2019.

Evans, Tim, Mark Alesia, and Marisa Kwiatkowski. "A 20-Year Toll: 368 Gymnasts Allege Sexual Exploitation." *Indianapolis Star*, February 8, 2018. https://www.indystar.com/story/news/2016/12/15/20-year-toll-368-gymnasts-allege-sexual-exploitation/95198724/. Accessed October 9, 2019.

"Following Larry Nassar Case, Congress Passes Bill Aiming to Protect Amateur Athletes From Abuse." *USA Today*, January 29, 2018. https://www.usatoday.com/story/sports/2018/01/29/congress-bill-aiming-protect-amateur-athletes-abuse/1077273001/. Accessed October 9, 2019.

Gilgoff, Dan. "Seeming Parallels Abound in Penn State, Catholic Church Abuse Scandals." *CNN Belief Blog*, November 10, 2011. http://religion.blogs.cnn.com/2011/11/10/seeming-parallels-abound-in-penn-state-catholic-church-abuse-scandals/. Accessed October 2, 2019.

Groppe, Maureen. "Trump Signs Law to Prevent Abuse of Athletes – A Response to USA Gymnastics Scandal." *Indianapolis Star*, February 14, 2018. https://www.indystar.com/story/news/politics/2018/02/14/trump-signs-law-prevent-abuse-athletes-response-usa-gymnastics-scandal/336879002/. Accessed October 9, 2019.

Haviland, Lyndon. "The Safe Sport Act Won't Prevent Child Sex Abuse in Youth Sports," *The Hill*, November 14, 2018, https://thehill.com/opinion/white-house/416659-the-safe-sport-act-wont-prevent-child-sex-abuse-in-youth-sports. Accessed October 9, 2019.

Hindi, Saja. "51 Women, Girls Sue U.S. Olympic Committee in Federal Court in Colorado For Failing to Stop Sexual Abuse by Larry Nassar." *Denver Post*, March 15, 2019. https://www.denverpost.com/2019/03/15/us-olympic-committee-larry-nassar-lawsuit-colorado. Accessed October 9, 2019.

Hruby, Patrick. "What the Catholic Church Can Teach Us About the Penn State Scandal." *Atlantic*, November 16, 2011. https://www.theatlantic.com/entertainment/archive/2011/11/what-the-catholic-church-can-teach-us-about-the-penn-state-scandal/248588/. Accessed October 2, 2019.

Jesse, David. "MSU President Engler: Nassar Survivor May Get Kickbacks From Lawyers." *Detroit Free Press*, June 13, 2018. https://www.freep.com/story/news/local/michigan/2018/06/13/msu-larry-nassar-rachael-denhollander/699307002/. Accessed October 9, 2019.

Jenkins, Sally. "The USOC Needs a Leader Who Cares More About Athletes Than Expense Accounts." *Washington Post*, July 5, 2018. https://www.washingtonpost.com/sports/olympics/the-usoc-needs-a-leader-who-cares-about-athletes-more-than-expense-accounts/2018/07/03/9554ded8-7ae5-11e8-80be-6d32e182a3bc_story.html?utm_term=.c36ccc3f7c44. Accessed October 9, 2019.

Jurkowitz, Mark. "Globe's Articles on Priests Spurred Scrutiny Worldwide." *Boston Globe*, April 8, 2003. http://archive.boston.com/globe/spotlight/abuse/extras/pulitzers2.htm. Accessed December 10, 2018.

Korn, Melissa. "Pressure Mounts on Harvard's All-Male Clubs to Admit Women." *Wall Street Journal*, April 14, 2016. https://www.wsj.com/articles/pressure-mounts-on-harvards-all-male-clubs-to-admit-women-1460626203. Accessed October 9, 2019.

Kozlowski, Kim. "How John Engler's MSU Reign Fell Apart." *Detroit News*, January 29, 2019. https://www.detroitnews.com/story/news/education/2019/01/29/how-john-engler-michigan-state-university-reign-fell-apart/2604186002/. Accessed October 9, 2019.

Linder, Chris, Jess S. Myers, Colleen Riggle, and Marvette Lacy. "From Margins to Mainstream: Social Media as a Tool for Campus Sexual Violence Activism." *Journal of Diversity in Higher Education* 9, no. 3 (2016): 231–244.

Logan, Kelsey and Steve Cuff. "How to Help Parents Cover Their Bases When Choosing a Sports Program." *AAP News*, February 26, 2019. https://www.aappublications.org/news/2019/02/26/sports022619. Accessed October 9, 2019.

Macur, Juliet. "Steve Penny, Former U.S.A. Gymnastics Chief, Arrested on Evidence Tampering Charge." *New York Times*, October 18, 2018. https://www.nytimes.com/2018/10/18/sports/steve-penny-gymnastics-arrest-tampering.html. Accessed October 9, 2019.

Madden, Pete and Cho Park. "Figure Skater to Congress: I Reported Sexual Abuse and Was Ignored." *ABC News*, April 18, 2018. https://abcnews.go.com/Sports/figure-skater-congress-reported-sexual-abuse/story?id=54564738. Accessed October 9, 2019.

McPhee, Joan and James P. Dowden. "Report of the Independent Investigation: The Constellation of Factors Underlying Larry Nassar's Abuse of Athletes." *Ropes & Gray*. Accessed March 14, 2019. https://www.ropesgray.com/-/media/Files/USOC/ropes-gray-full-report.pdf. Accessed October 9, 2019.

"Measuring the #MeToo Backlash." *The Economist*, October 20, 2018. https://www.economist.com/united-states/2018/10/20/measuring-the-metoo-backlash. Accessed October 9, 2019.

Mencarini, Matt. "Inside the Investigation and Prosecution of Larry Nassar." *Lansing State Journal*, April 7, 2018. https://www.lansingstatejournal.com/story/news/local/2018/04/05/larry-nassar-inside-prosecution-investigation/472506002/. Accessed October 9, 2019.

Mencarini, Matt. "MSU to Pay for Lou Anna Simon's Defense as Legal Bills for Larry Nassar Scandal Near $20M." *Lansing State Journal*, January 23, 2019. https://www.lansingstatejournal.com/story/news/local/2019/01/23/larry-nassar-lou-anna-simon-msu-michigan-state-bills/2645371002/. Accessed October 9, 2019.

Me Too Movement. "History & Vision." Accessed March 5, 2019. https://metoomvmt.org/about/#history.

Moskovitz, Diana. "SafeSport, the USOC's Attempt to Stop Child Abuse, is Set Up to Fail – Just Like it Was Supposed To." *Deadspin*, July 24, 2018. https://deadspin.com/safesport-the-usocs-attempt-to-stop-child-abuse-is-se-1826279217. Accessed October 9, 2019.

Nawyn, Stephanie and Amy Bonomi. "Inside MSU: Taking Risks to Improve Climate." *Journal of American College Health* (2018) DOI: 10.1080/07448481.2018.1472604.

Nissen, Jack. "Thousands Head to MSU in Wake of Scandal," *Detroit News*, February 1, 2018, https://www.detroitnews.com/story/news/local/michigan/2018/02/01/msu-trustee-forum-larry-nassar-scandal-kellogg-center-msu-michigan-state-university/110028966/. Accessed October 9, 2019.

O'Brien, Rebecca Davis. "U.S. Investigates F.B.I. Response to Gymnasts' Sex Abuse Claims." *Wall Street Journal*, September 4, 2018. https://www.wsj.com/articles/u-s-investigates-fbi-response-to-gymnasts-sex-abuse-claims-1536103576. Accessed October 9, 2019.

O'Connor, Madison. "President Simon, Trustees Apologize to Survivors, Say Cover-Up False," *The State News*, December 15, 2017. https://statenews.com/article/2017/12/msu-apology-to-survivors-coverup-allegations-false. Accessed October 9, 2019.

Parker, Najja. "Who is Tarana Burke? Meet the Woman Who Started the Me Too Movement a Decade Ago." *Atlanta Journal-Constitution*, December 6, 2017. https://www.ajc.com/news/world/who-tarana-burke-meet-the-woman-who-started-the-too-movement-decade-ago/i8NEiuFHKalvBh9ucukidK/. Accessed October 2, 2019.

Pérez-Peña, Richard. "In Report, Failures Throughout Penn State." *New York Times*, July 12, 2012. https://www.nytimes.com/2012/07/13/sports/ncaafootball/in-freeh-report-on-sandusky-failures-throughout-penn-state.html. Accessed October 2, 2019.

Robles, Frances. "Former President of Costa Rica is Accused of Assault." *New York Times*, February 5, 2019. https://www.nytimes.com/2019/02/05/world/americas/oscar-arias-sanchez-sexual-assault.html. Accessed October 9, 2019.

Siemaszko, Corky. "More Ohio State Wrestlers Say Rep. Jim Jordan Knew About Sexual Abuse When He Was Coach." *NBC News*, July 6, 2018. https://www.nbcnews.com/news/us-news/fourth-ohio-state-wrestler-says-rep-jim-jordan-knew-about-n889071. Accessed October 9, 2019.

Siemaszko, Corky. "Powerful GOP Rep. Jim Jordan Accused of Turning Blind Eye to Sexual Abuse as Ohio State Wrestling Coach." *NBC News*, July 3, 2018. https://www.nbcnews.com/news/us-news/powerful-gop-rep-jim-jordan-accused-turning-blind-eye-sexual-n888386?cid=sm_npd_nn_tw_ma. Accessed October 9, 2019.

Solnit, Rebecca. "Our Words Are Our Weapons." *Guernica*, June 2, 2014. https://www.guernicamag.com/rebecca-solnit-our-words-are-our-weapons-2/. Accessed October 2, 2019.

Sutelan, Edward. "Strauss Investigation 'Nearing its Conclusion' as Mediation Search Continues." *The Lantern*, February 22, 2019. https://www.thelantern.com/2019/02/strauss-investigation-nearing-its-conclusion-as-mediation-search-continues/. Accessed October 9. 2019.

Tackett, Michael. "Women Line Up to Run for Office, Harnessing Their Outrage at Trump." *New York Times*, December 4, 2017. https://www.nytimes.com/2017/12/04/us/politics/women-candidates-office.html. Accessed October 9, 2019.

"Thune and Nelson Statements on Passage of Safe Sport Authorization." U.S. Senate Committee on Commerce, Science and Transportation (press release). January 30, 2018.

https://www.commerce.senate.gov/public/index.cfm/2018/1/thune-and-nelson-statements-on-passage-of-safe-sport-authorization. Accessed October 9, 2019.

Tucker, Heather. "USA Gymnastics Says It Will Not Fine McKayla Maroney If She Speaks Out Against Larry Nassar." *USA Today*, January 16, 2018. https://www.usatoday.com/story/sports/olympics/2018/01/16/usa-gymnastics-mckayla-maroney-larry-nassar/1039025001/. Accessed October 9, 2019.

Weatherred, Jane Long. "Framing Child Sexual Abuse: A Longitudinal Content Analysis of Newspaper and Television Coverage, 2002–2012." *Journal of Child Sexual Abuse* 26, no. 1 (2017): 3–22.

Weiss, Sasha. "The power of #YesAllWomen." *New Yorker*, May 26, 2014. https://www.newyorker.com/culture/culture-desk/the-power-of-yesallwomen. Accessed October 2, 2019.

Wells, Kate. "'Time is Up,' Protestors Tell MSU's Leaders at 'Resignation Rally.'" *Michigan Radio*, April 21, 2018. https://www.michiganradio.org/post/time-protestors-tell-msus-leaders-resignation-rally. Accessed October 9, 2019.

Wertheim. John L. and David Epstein. "This is Penn State." *Sports Illustrated* 115, no. 20 (2011): 40–53.

West, Lindy. "Why is Fixing Sexism Women's Work?" *New York Times*, January 3, 2018. https://www.nytimes.com/2018/01/03/opinion/why-is-fixing-sexism-womens-work.html. Accessed October 9, 2019.

"What Group of People is Most Hostile to #MeToo?" *The Economist*, January 10, 2019. https://www.economist.com/united-states/2019/01/12/what-group-of-people-is-most-hostile-to-metoo. Accessed October 9, 2019.

Wolcott, R.J. "#MeToo Founder Tarana Burke Speaks at MSU: 'This is a Survivor's Movement.'" *Lansing State Journal*, April 20, 2018. https://www.lansingstatejournal.com/story/news/local/2018/04/19/metoo-msu-burke/534083002/. Accessed October 9, 2019.

Zacharek, Stephanie, Eliana Dockterman, and Haley Sweetland Edwards. "The Silence Breakers." *Time Magazine*, December 18, 2017. http://time.com/time-person-of-the-year-2017-silence-breakers/. Accessed October 9, 2019.

Francesco Collura
8 Hegemonic Masculinities and the Fear of Being Gay in the NHL

In the realm of professional male sports, coming out as gay can be considered a taboo subject. Society and the sporting environment at large create and reproduce hegemonic masculine ideologies that can result in homophobia. Despite the prevalence of homophobia in sport, almost all of the major North American professional male sports leagues have shared the experience of a player coming out and identifying as gay. These leagues include the National Basketball Association (NBA), the National Football League (NFL), Major League Baseball (MLB) and Major League Soccer (MLS). The only major league that has not had a player openly identify as gay is the National Hockey League (NHL). While this is problematic, what constitutes an even greater issue is the fact that the NHL is partnered with the You Can Play Project (YCPP), which is an organization that attempts to guarantee safety and support from homophobia if players decide to come out as gay.[1] Having the NHL support this type of organization indicates the NHL's awareness of the possibility of homosexual players in its league. However, not having any player, current or former, come out as gay shows that there must be reasons to why players are so reluctant to come out in the NHL. Having said that, I posit that while the YCPP aids in creating a safe environment for LGBTQ+ athletes, the NHL's heteronormative patriarchal environment has a hegemonic masculine hold on athletes from identifying or exhibiting 'un-masculine' behaviors that could harm the NHL's hyper-masculine reputation as an aggressive league.

The methodological framework that I applied to this research paper primarily focuses on addressing issues that have been raised in the documentary film *The Legacy of Brendan Burke* (2010). These issues will provide a basic explanation of what NHL players currently experience with regards to homophobia, whether it be on the ice, in the locker room, in the media, or in other scenarios. This film will serve as a starting point to discuss theories and concepts that potentially create and reinforce this patriarchal governing body within the NHL. The theories and concepts I will examine include masculinity, homophobia, locker-room talk, media reception, societal and political policies and negative

---

[1] Mike Murphy, "Women's Hockey Leagues NWHL, CWHL Set Example for Inclusivity in Sports," *SportingNews*, November 22, 2017, Para. 3. Accessed December 12, 2018. http://www.sportingnews.com/ca/nhl/news/nwhl-cwhl-nhl-harrison-browne-lauren-dahm-kelsey-koelzer-anya-battaglino/1m17lgodt2aig14h8avfypnfg3.

https://doi.org/10.1515/9783110679397-008

implications and repercussions that may surface from coming out. This is important, as it will lay the fundamental groundwork for understanding why the NHL currently experiences issues surrounding an athlete's sexuality. In doing so, this will provide a greater understanding as to why NHL players feel the need to suppress their sexuality in a league that is partnered with an organization aimed at openness and acceptance. This research is important because it will contribute to the broader literature on mediated sports culture since it aims at giving context to an issue that receives minimal attention in the NHL and hockey culture on a larger scale. Considering that the NHL is the only league without an openly gay player, it is clear that there are deeper issues at play.

The documentary film, *The Legacy of Brendan Burke*, focuses on the life of Brendan Burke, son of NHL General Manager Brian Burke. More specifically, the film examines Brendan Burke's struggle with his sexuality. This struggle was largely due to his close affiliation with the hockey environment. Since men's hockey has never been a site of LGBTQ+ inclusivity, Burke's family ties with the NHL in addition to serving as student manager on the Miami University hockey team stirred up fear and anxiety about coming out as gay.[2] While the film primarily focuses on Brendan Burke's life and personal battles, the documentary also focuses on an overarching theme of homosexuality and homophobia within the NHL. For instance, the film mentions that there are gay players within the league who are discouraged from coming out due to fear and negative ramifications that may follow as a result. The film touches upon this when it mentions that players frequent gay bars and oftentimes run into one another. Instead of being pillars of support for each other, the players simply lower their heads and avoid the general conversation of being gay in hockey. When Burke came out, this fear of rejection faded since his family and teammates accepted him.[3] Considering the positive response from his family and teammates, it is surprising that the NHL has never had an openly gay player. Therefore, something must be holding professional male hockey players from coming out publicly.

After the death of Brendan Burke, the Burke family worked together to create the YCPP organization, which seeks to create "awareness and acceptance of gay athletes."[4] To achieve this, the project aims at "promoting equality, respect

---

[2] *The Fifth Estate*, episode 10, "The Legacy of Brendan Burke," directed/written/performed by Julian Sher, aired November 26, 2010, on CBC. Accessed December 12, 2018. http://www.cbc.ca/fifth/episodes/2010-2011/the-legacy-of-brendan-burke.

[3] Ibid.

[4] Cheryl A. MacDonald, "Masculinity and Sport Revisited: A Review of Literature on Hegemonic Masculinity and Men's Ice Hockey in Canada," *Canadian Graduate Journal of Sociology and Criminology*, 3, no. 1 (2014): 96.

and safety for athletes regardless of their sexual orientation or gender identity."[5] In hockey, the YCPP was first adopted by the Canadian Women's Hockey League (CWHL) in December 2012, and then by the NHL four months later in 2013.[6] While one of the goals of the YCPP is to promote equality, the experiences from the women and men's leagues have differed greatly. For example, the NHL has never had an openly gay player while women's hockey has had many. Boston Blades goaltender, Lauren Dahm, states: "When you come to the rink, you're a hockey player. There's never any judgment when it comes to that kind of stuff."[7] This is significant as it plays true to the attitudes surrounding women's hockey. Men's hockey on the other hand has struggled with various homophobic incidents on and off the ice. There is an interrelationship here with fan culture in the sense that both the men and women's leagues have had "dramatically different track records."[8] In the men's game, fan culture tends to exemplify a very hyper-masculine form while the women's game is much more respectful to athletes in many aspects. For example, Harrison Browne, the first transgender athlete in the National Women's Hockey League (NWHL) goes on to say, "If you're gay, straight, bisexual or transgender, it doesn't matter. We're not defined by that in women's sports and women's hockey. We're defined by our skill level, our work ethic, our character and how good of a teammate we are."[9] Brown's quote resonates on many levels. While athletes should be defined by their skill, work ethic and character, it is sadly not the case in men's hockey. This is important as it provides an intersectional understanding on how women's hockey is more open and accepting of the LGBTQ+ community in comparison to men's hockey. Having the NHL partner with the YCPP seems out of place considering no player has come out. It seems as though this professional relationship is only a façade to deter the general publics understanding of homophobia within the NHL.

According to sport and sexuality expert, Brian Pronger, sports create an expression of orthodox masculinity, which can be understood through violence, struggle, and aesthetics.[10] Sports such as hockey and football exhibit violence and aggression while baseball and tennis are considered less masculine sports because they struggle with opponents without perpetrating violence.[11] The least masculine sports then are those that require the least amount of aggression such

---

5 Murphy, "Women's Hockey Leagues," Para. 3.
6 Ibid.
7 Ibid., Para. 5.
8 Ibid., Para. 3.
9 Ibid., Para. 10.
10 Brian Pronger, *The Arena of Masculinity* (Toronto: University of Toronto Press, 1992), 19.
11 Ibid.

as diving or figure skating.¹² Having said that, traditional masculinity is predicated on 'un-feminine' behavior. This means that heterosexuality is coded to be masculine while homosexuality is coded as feminine since it does not align with aggression. It is clear then that sports with hyper-masculinity through "violence and fighting" seem to attract more viewers and general attention.¹³ Considering Canadian national identity is tied to men's ice hockey, it is no wonder that certain forms of masculinity are favored over others. For instance, the "hard hitting, fearless and aggressive play" is much more privileged over what is considered effeminate in hockey such as "skating, passing and other skilled maneuvers."¹⁴ Having players, past and present, endorse this logic plays into the patriarchal system set up within the NHL. This is problematic since it essentially stigmatizes non-violent or non-aggressive mannerisms as deviant. Therefore, gay players are hesitant to come forward since they would expose this myth of a hyper-masculine hockey environment. Pronger sums this up perfectly when he states:

> That there are homosexual men hiding on major league baseball teams, as the stars of the National Hockey League, or as the bright lights of national Olympic teams is not a great concern to sports officials or the public. By keeping their homosexuality a secret, they are endorsing the significance of their sports as orthodox masculine heterosexual and patriarchal institutions. What is intolerable is if they make it known that they are gay, because this would expose the mythic relationship of masculinity and sports.¹⁵

This quote highlights that the sport governing body, whether it be the NHL or any other, does not strive for creating an inclusive space for LGBTQ+ athletes. While the NHL may be partnered with the YCPP, there is nothing done to create openness and acceptance towards gay players. This is the case since their identities do not align towards the hyper-masculine logic of hockey culture because coming out as gay would then downplay the NHL as an aggressive, violent, masculine league.

According to Kristi Allain, hockey players are expected to be humble and polite off the ice and warriors willing to fight for their team on the ice.¹⁶ When Sidney Crosby entered the NHL, it was believed that he would draw on this romanticized vision of "Canadian hockey identity."¹⁷ However, Crosby's masculinity has been challenged on multiple occasions. According to many commentators

---

12 Ibid.
13 Ibid., 22.
14 Kristi A. Allain, "Kid Crosby or Golden Boy: Sidney Crosby, Canadian National Identity, and the Policing of Hockey Masculinity," *International Review for the Sociology of Sport*, 46, no. 1 (2010): 13.
15 Pronger, *The Arena of Masculinity*, 118.
16 Allain, "Kid Crosby or Golden Boy," 4.
17 Ibid.

and fans, Crosby is seen as a "whiner" since he embellishes plays to draw penalties against opposing teams and garner the referee's attention.[18] Crosby has even been criticized by elite hockey personalities for not playing an appropriate role considering his age and status as a young player.[19] For instance, Don Cherry states: "No kid should have as much to say as he's got to say, yapping at the referees, doing the whole thing."[20] It is then evident that while Crosby possessed certain forms of masculinity during his youth, he also exhibits 'un-masculine' traits, which is seen as unacceptable since it does not conform to the Canadian national hockey identity.

Hegemony is a term developed by Antonio Gramsci (1891–1937), which refers to a form of dominance that is considered natural.[21] Hegemonic masculinity, according to Raewyn W. Connell's 1995 concept, is a theory concerned with "the mechanisms by which a hierarchy is created and legitimized."[22] Connell defined hegemonic masculinity as a culturally ideal form of masculine character, which connected masculinity to toughness as well as the "subordination of women" and "marginalization of gay men."[23] Therefore, hegemonic masculinity privileges certain types of masculine traits within the domain of sport and disadvantages others that do not abide with the characteristics. Male athletes are "constructed to exhibit, value, and reproduce traditional notions of masculinity."[24] Gay athletes on the other hand are unaware of the "blind acceptance" to some of the virtues sport exhibits.[25] Furthermore, mainstream sports are explicitly hostile towards LGBTQ+ presence.[26] This leaves gay athletes at a crossroads because they have simply embraced this orthodox model with hegemonic underpinnings. In doing so, they cannot explore their own sexualities and challenge the stigmatization of homosexuality in sport since the system continues to function without being questioned.[27]

---

18 Ibid.
19 Ibid.
20 Ibid.
21 Eric Anderson, *In the Game: Gay Athletes and the Cult of Masculinity* (Albany: State University of New York Press, 2005), 21.
22 Eric Anderson, *21st Century Jocks: Sporting Men and Contemporary Heterosexuality* (Winchester: Palgrave Macmillan, 2014), 38.
23 David Nylund, "When in Rome: Heterosexism, Homophobia, and Sports Talk Radio," *Journal of Sport and Social Issues*, 28, no. 2 (2004): 139.
24 Anderson, *21st Century Jocks*, 58.
25 Anderson, *In the Game*, 37.
26 Ibid., 42.
27 Ibid., 111.

Ice Hockey acts as a site of socialization among men.[28] According to media critics and gender scholars, there are five distinctive features of hegemonic masculinity where this socialization occurs. This includes "physical force, occupational achievement, patriarchy, frontiermanship, and heterosexuality."[29] Sports in general and contact sports more specifically are a place where hegemonic masculinity is reproduced and defined.[30] According to Eric Anderson, certain sports influence how masculinity gets constructed such as hockey or football.[31] Cheryl MacDonald sees male athletes as encompassing a traditional/brawny personality trait, which allows players to engage in harmful misogynistic jargon.[32] Therefore, hegemonic masculinity in sport explains the problematic behavior of homophobia that arises. Hegemonic masculinity creates interpersonal relationships between teammates.[33] Players who are close to one another are comfortable joking around "in a homosexual manner" and engage in homophobic "verbal jokes."[34] While these jokes may be used to target people close to them, it can be harmful for those dealing with their sexual identities. Furthermore, these homophobic jokes/slurs can also be used to intentionally harm and insult opponents.[35] These jokes are deliberately used to feminize or victimize the targeted individual.[36] This idealized form of masculinity contributes to creating an unsafe environment for gay athletes. Hence, hegemonic masculinity can be seen as one of the factors hindering athletes from coming out as gay.

A consequence of hegemonic masculinity in hockey is that athletes are expected to act and be "aggressive, stoic, competitive, independent, to show little emotion, and to police the maintenance of these traits amongst themselves, especially in the context of the game."[37] These athletes are encouraged to embody this type of masculinity from a very young age.[38] This is done in order to carry on these ideologies, as they become immersed in sport throughout adulthood. This is historically significant since organized sports were created as a "homosocial sphere" in order for men to enact their masculine characteristics/practices in

---

28 MacDonald, "Masculinity," 95.
29 Nylund, "When in Rome," 139.
30 Eric Anderson, "Openly Gay Athletes: Contesting Hegemonic Masculinity in a Homophobic Environment," *Gender and Society*, 16, no. 6 (2002): 860.
31 Ibid., 864.
32 MacDonald, "Masculinity," 96.
33 Ibid., 99.
34 Ibid., 104.
35 Ibid.
36 Ibid.
37 Ibid., 96.
38 Ibid., 99.

their own space away from the threat of supposed femininity.[39] Therefore, since hockey players are assumed to behave in a hetero-masculine way, heteronormativity plays a role within the NHL. In turn, these beliefs prevent heterosexual athletes from being contaminated by the homosexual stigma.[40] In doing so, they do not lose their so-called masculine traits hockey players are expected to possess. It also reconfirms the hetero-normative patriarchy within the NHL since homosexuality is equated with femininity, meaning that gay NHL players are not masculine enough to play the sport.[41] Silencing gay athletes enables heterosexual athletes to deny a feminine nature in the sport and avoid the risk of being outperformed by gay athletes who embody this feared femininity.[42] While it may be common for heterosexual athletes to flaunt their sexuality in public, this hetero-normative stronghold deters gay athletes from doing the same.[43] Hence, gay athletes within the NHL are sculpted to act a certain way (by remaining closeted) in order to perform this idealized masculine behavior that is expected of them.

Homophobia is defined as "a prejudice, fear, aversion, or discrimination toward homosexuals."[44] While openly gay athletes exist within the sporting world, "the nature of sports is still surrounded by homophobia" through the use of derogatory slurs among coaches and athletes.[45] By engaging in these derogatory slurs, sport becomes an area where heterosexuality is favored while homosexuality is targeted by these slurs. According to Eric Anderson, hegemonic masculinity is highly prevalent during periods of high homophobia.[46] For instance, in these cases, men are expected to raise their masculine capital by expressing sexist and homophobic attitudes and their heterosexual capital by objectifying women.[47] For example, in the 1977 film *Slapshot*, a hockey-based movie, players refer and taunt one another by using slurs such as "faggot" or "fag."[48] This is problematic since it becomes commonplace for exhibiting homophobic behavior. According to Mike Murphy, men's hockey has a problem with inclusivity towards minorities.[49] News headlines

---

39 Ibid.
40 Anderson, *In the Game*, 117.
41 Ibid.
42 Ibid.
43 Ibid.
44 Derek Fenwick and Duncan Simpson, "The Experience of Coming Out as a Gay Male Athlete," *Journal of Sport Behaviour*, 40, no. 2 (2017): 132.
45 Ibid.
46 Anderson, *21st Century Jocks*, 39.
47 Ibid.
48 Dayna B. Daniels, "Gender Slurs: Motivation Through Misogyny In Sports Films," in *Sexual Sports Rhetoric*, ed. Linda K. Fuller (New York: Peter Lang Publishing Inc., 2010), 228.
49 Murphy, "Women's Hockey Leagues," Para. 1.

of hate speech, whether it be racial or homophobic has become commonplace within the NHL.[50] Although there have been fines, statements and even suspensions from the league in an effort to end this, it continues to exist.[51] Athletes who act in a hyper-masculine manner attempt to nullify the possibility of gay athletes existing in sports, even though they are aware that gay men exist throughout society.[52] Therefore, homophobia is instilled in many athletes on a personal level. The expectation to behave like "men" meaning acting straight and adhering to standards of normalized behavior is common practice.[53] This is especially significant in athletic settings where men are expected to "butch it up."[54] This relates to the *Legacy of Brendan Burke* because players are hiding their sexuality since they are well aware of the social setting they are a part of. In turn, this also demonstrates that 'un-masculine' behavior is equated with homosexuality and seen as a threat to the aggressive nature of the NHL and the male hockey environment as a whole.

According to Eric Anderson, homohysteria is a term used to define "men's fear of being homosexualized" through certain associations with feminine behavior.[55] This inadvertently works in the reverse way for women in sport. Here, heterosexual women involved in sport are assumed to be lesbians.[56] As a result, this term is linked and can be seen as an extension of homophobia. In order for homohysteria to exist, Anderson posits three factors that must coincide with one another. These factors include:

1. The mass cultural awareness that homosexuality exists as a static sexual orientation within a significant portion of the population;
2. a cultural *zeitgeist* of disapproval toward homosexuality; and
3. disapproval of men's femininity or women's masculinity, as they are associated with homosexuality.[57]

These factors are predominant in the male hockey environment since hockey is a hyper-masculine space that displays athletic prowess and male dominance. Having a male hockey player associated with feminine behavior will de-legitimize that individual as athletically skilled in the sport. It will also undermine their physical capability of competing against others. As a result, 'un-masculine' behavior is

---

50 Ibid.
51 Ibid.
52 Anderson, *In the Game*, 117.
53 Pronger, *The Arena of Masculinity*, 262.
54 Ibid.
55 Anderson, *21st Century Jocks*, 42.
56 Ibid., 43.
57 Ibid., 42.

seen as unacceptable. Therefore, this reinstates homophobic undertones throughout hockey as it ensures a regulation of behavior.

Hegemonic masculinity requires that male athletes maintain 100% heterosexual desires and behaviors and continually prove their heterosexuality.[58] Homophobic environments exemplify this through homophobic discourse through the use of anti-gay slurs.[59] This plays a major role in what is often understood as locker-room talk. According to Helen Lenskyj, hetero-normative assumptions are used to validate heterosexism and homophobia on the playing field and in the locker room.[60] For example, in a *BBC HARDtalk* interview, Robbie Rogers explains the difficulties he endured as an MLS soccer player while he remained closeted about his sexuality.[61] Rogers goes in-depth about the ways in which teammates and coaching staff would casually use homophobic slurs without understanding the affect that may have had on certain players by simply assuming the default sexuality.[62] These misogynistic comments are enacted by various athletes, coaches and even fans in order to "put down" in most cases or even motivate athletes to act more masculine by training harder and striving for success to prove their masculine and heterosexual capital.[63] Furthermore, locker-room talk enables homohysteria by implying that some athletes lack masculinity.[64] In these cases, athletes are called to question their sexuality for unruly behavior in the eyes of masculinity. This is problematic as it serves as a gateway to enabling homophobic discourse in the domain of professional sport. Hence, the presence of a gay man in a team-based environment could "challenge many well-constructed myths" of what a male player should be and act like.[65] Since sports such as hockey are seen as "overtly masculine" and culturally understood to be played by heterosexual men, the idea of having gay athletes in the locker room is daunting for those who "share homo-social encounters on and off the field and in the locker room."[66] By this, heterosexual players may fear criticism for being outperformed by a player who socially lacks these idealized masculine traits. This heterosexual fear of gay athletes

---

[58] Anderson, *In the Game*, 22.
[59] Ibid.
[60] Helen Jefferson Lenskyj, *Out On The Field* (Toronto: Women's Press, 2003), 6.
[61] *BBC HARDtalk*, episode 10, "Robbie Rogers – Footballer," directed/written/performed by Carey Clark, aired January 26, 2015, on BBC, http://www.bbc.co.uk/programmes/n3csw9ld. Accessed December 12, 2018.
[62] Ibid.
[63] Daniels, "Gender Slurs," 228.
[64] Ibid
[65] Ibid.
[66] Ibid.

adds to this problem. It creates a state of disapproval towards sexual minorities and regulates this behavior in the broader hockey league. Thus resulting in a lack of players openly identifying as gay by remaining silent about their minority identity.

When a professional athlete decides to come out as gay, they generally do so through a mainstream media outlet where they can be heard. While sport is an institution that preserves hegemonic masculinity, so to does mass media.[67] Sport fans, professional athletes, and young reporters are generally much more accepting of homosexuality than veteran sport reporters who receive mainstream media coverage.[68] With that being said, these sport media outlets have a poor track record of promoting homosexuality as something positive within the realm of sports culture. According to David Nylund, the media coverage of athletes in sport reinforces traditional masculinity in a variety of ways.[69] These ways include the privileging of masculine behavior and imagery over feminine or homosexual behavior and imagery, the masculine image as "natural or conventional," and through disparaging "strong females or homosexuals."[70] This is problematic since it creates a system of normalized behavior as to how athletes should behave. This results in systemic homophobia since it determines forms of acceptable masculinity.

One of the primary outlets that have reinforced hegemonic masculinity as the norm includes Jim Rome's radio talk show, *The Jim Rome Show*. According to Nylund, Rome embodies an aggressive form of masculinity.[71] One example of this aggressiveness stems from a 1994 interview with NFL quarterback for the New Orleans Saints, Jim Everett. Rome continuously called him Chris in relation to the female tennis star Chris Evert thereby implying that the quarterback lacked rugged masculinity and toughness.[72] Another example of Rome's misogynistic comments occurred in 2001 when the editor in chief of *Out* magazine, Brendan Lemon stated that he was in a relationship with a MLB player.[73] Although Lemon never stated his partner's name, Rome took it upon himself to create a monologue regarding gay athletes in professional male sports across the major North American sports

---

[67] Kian, Edward M. "Sexuality in the Mediation of Sport," in *Routledge Handbook of Sport, Gender and Sexuality*, eds. Jennifer Hargreaves and Eric Anderson (New York: Routledge, 2014), 463.
[68] Ibid., 464.
[69] Nylund, "When in Rome," 140.
[70] Ibid.
[71] Ibid., 141.
[72] Ibid.
[73] Ibid., 152.

leagues and the problems that may arise.[74] He invited Eric Davis, a MLB veteran to the show to get an insider perspective on the issue.[75] Their interview went as follows:

> Rome: "What would happen if a teammate of yours, or any baseball player, would come out of the closet and say, 'I am gay?' What would the reaction be like? How badly would that go?"
>
> Eric: "I think it would go real bad. I think people would jump to form an opinion because everybody has an opinion about gays already. But I think it would be a very difficult situation because with us showering with each other . . . being around each other as men. Now, you're in the shower with a guy who's gay . . . looking at you . . . maybe making a pass. That's an uncomfortable situation. In society, they have never really accepted it. They want to come out. And if that's the cause fine but in sports, it would definitely raise some eyebrows. . . . I don't think it should be thrown at 25 guys saying, 'yeah I am gay.'"
>
> "[Rome changes the subject . . . no follow-up]"[76]

According to OutSports.com, a website that is catered to an LGBTQ+ sport fan audience, Rome is referred to as "the commentator who makes a name for himself by saying stupid things with an obnoxious style, that for some reason, attracts many straight sports fans."[77] The media industry in the sporting context functions in a way that creates pleasure through oppressive ideologies towards minority groups.[78] This is problematic on a variety of levels. We can see some connection to Jim Rome and Don Cherry on *Coaches Corner*. Cherry embodies this hyper-masculine attitude that Rome exhibits throughout his show. According to Cherry, "hockey players should be polite and unassuming, especially in their dealings with the public, but also be willing to take action by dropping their gloves and defending their teammates while on the ice."[79] On multiple episodes of *Coaches Corner*, Cherry praises these tough Canadian hockey players "who are willing to fight and pay a physical toll for their sport."[80] On one occasion he states, "He just takes the body and he's ready for anything."[81] Cherry often credits and lauds the nitty-gritty hockey players without much skill, by favoring players such as Dion Phaneuf over Sidney Crosby. Having well-known media hosts display their views in this manner legitimizes the

---

74 Ibid.
75 Ibid.
76 Ibid., 153.
77 Ibid., 142.
78 Ibid., 139.
79 Allain, "Kid Crosby or Golden Boy," 9.
80 Ibid.
81 Ibid.

hegemonic ideologies embedded within the NHL. Since they do not attempt to create openness and acceptance towards the LGBTQ+ community, they ignore the larger issues regarding homosexuality in hockey since it is not seen as a prevalent discussion. When the discussion does arise, as it did on Rome's show, it is discussed in the ways it affects the heterosexual players, but never in a way that is understood from the minority perspective. In addition, this will have a major impact on audiences and may directly affect their opinion on these issues that arise. In doing so, fans also fall victim to the media's reaffirmation of hegemonic masculinity and homophobia in team-based sports that embody this aggressive style of play.

When NFL running back, David Kopay, came out in 1975, it was assumed that this would reduce bigotry in male team-based sports across North America.[82] Yet, years after Kopay came out, he claimed that "many on-field brawls still result from players' being called 'fag,' a sign of continued intolerance ... He says that obstacles lie with franchise owners, who believe openly gay players will lose them money through diminished sponsorship ratings."[83] Toby Miller notes that gay football players in particular have extensive clauses in their contracts that prescribe public behavior and prohibit attendance to gay bars.[84] While Miller specifically examines issues within football, this can also relate to other team-based sports such as hockey. For instance, Leigh Steinberg, an NHL agent, has indicated "it is easier to win endorsement deals for an athlete who has committed a felony than for one who has committed fellatio."[85] Steinberg's comment is highly problematic. Not only does it raise awareness of homophobic attitudes within the sport governing body, it states that criminalized behavior is much more acceptable within the sporting environment than homosexuality. Although this article was written in 2001, sports have not come very far in achieving LGBTQ+ equity. While some athletes have come out in the MLB, NFL, NBA, and MLS since then, the NHL must continue to endorse this ideology if no one has identified as queer.

Coaches can even be held responsible for this problem. For instance, in *ESPN's* 1998 "Gays in Sports" episode, NFL running-back coach for the Arizona Cardinals, Johnny Roland, said "you try to sell your team on being tough, rough, hard-nosed football team and I assume if someone was of that persuasion [gay], I am not sure of his toughness."[86] Here, you see a coach doubt the suitability of gay players holding up and retaining the rugged masculinity that is expected from that sport. Having ideas of hegemonic masculinity in place reinforces these stereotypes and

---

82 Toby Miller, *Sportsex* (Philadelphia: Temple University Press, 2001), 67.
83 Ibid.
84 Ibid.
85 Ibid., 68.
86 Ibid.

questions the ability and suitability for gay men in team sports. Like American football, the same can also be said for hockey, where players are supposed to appear hyper-masculine in order to preserve the ideals of the game.

According to Derek Fenwick and Duncan Simpson, the largest concern among gay male athletes is the fear of being "outed" to their teammates and coaches.[87] Hence these athletes try to hide their sexuality in order to fit in rather than face rejection or negative ramifications. Much of this fear is highlighted through the use of homophobic slurs or verbal hatred towards gay people.[88] This is mostly emphasized through locker-room talk, but it is also quite prevalent in the media. This fear of rejection creates uncertainty and anxiety amongst these athletes.[89] This type of fear results in hiding/remaining closeted. Furthermore, this can be considered a greater issue within the sporting context because sport governing bodies have done very little to create an open and safe space. While the NHL has made a partnership deal with the YCPP, this is clearly not enough to aid LGBTQ+ athletes, as it only serves as a symbolic relationship with the NHL. This also falsely implies that the NHL, and broader professional hockey culture is inclusive and welcoming of multiple sexualities.

The Don't Ask, Don't Tell American military policy enacted under former President Bill Clinton in the 1990s silenced soldiers with a threat of discharge if their non-hetero-normative sexuality was expressed. Essentially, this policy posits, "we know it exists, but we're not going to recognize it or talk about it."[90] There is a connection between this former military policy, the sporting environment within the NHL and greater homophobic culture at large. Sport is a realm that exhibits a lot of heterosexual hegemony, meaning that this hinders gay athletes from freely discussing their homosexuality as heterosexuals do.[91] It also shows that heterosexuality is "charmed" and homosexuality is "deviant."[92] This sees heterosexuality as much more acceptable and understandable in comparison to homosexuality. The mere fact that sport mirrors a former political policy that hindered LGBTQ+ people from expressing themselves contributes to gay athletes remaining in the closet. Since the sporting environment exhibits anti-gay attitudes, athletes must remain discreet in order to fit in rather than be exploited.

Society is experiencing a cultural shift from being homophobic to stigmatizing homophobia. This has occurred by multiple influences through a decrease

---

87 Fenwick and Simpson, "Experience," 133.
88 Ibid., 139.
89 Ibid., 147.
90 Anderson, *In the Game*, 112.
91 Ibid.
92 Ibid.

in religiosity, LGBTQ+ social activism, and an increasing amount of LGBTQ+ people coming out socially.[93] With events such as Gay Pride, the need to conform begins to diminish.[94] An increasing number of professional sport teams, some of which are part of the NHL, host Pride events in order to recognize their diverse fan base.[95] Some athletes are even partnered with the "It Gets Better Project" which was created by Dan Savage as an anti-bullying campaign.[96] High-profile athletes have showed their support such as Sean Avery or Steve Nash, not only in a sporting context, but also on a wider scale.[97] While this is progressive, more must be done and is required in the campaign against homophobia in sport.[98] If hegemonic masculinity is predicated upon homophobia, and homophobia is the "chief policing agent against behaviors coded as feminine", the reduction of cultural homophobia would result in a major change through the way masculinity is "constructed and maintained."[99] Thus, the cultural reduction of homophobia will have a major impact on the attitudes within the sporting community and society at large. What is truly significant however is that fact that sport scholar, Brian Pronger, discussed this need to conform beginning to diminish nearly 30 years ago. Yet, the very need to have a discussion on this topic is still quite prevalent. Why is it that homosexuality is still a major concern within the NHL? In a sense, while we may exhibit less homophobic attitudes than we once did in the past, homophobia still exists and constitutes a major issue within the NHL, even if it is not overtly present, due to the fact that the league has never had an openly gay player come forward about their sexuality.

On April 29, 2013, Jason Collins became the first active male athlete to come out as gay in the five major male team-based sports in North America.[100] Andrew Billings, Leigh Moscowitz, Coral Rae, and Natalie Brown-Devlin's study examined Twitter posts and newspaper responses over three time periods following Collins coming out. Collins' was primarily seen as a trailblazer since he transcended certain stereotypes regarding gay athletes since he typified masculinity, he was African American, and a devout Christian.[101] Results indicate that

---

93 Anderson, *21st Century Jocks*, 40.
94 Pronger, *The Arena of Masculinity*, 262.
95 Nigel Jarvis, "The Inclusive Masculinities of Heterosexual Men within UK Gay Sport Clubs," *International Review for the Sociology of* Sport, 50, no. 3 (2015): 283.
96 Ibid.
97 Ibid.
98 Ibid., 284
99 Anderson, *21st Century Jocks*, 14.
100 Andrew C. Billings, Leigh M. Moscowitz, Coral Rae, and Natalie Brown-Devlin, "The Art of Coming Out: Traditional and Social Media Frames Surrounding the NBA's Jason Collins," *Journalism and Mass Communication Quarterly*, 92, no. 1 (2015): 142.
101 Ibid., 153.

Collins received overwhelming support over the two media platforms.[102] Other male athletes had already been out for decades in single-person sports, while women have tended to come out in both team and single-person sports and men in team sports only after they have retired.[103] This overall congratulatory and supportive tone however runs the risk that homophobia is no longer an issue and coming out symbolizes full acceptance and equality.[104] The same can also be said when Welsh rugby star, Gareth Thomas, Irish Hurler, Donál Og Cusack, English cricketer Steven Davies, Swedish footballer Anton Hysén, and MLS player Robbie Rogers came out as gay through the media since they were all acknowledged and welcomed by their fellow players and staff.[105] However, while these few incidents of coming out did occur, others received some form of negative responses. Take Michael Sam for instance and his 2014 decision to come out during the NFL draft and the ramifications he has faced as a result.[106] Not only did Sam receive media backlash and criticism for being affectionate to his same-sex partner at the time, he is no longer part of an NFL team. While we may never know the true incentives to whether or not Sam was good enough to play for the league, some of this has to be predicated on patriarchal attitudes exhibited within the sporting body. Even though this may be considered an isolated incident within the NFL, it is interesting to point out that no professional athlete in a team-based sport has come out since Sam. This paper was written in early 2018 before MLS player Collin Martin came out publicly – and now remains the only openly out male athlete in North America's top five team-based sporting leagues. Considering the athletes mentioned above were well into the pinnacle of their careers and nearing retirement, attitudes towards them clearly differed since they were exiting the sporting world, whereas Sam was just about to enter. Hence, the issue of players coming out and being open about their sexual orientation must be larger than the NHL. Having said that, the NHL's affiliations with the YCPP, hosting pride nights, or even players endorsing the "It Gets Better Project" does not align with a players fear to come out and openly identify as LGBTQ+. Therefore, the NHL's sport governing body must have a hold on these athletes from tarnishing the aggressive reputation of the league.

Overall, the NHL's stronghold of hegemonic masculine ideals contributes to having professional hockey players remain in the closet. While the YCPPs aims

---

102 Ibid., 154.
103 Ibid., 142–143.
104 Ibid., 154.
105 Jarvis, "Inclusive Masculinities," 284.
106 Billings, Moscowitz, Rae, and Brown-Devlin, "Art of Coming Out," 156.

clearly attempt to bridge this gap by creating a much more inclusive space for professional athletes, the NHL's relationship with this organization is merely symbolic, otherwise players would be comfortable and open when discussing their sexual 'otherness.' This is only reinforced with the media through sport television/radio hosts such as Don Cherry or Jim Rome who exhibit a form of hypermasculinity and exemplify this ideology to players, and more importantly, the youth of tomorrow. On a broader spectrum, players may also be reluctant to join a list of 'out' players considering the treatment NFL draft pick Michael Sam received when coming out prior to becoming a professional. Perhaps athletes in general, and more specifically the NHL, may opt to come out like Jason Collins or Robbie Rogers well into their career once they have established themselves and have neared retirement in order to create a safety net for themselves. From an outsider perspective, it is clear that while the NHL creates events such as Pride nights or partners with associations such as the YCPP, more must be done in order for athletes to come out and feel comfortable discussing their sexuality in public in the way women's hockey and broader sports culture has done. Only then will the NHL be able to bridge the gap of becoming an inclusive league towards sexual minorities.

Works Cited

Allain, Kristi A. "Kid Crosby or Golden Boy: Sidney Crosby, Canadian National Identity, and the Policing of Hockey Masculinity." *International Review for the Sociology of Sport*, 46, no. 1 (2010): 3–22.

Anderson, Eric. *In the Game: Gay Athletes and the Cult of Masculinity*. Albany: State University of New York Press, 2005.

Anderson, Eric. "Openly Gay Athletes: Contesting Hegemonic Masculinity in a Homophobic Environment." *Gender and Society*, 16, no. 6 (2002): 860–877.

Anderson, Eric. *21st Century Jocks: Sporting Men and Contemporary Heterosexuality*. Winchester: Palgrave Macmillan, 2014.

Billings, Andrew C., Moscowitz, Leigh. M., Rae, Coral., and Brown-Devlin, Natalie "The Art of Coming Out: Traditional and Social Media Frames Surrounding the NBA's Jason Collins." *Journalism and Mass CommunicationQuarterly*, 92, no. 1 (2015): 142–160.

Clark, Carey, dir. *BBC HARDtalk*. Season 18, episode 10, "Robbie Rogers – Footballer." Aired January 26, 2015, on BBC. Accessed December 12, 2018. Retrieved from http://www.bbc.co.uk/programmes/n3csw9ld.

Daniels, Dayna B. "Gender Slurs: Motivation Through Misogyny In Sports Films." In *Sexual Sports Rhetoric*, edited by Linda K. Fuller, 217–231. New York: Peter Lang Publishing Inc., 2010.

Fenwick, Derek and Simpson, Duncan. "The Experience of Coming Out as a Gay Male Athlete." *Journal of Sport Behaviour*, 40, no. 2 (2017): 131–155.

Jarvis, Nigel. "The Inclusive Masculinities of Heterosexual Men within UK Gay Sport Clubs." *International Review for the Sociology of Sport*, 50, no. 3 (2015): 283–300.

Kian, Edward M. "Sexuality in the Mediation of Sport." In *Routledge Handbook of Sport, Gender and Sexuality* edited by Jennifer Hargreaves and Eric Anderson, 461–469. New York: Taylor and Francis, 2014.

Lenskyj, Helen J. *Out On The Field*. Toronto: Women's Press, 2003.

MacDonald, Cheryl A. "Masculinity and Sport Revisited: A Review of Literature on Hegemonic Masculinity and Men's Ice Hockey in Canada." *Canadian Graduate Journal of Sociology and Criminology*, 3, no. 1 (2014): 95–112.

Miller, Toby. *Sportsex*. Philadelphia: Temple University Press, 2001.

Murphy, Mike. "Women's Hockey Leagues NWHL, CWHL Set Example for Inclusivity in Sports." *SportingNews*, November 22, 2017. Accessed December 12, 2018. Retrieved from http://www.sportingnews.com/ca/nhl/news/nwhl-cwhl-nhl-harrison-browne-lauren-dahm-kelsey-koelzer-anya-battaglino/1m17lgodt2aig14h8avfypnfg3.

Nylund, David. "When in Rome: Heterosexism, Homophobia, and Sports Talk Radio." *Journal of Sport and Social Issues*, 28, no. 2 (2004): 136–168.

Pronger, Brian. *The Arena of Masculinity*. Toronto: University of Toronto Press, 1992.

Sher, Julian, dir. *The Fifth Estate*. Season 36, episode 10, "The Legacy of Brendan Burke." Aired November 26, 2010, on CBC. Accessed December 12, 2018. Retrieved from http://www.cbc.ca/fifth/episodes/2010-2011/the-legacy-of-brendan-burke

Contributors

Thomas Aiello is Associate Professor of History and African American Studies at Valdosta State University, Georgia. He has authored or edited numerous volumes on African American History and Sports History. His latest works include *The Battle for the Souls of Black Folk: W.E.B. DuBois, Booker T. Washington, and the Debate That Shaped the Course of Civil Rights* (Praeger, 2016) and *Jim Crow's Last Stand: Nonunanimous Criminal Jury Verdicts In Louisiana* (Louisiana State University Press, 2015).

Kathleen Bachynski is an Assistant Professor of public health at Muhlenberg College. She researches and teaches on topics in sports safety, epidemiology, public health ethics, and the history of medicine. She is the author of *No Game for Boys to Play: The History of Youth Football and the Origins of a Public Health Crisis* (University of North Carolina Press, 2019). She has also published articles in the *New England Journal of Medicine*; *Journal of Law, Medicine and Ethics*; *Injury Prevention*; *American Journal of Public Health*; *Neurology*; *Lancet Neurology*; *Journal of the History of Medicine and Allied Health Sciences*; *Journal of Safety Research*; *Health Affairs*; and the *Journal of Legal Aspects of Sport*.

Francesco "Frankie" Collura is currently a PhD student at Ryerson University in the Communication and Culture program. At the time of writing and presenting this conference paper, I was completing my MA at Ryerson University in the same program. My research explores minority populations in sports. I specifically focus on the LGBTQ+ community in order to develop an understanding as to why sexual and gender minorities face discrimination at a political and cultural level. This conference paper served as a gateway into my MA research and current PhD research in that it aimed at exploring how LGBTQ+ athletes negotiate their minority identities in hockey. This work has allowed me to understand how homophobia is a gendered experience and that certain sport cultures are either more or less accepting of LGBTQ+ athletes.

Thomas "Tom" Heenan teaches Australia and Sport Studies at Monash University's School of Languages, Culture, Literature, and Linguistics. He is the author of *From Traveler to Traitor: The Life of Wilfred Burchett* (2006) and with David Dunstan, *The Other Side of the Don: Episodes in a Life* (2015), a biographical study of the famous Australian cricketer, Sir Donald Bradman. With Dr. Salma Thani he has written on the increasing diplomatic and business roles that sport plays in the Gulf region. A sports columnist for the online Australian publication, *The New Daily*, he has also written for Fairfax and News Corp publications, and *The Conversation* and *Outlook India*. He has provided sport comment for Australian media outlets, as well as the BBC, Radio New Zealand and India's NDTV.

Nicole Hirschfelder is an Associate Professor at the American Studies Department of the University of Tübingen. She studied at Frankfurt University, University of Wisconsin-Madison, Tübingen and Yale University and was a visiting professor at the University of Maryland in 2016 and 2019. Her main areas of scholarship include the Civil Rights Movement, new social movements, figurational sociology as well as disaster studies. Her key publications include her monograph, *Oppression as Process: The Case of Bayard Rustin*, a co-edited volume, titled *Who Can Speak and Who Is Heard/ Hurt? Facing Problems of Race, Racism, and Ethnic Diversity in the Humanities in Germany*, and articles on the Black Lives Matter movement in German and English.

Frank Jacob is Professor of Global History at Nord Universitet, Bodø, Norway. Before he held positions at the City University of New York and Würzburg University, Germany. His main research interest are radicalisms, revolutionary movements and popular culture. One of his other relevant publications on sports is *Fußball: Identitätsdiskurse, Politik und Skandale*, co-ed. with Alexander Friedman (Kohlhammer, 2020).

Steve Marston is a scholar in the cultural-political history of sport. Trained in the field of American Studies, he focuses on the ways in which ideas about identity, (inter)nationalism, capitalism, and other issues circulate through the sport field. While earning graduate degrees from the University of Alabama (M.A.) and the University of Kansas (Ph.D), he addressed such topics as Barack Obama's deployment of sports on the 2008 campaign trail, baggy basketball shorts as hip-hop markers, and the making of identity and region through Heartland dirt-track auto racing. He has also incorporated this approach into his teaching, which includes courses on sport as well as other cultural fields. Steve is currently a Visiting Assistant Professor of History and American Studies at Trinity College in Hartford, Connecticut.

Steven A. Riess is a Bernard Brommel Distinguished Research Professor, *emeritus*, with the Department of History, Northeastern Illinois University, where he taught for 35 years. A graduate of New York University, with a Ph.D. in history from the University of Chicago, he has written several books, including *Sports in Industrial America, 1850–1920*, rev. 2nd ed.; *The Sport of Kings and the Kings of Crime: Horse Racing, Politics, and Crime in New York, 1865–1913*; *Touching Base: Professional Baseball and American Culture in the Progressive Era*, rev. ed.; and *City Games: The Evolution of American Society and the Rise of Sports*. He has also edited several books, including *A Companion to American Sport History*, which won the NASSH prize for best anthology in sport history for 2014. Steve is the former editor of the *Journal of Sport History*, and has edited for 25 years the Syracuse University Press series on "Sport and Entertainment."

Index

Activism 101–103, 106, 108–110, 115, 121
Activist(s) 102, 104, 106–108, 110, 111, 113–115
Albert Park 49, 50, 56
Alexander Pierre Tureaud 93
Althea Gibson 93
Amateur Athletic Union 75, 87
American Tennis Association (ATA) 84, 86, 87, 89, 91–93
Andrews, Daniel (Victorian Labor Premier) 53–55, 57, 59, 60
Andrews Government (Victorian Labor 2014) 54, 58
Anna Koll 81, 82
Athlete(s) 101–104, 107–116, 121
Aurora Downs 18
Australian Football League (AFL) 40, 51–54
Australian Grand Prix 47–49, 50, 51, 55–57, 61
Australian Grand Prix Corporation 49, 50, 56, 60
Australian Olympic Committee (AOC) 42, 43
Australian Open (tennis) 37, 39, 40, 41, 52, 53, 55

Balmoral Jockey Club 26–28
Barack Obama 121
Bidwill, Charles 22
Big Bill Tilden 76
Bill Tilden 79
Black liberalism 121
Black Lives Matter 104, 107–110, 124
Black Lives Matter activism 104
Black Lives Matter movement 5
Black radicalism 121
Bobby Riggs 82
Bracks, Steve (Labor Premier of Victoria 1999–2007) 51
Bracks Government (Victorian Labor 1999–2007) 52, 56
Brett Kavanaugh 143, 153, 160
Brumby, John (Victorian Labor Premier 2007–2010) 55

Brumby Government (Victorian Labor 2007-2010) 55
Bryan "Bitsy" Grant 79

Cahokia Downs 23
Cain, John (Labor Premier 1982-1990) 38, 40, 41, 43
Cain Government (Victorian Labor 1982-1990) 39–41, 42
Catholic Church 144, 145, 148
Channels 89
Chicago 4
Chicago Downs 21, 22
Chicago Thoroughbred Enterprises (CTE) 24, 25, 28–31
Choate, Clyde 23
City Park Tennis Club 80
Coates, John 43
Coles, Phil 43
[Colin] Kaepernick 103–109, 114, 115, 119
Collingwood Football Club (AFL) 52, 53
Coming out 168
Commodification of sports 3
Corbett, Jim 74

Davis Cup 82
DeLesseps Morrison 94
Denhollander 150, 152, 160
Docklands football stadium (naming rights-Etihad & Marvel stadium) 51, 52–54
Donald Trump 119, 144, 146, 147
Don Budge 79, 93
Don't Ask, Don't Tell 179
Dr. Blasey Ford 143
Dr. Christine Blasey Ford 143
Dryades Street YMCA 87, 89, 92
Dryades Y. 92
Dwight F. Davis 76

Ecclestone, Bernie (Formula One) 47–49, 50, 51, 56, 57
Edgar Brown 89
Ellsworth Vines 79, 81, 82
Emmet Paré 79

Eric Reid 104, 105
Everest Saitch 89
Everett, Marje L. 22, 24, 28–31

Fred Perry 81, 82

G. Stanley Hall 75
Gosper, Kevan 43
Grand Final (AFL) 39, 40
Gulick and Hall 75

Hamilton "Ham" Richardson 79
Ham Richardson 79
Harness racing 13–17
Harvey Weinstein 143, 144, 147, 148, 159
Hegemonic masculinity 171
Hegemony 171
Hillary Clinton 119
Homohysteria 174
Homophobia 167
Homosexuality 168
Hudson Conway (Melbourne Casino bid) 44, 46, 47
Hyper-masculine 167

Illinois Racing Board (IRB) 17, 20–22, 24–29, 32
International Lawn Tennis Challenge Cup 76
International Olympic Committee (IOC) 42, 43
Isaacs, Theodore 28–32
Isadora Channels 89

Jerry Sandusky 144, 145
Jim Jordan 157, 158
John Engler 152–154
Johnston, William H. 19, 20, 33

Kefauver, Estes 21, 22
Kennett, Jeff (Liberal Premier of Victoria 1992–1999) 44–49, 50, 51, 56, 57, 60, 61
Kennett Government (Victorian Liberal government 1992-1999) 49, 51
Kerner, Otto 4, 13, 26–33
Kirner, Joan 43

Larry Nassar case 5
Leander Perez 94
LeBron James 5, 119
Lee, Clyde 20
Levy, George M. 14–16, 18
Locker-room talk 175
Lulu Ballard 89
Luther Halsey Gulick 75

[Martin Luther] King [Jr.] 112
Mary Ewing Outerbridge 70
Maywood Park 16–18, 23, 24
McGuire, Eddie (Media personality & Collingwood Football Club president) 52, 53, 60
Media 102–108, 110, 115
Megan Rapinoe 3
Melbourne 5
Melbourne Cricket Ground (MCG) 37, 40, 52, 54
Melbourne Cup 39
Melbourne Park 48, 55
Melbourne Racing Club (MRC) 58
#MeToo movement 5
Michigan State 152, 156–158
Michigan State University 147, 150, 152, 159
Miller, William 22, 27, 30
MSU 151, 152, 154, 155
Muhammad Ali 101

Napthine Government (Victorian Liberal 2013–2014) 55
National Basketball Association 119
National Football League 119
National Hockey League (NHL) 6
National Tennis Centre 41, 48, 53, 55
Nehemiah Atkinson 92–95
New Orleans 5
New Orleans Lawn Tennis Club (NOLTC) 69–71, 75–80, 82–84, 87, 89, 92, 93, 95, 96
New York Athletic Club 75

Ogilvie, Richard 26, 29
Olympic Games 4, 42

Ora Washington 89
Orthodox masculinity 169, 170

Parks 106
Paul Powell shoebox scandal 4
Pierre Bourdieu 116
Powell, Paul 13, 17, 19, 20, 22–25
President Trump 155, 158
Protecting Young Victims from Sexual Abuse and Safe Sport Authorization Act 155
Protest 119

Rachael Denhollander 143
Reginald Weir 89
Richard Strauss 157, 158
Roosevelt Raceway 14, 15, 17
Rosa Parks 106
Rosemarie Aquilina 149, 150
Rostenkowski, Daniel 23

Safe Sport Authorization 156
Safe Sport Authorization Act 156
SBC Dominguez Barry (Melbourne Casino bid) 47
Serena Williams 101
Sexual minorities 182
Sheraton-Leighton (Melbourne Casino bid) 46, 47
Southern Lawn Tennis Association 78
Spectators 15
Sportsman's Park 19, 21, 23
Sprague, Russel 15
Spring Racing Carnival 58, 59
Stelle's 24
Stevenson, Adlai 20, 27
Suburban Downs 23
Sullivan, John L. 74
Suzanne Lenglen 76

Tarana Burke 145, 147, 154
Ted Thompson 89
The club 72
Thompson, James 30, 31, 33
Thomy Lafon 87
Thoroughbred racing 12, 13
Trump, Donald 61, 113–115
Tulane 78, 79, 81, 82

United States Lawn Tennis Association (USLTA) 69, 78, 81, 93
U.S. Olympic Committee 151, 152
USA Gymnastics (USAG) 147–151, 155, 158, 159
USOC 151, 152, 156
US Soccer Federation 3
US Women's Soccer Team 3

Victorian Major Events Corporation (VMEC) 43, 44, 48, 60
Victoria Racing Club (VRC) 58, 59

Wagering 18
Walker, Ron (VMEC, AGPC, Liberal Party, property developer) 43, 44, 46–50, 53, 55, 55, 56, 57, 59, 60, 61
Washington Park (WPTA) 25, 27, 31
Wiedrick, Irwin "Big Sam" 20, 21
Williams, Lloyd (property developer) 44, 46, 48, 58, 60
Wimbledon 70
Women's activism 108, 109
World Cups 4

Xavier 88, 89, 92
Xavier College 89
Xavier University 87

Yonkers Raceway 15–17

www.ingramcontent.com/pod-product-compliance
Lightning Source LLC
Chambersburg PA
CBHW020331170426
43200CB00006B/347